AF600436

The Political Activities of Detroit Clubwomen in the 1920s

Great Lakes Books

A complete listing of the books in this series can be found online at wsupress.wayne.edu

The Political Activities of Detroit Clubwomen in the 1920s

A Challenge and a Promise

Jayne Morris-Crowther

Wayne State University Press Detroit

17 16 15 14 13 5 4 3 2 1

Library of Congress Cataloging-in-Publication Data

Morris-Crowther, Jayne.

The political activities of Detroit clubwomen in the 1920s : a challenge and a promise / Jayne Morris-Crowther.

pages ; cm. — (Great Lakes books)

Includes bibliographical references and index.

ISBN 978-0-8143-3815-5 (cloth : alk. paper) —

ISBN 978-0-8143-3816-2 (ebook) (print)

1. Women political activists—Michigan—Detroit. 2. Women—Political activity—Michigan—Detroit. 3. Women—Societies and clubs—Michigan—Detroit. 4. Detroit (Mich.)—Politics and government. I. Title.

HQ1391.U5M67 2013

324'.30977434—dc23

2012035951

Some of the research in this book was published earlier under the title "Municipal Housekeeping: The Political Activities of the Detroit Federation of Women's Clubs in the 1920s," *Michigan Historical Review* 30 (Spring 2004): 31–57.

For John, Jack, and Geoff in loving appreciation

Contents

Acknowledgments

In this research I am the grateful beneficiary of outstanding historians, archivists, family, and friends.

I wish to thank the staff of the Burton Historical Collection at the Detroit Public Library. David Poremba, Cheri Gay, John Gibson, Barbara Louie, Janet Nelson, Lillian Stefano, Winston Johnson, Romie Minor, Jackie Lawson, and Anna Savvides tirelessly assisted me in every way possible. The staff at the Bentley Historical Library of the University of Michigan always provided quick and efficient service for my research needs. I am especially grateful for the assistance of Karen L. Jania. Lastly, the research librarian of the *Detroit News,* Linda Culpepper, answered my many e-mails promptly and with invaluable information. All of the above people share a dedication to Detroit's history and helped immeasurably.

I would like to extend my thanks to Dr. Leslie Page Moch, Dr. Richard Thomas, and Dr. Louise Jezierski, who spent endless hours reading drafts and conferring with me. Each has contributed his/her unique ability to this work. I am indebted to Dr. Maureen A. Flanagan, whose brilliant command of political, urban, and gender history pushed me to explore the nexus of those three fields. Her commitment to me was unfailing. She spent countless hours reading drafts and making suggestions. Our numerous hours in conference were both productive and enjoyable as she opened her home and hospitality to me many times. I consider myself most fortunate to have worked with such a fine historian.

The accomplished staff at Wayne State University Press has worked with me on this book over the last five years. They contracted expert reviewers whose insights and suggestions have made this a stronger and more interesting book. I am grateful to Kathryn Peterson Wildfong, editor in chief, who consistently supported this research from the beginning. I was extremely fortunate to have Jennifer Backer as my copyeditor.

Finally, I wish to thank my family and friends who supported this effort. My sister, Judith Morris Mullen, and my dear friend Susie Barr were always encouraging. I am grateful to my parents, the late Herbert and Helen Morris, who raised me in historic Quincy, Massachusetts, and shared their love for both books and history. I am most thankful for my family, John, Jack and Geoffrey Crowther, to whom this book is dedicated. They all patiently contributed in many ways. They were a constant reminder that what motivated Detroit clubwomen was a love of family. My husband, John, always respected my research and made many sacrifices, too numerous to mention. He facilitated my research trips to Detroit and, regardless of the hour, always assisted me with my many computer needs. His academic standards are the highest, and I still aspire to emulate his scholarship.

Introduction

"A Challenge and a Promise"
Michigan Woman 6 (August 1928), 5

In 1919, the *Detroit Times* reported that some city councilmen showed their "temerity" by opposing the wishes of Detroit's clubwomen. About forty of these clubwomen, recently enfranchised by a November state referendum, were demanding that a section of a public park be attached to a nearby girls' home. Instead the City Council voted to condemn the property for park purposes and thereby incurred the wrath of Detroit's white clubwomen. The newspaper praised the five councilmen who opposed the women as "bold, heroes of their convictions."

The article reveals something of both the nature of the activities of Detroit's clubwomen and the political atmosphere in which they worked. The *Detroit Times* showed a respect for the political influence of these women when they reported the "temerity" of those who opposed them. At the same time, the article praised those "heroes" for not yielding to the clubwomen's wishes. The women might have had political influence, but they were not in command. The implication was that the women were assertive and it took great courage to oppose them. Consequently, the men who voted against the clubwomen were, in fact, heroes.

In the coming decade, Detroit clubwomen continued to make political demands on city, county, and state officials. They wanted both to fit in and to alter the political landscape. As fully enfranchised citizens, both black and white clubwomen wanted their voices heard. They insisted that they stood for the public good but understood that to mean middle-class morality and traditional gender roles. Furthermore, they were convinced that as organized women, they spoke for all the women of the city. In spite of this conviction white clubwomen made little effort to understand or reach out to those of a different class or race. They were cautious but persistent, politically innovative but rarely radical. As with the Palmer Park vote, however, even with their high visibility, they often met with failure or, at best, limited success. The context of women's activities in organized club work, their misplaced assumptions, and the urban context of the city of Detroit help explain these limits. Despite these limits, as the 1920s progressed, black and white clubwomen worked to optimize their political effectiveness.

Detroit clubwomen lived privileged lives compared to their respective sisters. White clubwomen were middle-class to wealthy women with leisure time for club activities. Club meeting times varied but were often twice per month, with additional meeting time for the various committees within each club. White clubs usually met during the day, and the women were not paid for their many time-consuming club activities. In addition, clubwomen often had to pay for their own transportation or use their own automobiles for club business.

White clubwomen were often well educated and well connected to powerful men. Many white women had teaching degrees and were related (often married to) to business and civic leaders. For example, Delphine Dodge (Mrs. R. H.) Ashbaugh was the sister of automobile manufacturers John and Horace Dodge. Dorothea Steffens was married to the city comptroller, Henry Steffens Jr.

Similarly, black women's clubs drew their membership from middle-class women with significant social connections. Their husbands, too, came from the business and professional ranks. For instance, Mary McCoy was married to the inventor Elijah McCoy, and Beulah Young's husband, James, was Detroit's first black surgeon. Detroit's African American women often met at members' houses, which demanded appropriate decor and hostess responsibilities. Many prominent members of African American women's clubs were teachers and journalists as well. Their education and privileged position in the community enabled them to wield great influence in their clubs.[1]

As Detroit clubwomen inserted themselves in previously male-dominated public affairs, they contributed to an evolving concept of twentieth-century politics.[2] Through their voluntary associations, women opened up new possibilities for civic action. Because these associations occupied a unique position between the state and domestic life, they offered women the opportunity to participate in public life even without suffrage and can help us understand the connection between the public and private. Activist clubwomen seized upon and developed their own political culture within these spaces that, in turn, led them to develop political ideas and actions that differed from those of men in strictly male organizations.[3]

As the women developed their own unique beliefs, they displayed the political nature of their plans. They were interested in the reordering of power within the city and the role of citizens in that effort. Defining politics as "efforts to affect the distribution of power and resources in a state community," the women of Detroit were making appeals to the municipal government and were therefore acting politically.[4] They were taking their vision of their city and translating it into public policy. This urban, political, policy-oriented vision was at the heart of clubwomen's activism.[5] They found ways to wield power through a series of networks that brought reformers, political activists, and traditional women's organizations together on issues of common concern. The women in these networks stressed issues and not personalities. In their clubs they were more collaborative and less concerned with competition and prestige than were their male counterparts in Detroit. They also focused heavily on issues of economic security and humanitarian reform. In Detroit, while individual clubwomen were strong supporters of their respective political parties, the clubs themselves supported candidates of both parties based on their voting records. Women were not always trying to elect other women but concentrated on bringing women into existing institutional structures outside electoral politics. Detroit women worked very hard to secure the appointment of women to institutional boards, especially when those boards concerned women and children.[6]

Detroit is a particularly suitable city to use as the focus of a study of clubwomen's political activity in the 1920s. Its meteoric rise to industrial prominence coincided with women gaining the right to vote and the huge influx of black and foreign migrants into the city. Consequently there was a confluence of mass industrialization, mass immigration, and doubling the franchise. The economic, social, and political realities of the city were vastly different from what they had been only twenty years earlier.

From 1900 to 1920 Detroit grew from a small manufacturing city to an industrial giant, attracting laborers from the American South and around the world. By 1920 Detroit was more multiethnic and multiracial than ever before. As the social makeup and the economics of the city rapidly changed, the municipal politics had to change as well. The increase in sheer numbers of Detroiters demanded more city services. These changes were concurrent with the Progressive Era, which stressed a positive not passive government that was concerned about the welfare of its citizens. Black and white clubwomen supported a maternalist agenda and often Progressive ideas. They began to launch programs to protect women and children and their homes in this new urban industrial environment. Black women's situation was more complex. They strove for respectability and could not always depend on the government to provide services so they provided their own or worked for general uplift.

These enfranchised clubwomen operated during a period that has been largely neglected by historians of Detroit. There are several works on the Progressive Era in Detroit, but none of them includes the political activities of women.[7] Other historians have included Detroit women in their works but focus on post–World War II.[8] With the noted exception of Victoria W. Wolcott's excellent research on African American women, there has been scant attention paid to Detroit women during this period and almost none paid to women's political activity in Detroit.[9] This has led to the erroneous conclusion that in the early part of the twentieth century, only men were active in the area's politics. For example, the *Detroit News* described the crusade to reform the Detroit school board as the work of the Municipal League.[10] This explanation ignores the crucial role played by Detroit clubwomen, headed by Laura Osborn. Neglecting the role of women in these efforts and many others in Detroit politics not only lessens their achievements but also enhances the role of men in those activities.

Detroit women expanded their public activity and civic activism as the city became industrialized and urbanized. In doing so, they reflected similar activities throughout the country where women were influencing policies in their states and cities. Clubwomen were advocating comparable solutions to municipal problems that often put them in conflict with urban men, as witnessed in Detroit by the

Palmer Park vote. White clubwomen throughout the nation persisted in participating in public life and thereby challenged the male dominance of power in American cities. Women were instrumental in improving the health of city residents by advocating modern sewage removal and consequently made towns and cities healthier and more attractive. The growth of industrialization and urbanization encouraged educated, middle-class women throughout the United States to become civic activists.[11] Even in the politically rigid American South, women made an impact at the local level, challenging its gendered and political order.[12]

Nationally female reformers were joined by organized women throughout Michigan, particularly in Detroit, who were attending legislative hearings and sessions, as well as city council and school board meetings. They made their views known to policymakers and launched publicity campaigns to cultivate public support. They were especially concerned about the welfare of the family and the home. As Paula Baker explains, "many nineteenth century women found this vision of the home congenial: it encouraged a sense of community and responsibility toward all women and it furnished a basis for political action."[13] Women often stressed that they had a unique perspective in their position between the public and private spheres. Detroit women originally founded their voluntary associations for cultural, literary, and charitable purposes but found through cooperation that they could promote civic betterment.[14] During the expansion of the market economy, both women's and men's clubs provided an avenue for public action; many women's clubs influenced public policy even before women had the franchise.[15] These organized women were acting politically because they were involved in a struggle over power relations. Women strove for recognition of their public work and for expanding women's opportunities before suffrage.[16]

It was a gendered vision in Detroit and cities throughout the United States that clubwomen consequently translated into political action. Urban politics often provided the battleground on which men and women struggled for power and resources early in the twentieth century. Detroit clubwomen practiced "municipal housekeeping," a label that gave an air of respectability to otherwise unseemly public or political activity, but their programs often ran counter to those of men's groups in Detroit, which were mainly concerned with the financial bottom line.[17] Like women in Chicago, Detroit women answered the question "What is the public good?" differently than men did.[18] When women in Detroit campaigned for public bathhouses, aldermen were concerned with their expense, not with the benefits they would bring.

In Detroit, white clubwomen changed what constituted the concerns of the state. They made a private-public connection in their voluntary clubs and the public work they undertook well before they could vote. They looked to the municipal government to provide services arising from private needs like recreation and personal hygiene. Between 1901 and 1903 the Detroit Branch of the Council of Women campaigned successfully for municipal playgrounds. Clara B. Arthur, who was the president of the Detroit Federation of Women's Clubs (DFWC), as well as a member of the Detroit Equal Suffrage Association (DESA), led the fight for public bathhouses. She began this work in the early twentieth century and it came to fruition in 1906. Consequently, women championed "women's issues" and established themselves as legitimate political actors. For example, in 1912, Detroit women added social welfare as a legitimate concern for public debate in their support for mothers' pensions.

As Detroit women emphasized the public-private connection, they were demonstrating one of the fundamental elements of "municipal housekeeping": the connection between the home and the city. The rapid urbanization of Detroit made sanitation issues, which directly connected the home with the city, of paramount concern to clubwomen. Public officials, recognizing this connection and clubwomen's willingness to help, often appealed to them in efforts to create a cleaner environment in Detroit. For example, clubwomen both initiated and participated in clean food, anti-vermin, and smoke abatement campaigns. In this regard, they experienced varying degrees of success.

Detroit clubwomen pursued a "womanly" politics, meaning one that focused primarily on the needs of women. This work was independent from that of men but still necessary to represent the needs of everyone. One of the reasons women sought the vote was because industrial capitalism had changed the nature of women's work, making it more public. Some women worked outside the home in the waged workforce but were poorly understood by white clubwomen who, in any case, still advocated state policy that affected working women. Women who remained in the home, outside the waged workforce, still depended on public policies to provide services and protections for that home.[19]

While African American clubwomen were also connecting the private with the public, they could not depend on the government for social welfare. Their complex position in terms of class, race, and gender gave them a unique perspective on reform. Black clubwomen's strategy for reform began with a campaign to prove they were worthy of respect. They believed that if they proved they were morally equal to white women, they, too, would be able to press for social reform. Undergirding their policies was a firm belief that respectable bourgeois behavior would further themselves individually and their race as a whole. In this effort, several black clubwomen established homes, such as Detroit's Second Baptist's Christian Industrial Home in 1904. This facility provided clean, safe room and board for young single girls. African American clubwomen enlisted volunteers and sought money from the black community for these institutions.[20] Black women reformers were often members of such organizations as the National Association of Colored Women (NACW). Their campaign for welfare was inextricably tied to equal rights. They held their national convention in Detroit in July 1906, where they issued a resolution protesting Jim Crow laws in public transportation. It read: "Resolved: That we unite in advising our people to refrain so far as possible from using these conveyances where discrimination exists."[21] As a whole, African American clubwomen focused on respectability and general uplifting programs in health, education, and day care.[22]

In Detroit as elsewhere in the United States, the perception of urban problems and the solutions women generated for them have gendered connotations. Reforming women believed mothers had a crucial role in raising good citizens, a role that became even more pivotal in the face of a rapidly changing urban and industrialized world. Clubwomen believed that because they were part of the educated elite, they were in the best position to determine the "proper" way to raise children.[23] They therefore championed new protective labor legislation for women and children, educational reform, food inspection, and crime prevention. Detroit clubwomen saw themselves as concerned citizens with the responsibility to act on behalf of those less fortunate and believed the city was the responsibility of both men and women. They offered a unique vision for Detroit based on gendered ideas that would benefit all residents.

Like other organized middle-class clubwomen across the country, Detroit women seldom advocated radical political change or understood the inequities of the wage system. Rather, they were concerned with how the wage system placed a disproportionate burden on women, which led white clubwomen to advocate social welfare in the early decades of the twentieth century.[24] Working through their voluntary clubs, women promoted social welfare legislation that emanated from their vision of maternalism. This vision emphasized a woman's role as a mother; clubwomen believed that the common bond among all women was motherhood. Maternalism was translated into public policy through such federal programs as the Federal Children's Bureau, which investigated issues like the birthrate, infant mortality, child labor, and children in the court systems. Clubwomen supported state programs like Mothers' Pensions, which provided monthly stipends for mothers without financial support.[25]

Regardless of their focus, both black and white clubwomen were doing political work while still disenfranchised. Thus research on enfranchised women in the 1920s must be connected to women's earlier activities: women continued to work together in voluntary associations (many of which had been formed for political purposes) even after gaining the vote. Disenfranchised Detroit women had created a separate political culture from that of men. Furthermore, in the 1920s women's voluntary associations multiplied. Detroit clubwomen continued to pursue interest-group politics in such organizations as the Twentieth Century Club, the League of Women Voters, the Detroit League of Catholic Women, the Detroit New Century Club, the Progressive Civic League, and the African-American Detroit Study Club. While many women were in associations, no one group spoke for all women and there was no "women's bloc" in politics. Women's political efforts were as varied as men's. Clubwomen often banded together to support issues of common interest, but they did not always agree on the same policy. For example, in Michigan not all women supported women's suffrage, and club members disagreed about the idea of furthering equal rights for women.[26]

Many of Detroit women's clubs were loosely organized into the DFWC. Primarily, but not exclusively, a white women's organization, in the 1920s the DFWC represented 15,000 women in 107 clubs. The clubs were devoted to artistic, literary, philanthropic, or civic agendas. They chose to become federated so that they could, if they desired, speak with one voice. Its constitution and bylaws stated that "Its object is to bring into communication the various clubs of Detroit as a means of prosecuting any work of common interest, but no club entering the Federation shall thereby lose its independence in aim or method or be committed to any principles or method of any other club."[27] The leadership of the DFWC came from the various member clubs, and the individual clubs occasionally withheld support for DFWC decisions. The DFWC dissented from the nationwide racial policy of the General Federation of Women's Clubs (GFWC) and accepted two African American women's clubs, the Detroit Study Club and the Entre Nous Club. In doing so, they risked eviction from the GFWC but took advantage of a "subtle evasion clause," which was used occasionally at the local level.[28] The DFWC seldom questioned the American political or economic system, but it did support women's political engagement. Thus the members of the DFWC provide a glimpse into the political activities of Detroit's clubwomen.

By the 1920s there were eight African American clubs in Detroit: Willing Workers, Detroit Study Club, Lydian Association, In As Much Circle of King's Daughters, Labor of Love Circle of King's Daughters, West Side Art and Literary Club, Altar Society of the Second Baptist Church, and the Earnest Workers of the Second Baptist Church. On April 8, 1921, they joined to form the Detroit Association of Colored Women's Clubs. Their first president was Veronica Lucas, and their purpose was to assist the black community. They represented black families in issues related to housing, employment, health, and orphans, and were opposed to alcoholism and illiteracy.[29]

The political activities of all Detroit's middle-class clubwomen illuminate the complexity of equal political participation for women after suffrage. Other studies concentrate on cities that were well established before the immense changes of mass industrialization. This book concentrates on political work because it highlights the difficulty of equal political participation when viewed at the nexus of both urban and gendered variables. Women's political work predated their franchise and therefore created a situation that set patterns of political activity that endured after suffrage.[30] In this regard they changed how people behaved politically. They pioneered new lobbying techniques such as personal interviews and investigations and practiced grassroots politics outside the party system. Detroit clubwomen had their greatest success in public (not partisan) political education and grassroots organizational activity. Moreover, the context of urbanization structured the political work of women in their specific cities. Detroit offered its clubwomen an urban environment where municipal government was in flux. At the same time, the legitimate concerns of the city government changed. In the early twentieth century organized women concluded that the problems associated with congested, urban living could be and should be solved by the municipal community.[31] The political environment in Detroit was further influenced by the city's unique economic situation. Detroit had become the third largest manufacturing city in the country, dominated by the automobile industry. Powerful business leaders had commensurate political power.[32] Lastly, the political milieu of the Progressive Era sought municipal answers through impartial experts and scientific inquiry and viewed the political parties as self-serving rather than serving the public. This offered possibilities as well as limitations for enfranchised clubwomen.

These thoughtful, educated, and well-organized women tried to affect public policy, but their success was limited. Their political success before the franchise encouraged them to continue the same organizational and methodological tactics. Although white clubwomen believed they spoke for all women, they rarely, if ever, allied with African American women with similar agendas. This inconsistency often meant that two groups of women ran parallel agendas. In Atlanta and North Carolina, black and white clubwomen banded together over common causes during this time period; this never happened in Detroit.[33] Both black and white clubwomen held the erroneous assumption that they spoke for a much larger group of women than they actually did. Black clubwomen believed they spoke for all black women, and white clubwomen thought they spoke for all women. Both groups, therefore, pursued policies founded upon false assumptions. White women were reluctant to work with like-minded black women in Detroit because the increasing racism of the city (and of the clubwomen themselves) overshadowed their similar commitments to bourgeois, Victorian values. White clubwomen did not speak of race because they saw it as a great divider, and it repudiated their claim to speak for all women.

Lack of access to both political decision making and business interests hurt the civic effectiveness of both black and white clubwomen. Their limited success was due to their lack of business influence in the city and to gendered stereotypes regarding the proper roles of men and women. Clubwomen's goals, as articulated in their writings, were often at odds with newspapers' presentation of them. Unless a newspaper supported one of the clubwomen's crusades, such as anti-gambling, both black and white newspapers printed club activities in the society section and usually only once a week. This was an especially pressing concern to African American women, whose presence and accomplishments were completely ignored by the major Detroit newspapers. Despite all of this adversity, Detroit clubwomen continued their political participation.

In the 1920s Detroit absorbed the economic consequences of mass industrialization, the political consequences of doubling the franchise, and the social consequences of mass migration into the city. Both black and white clubwomen attempted to alter the way in which the city responded to these challenges. They first sought to maximize their political clout with their full use of the franchise. Believing that "Democracy is not a spectator sport," they sought to educate voters and get them to vote.[34] Politicians at first feared their numbers as the newspapers reported large turnouts of women at the polls. This book and others show that the real impact of women's franchise powers was seen at the local level. But the threat that women might vote en masse at least turned the attention of politicians toward the issues women were advocating.[35] As a result, they often sought clubwomen's advice on matters pertaining to women and children. Clubwomen sought and received protection for mothers through pensions and infant health care information. They also successfully advocated policies to protect children in the labor force but failed to eliminate child labor.

Clubwomen feared many of the social consequences of urbanization so they took a lively interest in matters of crime and punishment. Their work had little effect on vice but they did help make significant changes to the judicial system; white clubwomen were instrumental in the creation of the Women's Division of the Police Department. Women also knew that the realities of a modern, urban environment held hazards for the home. They worked for consumer product protection, movie censorship, and cleaner air. They launched safety campaigns and supervised playgrounds to protect pedestrians and children. In these matters they had some success. They were consistently engaged in the contentious issues of water, sewage, and transportation but failed to advocate any policy.

Throughout the decade Detroit clubwomen, black and white, were convinced that their political views were important and necessary for the newly industrialized, urbanized Detroit. They were engaged politically in municipal affairs and consistently challenged the political male domination of Detroit politics. They fought uphill battles as they advocated policies that they believed would help women and children, and they fiercely defended the home against the dangers of an urban environment. Throughout all these campaigns they insisted that their voices be heard on an equal basis as those of men. As civic-minded women, they considered their commitment to Detroit both a challenge and a promise.[36]

1

Early Twentieth-Century Detroit and the Beginning of Women's Activism

"The Growing Power of Women's Clubs in Detroit"
Detroit News Tribune, February 18, 1906

In the early twentieth century Detroit was a dynamic city undergoing rapid industrialization and an accompanying population boom, making the city more heterogeneous than it had been in the nineteenth century. There was increased demand for city services, as the city had greater municipal responsibility to provide police and fire protection, clean water and waste removal, education, and transportation for a much larger population. But the decentralized, corrupt city government was poorly equipped to meet the challenges of its newly acquired urban and industrial condition. This led concerned individuals, such as businessmen and clubwomen, to confront these challenges. Although early twentieth-century Detroit's municipal affairs were dominated by men, Detroit's black and white middle-class women used their clubs and associations to promote public policies they believed were necessary for the welfare of Detroit's citizens. Detroit historians have largely ignored this important part of early Detroit politics. Women began tentatively but grew more confident as they became convinced their voices needed to be heard. Thus Detroit's clubwomen increasingly attended public hearings, met privately with policymakers, and launched publicity campaigns to turn their plans into municipal policy.

Michigan women had a long history of female activism both in the suffrage campaign and within Detroit. When the effort for women's suffrage failed at the 1874 state convention, there was no state organization representing women's suffrage, but the Detroit Equal Suffrage Association (DESA), founded by Helen Jenkins in 1875, carried on the suffrage work. In 1884, woman's suffrage was reorganized statewide into the Michigan Equal Suffrage Association (MESA). A year later under the leadership of Mary L. Doe of Bay City, women attempted unsuccessfully to get a state law passed that would grant municipal suffrage to women who were taxpayers.[1] In Detroit, however, an 1889 city charter amendment gave mothers of minor children the right to vote in school elections. The state conferred municipal suffrage for women in 1893, but it was struck down by the Michigan State Supreme Court on the grounds that "the Legislature had no right to create a new class of voters."[2]

The struggle for suffrage was one part of the growth of Detroit women's associations in the late nineteenth and early twentieth centuries. The first Detroit women's club was founded in 1873 by Frances Newberry (Mrs. John) Bagley. The charter members were Mrs. Brearley, Sarah Webster (Mrs. J. T.) Stevens, Elvira Wilkinson (Mrs. W. H.) Allen, Mrs. Albert Hill, Miss S. A. Brearley, Lydia Hopkins, and Elizabeth Dwight. They organized to share literary and cultural interests. Twenty-one years later, the Twentieth Century Club was founded and claimed as members some of the most civic-minded clubwomen in early twentieth-century Detroit. Its members included Stella Krebs (Mrs. Carl) Brumme, Adaline Dunlap (Mrs. Charles Hague) Booth, Mrs. Hermon Sanderson, Mary Egan (Mrs. J. Hal) Livsey, Harriet Robinson (Mrs. William A.) McGraw, Mrs. William Robinson, Clara Arthur, Emma (Mrs. Charles) Fox, and African American clubwoman Mary (Mrs. Elijah) McCoy.[3]

In 1895, Detroit clubwoman Frances Margah, president of the Detroit Review Club, thought women could be a greater power in the community if they banded together. She asked Frances Bagley, as a member of Detroit's oldest women's club, to propose a federation of women's clubs. Subsequently the Detroit Review Club, Twentieth Century Club, Detroit Woman's Club, Woman's Historical Club, Clio Club, Wednesday History Club, Hypathia, and Zatema Club formed the Detroit Federation of Women's Clubs (DFWC).[4] Its bylaws simply stated that the women wanted to understand each other's work, to provide more unified thinking, and consequently to make their efforts more effective.[5]

At the same time, African American women were forming their own clubs in Detroit. In 1895 Mary McCoy founded the first Detroit

African American women's club: In As Much Circle of King's Daughters and Sons Club. McCoy was known as the "Mother of Clubs" in Detroit and was also a member of the Lydian Association of Detroit, Guiding Star Chapter Order of the Eastern Star and the Willing Workers.[6] She was the only African American charter member of the Detroit Twentieth Century Club and was also a member of the National Association for the Advancement of Colored People (NAACP). She founded the Phyllis Wheatley Home for Aged Colored Women in Detroit and was sometimes called the "best known woman of Detroit."[7]

Throughout the state, black women who had attended the 1898 meeting of the National Association of Colored Women (NACW) founded the Michigan State Association. Its first president was Women's Christian Temperance Union (WCTU) member Lucy Thurman. Other members included Mary McCoy, Delia Barrier, M. C. Johnson, Frances Preston, Elida Price, Veronica Lucas, Fanny Richards, Meta Pelham, Lola Gregory, Lucile Owen, and Mollie Lewis.

In the early twentieth century, as Detroit was on the verge of a massive urban and industrial development, Detroit women expanded their public activity and civic activism. Women throughout Michigan and particularly within Detroit were concerned about the welfare of the family and the home. Because they were outside the franchise, they used their clubs and associations as vehicles for their civic action. In Detroit, women identified themselves in a nongendered way as concerned citizens, but much of what they advocated supported traditional gender roles and middle-class morality. Still, they believed the city was the responsibility of both men and women, and these women offered a unique vision for Detroit. Moreover, as organized women, they believed they spoke for the unorganized women as well. Clara Arthur's pre-franchise booklet *Progress of Michigan Women* claimed that within the state, "wise laws came from the untiring activity of Michigan women interested in the development of their sex and the need of the state for women's counsel."[8]

Women's counsel was not always appreciated; Detroit clubwomen's political activism thus had to be creative and persistent. Men considered women political outsiders and often disparaged their political activity. In Detroit and in other U.S. cities, women pioneered nonvoting political pressure techniques such as public education and petitions. They used scientific research and the advice of experts to demonstrate that their reforms were worthwhile and necessary. For example, when Detroit's white clubwomen advocated public baths, they cited favorable evidence from public health officials. Women's clubs were also places where women could develop the leadership, organizational, and communication skills necessary for public activism.[9] While white women of Detroit shared a common ideology and methodology with other civically active clubwomen, the extraordinary growth of Detroit heightened the sense of urgency.

The DFWC originally endorsed proposals that originated outside the federation. Gradually club members found they could initiate proposals themselves and promote their own ideas about how to make Detroit a safer, healthier, more progressive city.[10] One idea that women advocated to meet this goal was public playgrounds. In 1899, Clara Arthur, a former teacher and founding member of the Michigan Equal Suffrage Association fours years earlier, presented a paper before the Philanthropy and Reform Department of the Twentieth Century Club about the need for playgrounds. Arthur explained that Detroit's poor children had no place to play except in the streets and noted that some cities such as Boston provided designated play areas for children.[11]

The campaign for municipal playgrounds originally proposed by Arthur began in 1901 under the leadership of the Detroit Branch of the Council of Women. This council was an eclectic group of women's clubs that did not include the DFWC but did include some of its members such as the DESA, the City Union of King's Daughters, the Women and Children's Protective Association, the La Tour Hive of the Lady Maccabees, the Mothers' Kindergarten Circle, the Women's Independent Voters' Association, the WCTU, the Mothers' Club of the Hancock School, Detroit Sorosis, Per Gradis, and the Detroit Woman's Club. The council originally requested an empty city lot on Riopelle Street for a playground, but the City Council refused. The women then successfully appealed to the Detroit school board for the use of the Russell School yard and basement for the summer of 1901. Clara Talbot (Mrs. John) Hickey led a committee of women who went door-to-door soliciting the necessary twelve hundred dollars to run the playground. They had to secure funding again the next year because the city refused to provide money for a "fad." Prevailing opinion held that playgrounds were part of private charity, but the playground crusaders believed it was the city's responsibility. In the effort to change public opinion, the white clubwomen launched an educational campaign. They wrote hundreds of letters to organizations, newspapers, and city officials to raise public awareness of this issue. They made and sponsored numerous speeches. S. V. Tsaroff, a noted expert in playground education, lectured in Detroit at their request. In 1903, the women presented a petition to the Detroit Board of Education with fourteen thousand names. The board finally acquiesced and procured money from the City Council for playgrounds.[12]

The Detroit clubwomen's playground crusade stands at the intersection of various class, ethnic, and maternal considerations. As businessmen became increasingly concerned about their employees' free time, recreation took on a new meaning. These businessmen championed programs like the Safe and Sane Fourth of July celebrations and, more important, Prohibition.[13] Luther H. Gulick Jr., the first president of the Playground Association of America, said, "the organization of leisure is just as important and technical a matter as the organization of industry."[14]

Women were simultaneously trying to enact laws to protect children from labor exploitation. As children were gradually freed from the labor force, clubwomen feared that petty crime arose from unsupervised children.[15] Clubwomen were also concerned about the kind of child-rearing taking place in working-class homes and ethnic environments.[16] The DFWC ran a special program for the daughters of immigrants as part of its Americanization program.[17] Clubwomen's increasing emphasis on supporting their vision of motherhood through state programs emboldened them to champion playgrounds and supervised play.[18] Consequently, reformers in the Progressive Era saw the city streets as an improper environment for children's play. Instead, they advocated supervised municipal playgrounds.

White clubwomen agreed with Lillian Wald, a noted children's advocate, who believed that supervised play was the best way to head off juvenile crime. In the coming years, Detroit clubwomen continued to support the playground effort. The DFWC even helped pay the salary of the first municipal swim teacher in Detroit. The campaign for playgrounds eventually evolved into the Detroit Municipal Recreation Committee in 1914 and acquired a national reputation for its quality.[19]

At about the same time the playground campaign was under way, the DFWC formed a committee to urge city officials to build a public bathhouse. Under the leadership of Clara Arthur, clubwomen faced formidable opposition on this issue. But Arthur had significant networking ability with Detroit's white clubwomen.[20] The *Detroit Free Press* supported the idea of public baths but felt the city should have a comprehensive plan for parks, playgrounds, convenience stations, and so forth, and that these initiatives should be included in an annual budget and not simply be done piecemeal. The *Free Press* believed this was a better system than "the gratification of the personal desires of well-meaning individuals or organizations."[21]

But the DFWC persevered and sent a letter to the City Council on behalf of its two thousand members, noting that thirty-six U.S. cities had public baths and that more were in the works throughout the country. In addition, the DFWC noted that the Federal Bureau of Labor claimed that baths elevated the material and moral tone of workers. The clubwomen cited health officials who argued that inadequate bathing facilities were a public health menace.[22]

When clubwomen appealed to the aldermen for assistance, they were told people could always bathe in the river. After several years, however, the city fathers grew tired of the "pestering women" and in 1906 they appropriated $20,000 for the first public bathhouse in Detroit. It opened in 1908 on Erskin Street, east of Russell, and was appropriately named the Clara Arthur Bath House. The women also successfully campaigned for showers in some of the public schools.[23]

Pre-franchise clubwomen of Detroit were also interested in issues pertaining to children in general. They lobbied successfully to raise the working age from twelve to fourteen. They then tackled the issue of raising the age of dismissal for destitute, noncriminal children housed in the Coldwater State Public School for Dependent Children to fourteen because the only options available to these children upon their departure from the school at age twelve were entering a poorhouse or going to jail.[24] Legislators did not want to spend the money to house the children for two extra years, but the clubwomen of Detroit lobbied relentlessly to raise the dismissal age to fourteen. One state senator remarked as he saw the women returning to the capitol, "Well there are those women again. They do not know when they are insulted." Still, the women kept working.[25] Clubwomen lobbied business and professional men to support the older dismissal age. They secured favorable publicity in the *Detroit Journal, Detroit Free Press,* and *Detroit Tribune.* They questioned the validity of the legislators' claim that it would be too expensive to house children for another two years. Finally, in 1907 after seven years of lobbying, the dismissal age at Coldwater was raised to fourteen.[26]

This success and others earned Detroit's white clubwomen the reputation of having political clout, especially on issues pertaining to women and children. In 1906, the *Detroit News Tribune* wrote a story titled "The Growing Power of Women's Clubs in Detroit." It claimed that the "power of clubwomen has been steadily growing." The article was written in response to a recent assertion of an eastern college president who had said that women's clubs did more harm than good. The *Detroit News Tribune* listed both the civic achievements of clubwomen as well as their current projects.[27]

The efforts of Detroit's clubwomen reflected similar activities of organized American women nationwide who used motherhood and its accompanying respect as a wedge into municipal politics. Disenfranchised American women who operated outside partisan politics appealed to traditionally accepted gendered roles of women and motherhood. The rhetoric was effective and rose above party politics to concepts like universal motherhood. Once this concept was politically accepted, organized American women in Detroit and elsewhere used it to advocate a vast array of municipal and state policies that often had class, ethnic, and racial implications.[28] While some historians consider this strategy as limiting, others believe women succeeded in establishing an American maternalist social policy.[29]

Detroit clubwomen not only were pursuing a maternalist agenda but, like the members of the Women's City Club of New York and other American women's clubs, were emphasizing the connection between family and community in their reform work—they focused on "social" or "human" issues. Detroit's clubwomen, like their sisters in other American cities, sought to improve the quality of life for all of the city's residents.[30] They promoted a municipal responsibility that responded to the broader needs of its citizens. At the same time, the industrialization of Detroit was spawning a new and powerful business elite determined to put municipal responsibility in their hands alone, not let it extend to the working class. By 1920, automobile manufacturing was the leading industry of Detroit. Consequently the wealthy auto barons, along with other big businessmen, dominated Detroit's municipal affairs. Automobile manufacturers and other businessmen formed organizations such as the Municipal League in 1902 "to promote business-like, honest and efficient conduct in municipal affairs."[31]

As the automobile industry grew in Detroit, the city was filled with increasing numbers of foreign, unskilled, and semiskilled workers.[32] Growing class stratification, the large number of migrants in Detroit, and an exaggerated fear of socialism and labor radicalism led the city's great industrialists to work together to impose social order on the community. The big businessmen intended for this new social order be based on a unified workforce. They used welfare capitalism and Americanization programs to establish this.[33]

Businessmen had many opportunities to make their needs clear in the city of Detroit.[34] Members of organizations like the Municipal League joined with Progressive Republicans to direct political and economic reform in Detroit. They believed that efficient government would cut costs and create a better business climate by freeing capital for investment, thereby attracting industry and customers to Detroit. Threatening this vision, however, was a series of political scandals. These generally involved election fraud but sometimes involved graft. Before charter reform, Detroit was governed by a weak mayor with a City Council consisting of two aldermen from each of the city's twenty-one wards elected on a partisan ballot. According to historian Sidney Fine, the dominant influence was "easy going, inefficient and in a petty way corrupt."[35] Both the Democrats and Republicans cooperated to prevent the election of local reform candidates, especially in the Common Council. In addition to election fraud, there were scandals involving financial gains for officeholders and financial losses for the city. The endemic corruption of Detroit even involved the city's school system. Of particular concern to women were scandals involving the bribery of school board members by book agents, furniture dealers, and contractors, which led to a call to change the procedure for electing school board members.[36]

Detroit clubwomen supported school board reform because it reflected their concern with the quality of children's education.[37] As was the case throughout the country, clubwomen worked for better enforcement of attendance laws and to lengthen attendance requirements from age fourteen to age sixteen. Fourteen-year-olds could leave school for work if their family needed the income. White clubwomen also successfully campaigned to have truant officers placed under the school board and not the city government.[38] Clubwomen campaigned for higher salaries for teachers as well as the retention of art and music teachers. While they were defending the creative arts teachers and endorsing better salaries, Detroit's white clubwomen realized that the city needed fundamental school board reform. The Board of Education for the city of Detroit was made up of eighteen school inspectors, one elected from each ward. The members were oftentimes uneducated and only interested in the bribes from the furniture and book dealers. In 1912 Laura Freele (Mrs. Francis) Osborn of the Twentieth Century Club led the way to reform the school board to a smaller, nonpartisan, at-large one. She co-opted the support of MESA to help educate the public for reform. Clubwomen went door-to-door, made speeches, and wrote letters. The Michigan state legislature responded by passing a bill for small, nonpartisan city school boards. Those who opposed this questioned the constitutionality of the bill, but the courts upheld it.[39]

Led by Osborn, Detroit's white clubwomen began a crusade to educate the public about the advantages of a smaller board; they worked with the Municipal League and the *Detroit News* to publicize their efforts. The Twentieth Century Club's Education Committee printed two thousand copies of a pamphlet titled "Children First."[40] Detroit voters, perhaps aided by votes of women eligible to vote as property owners and parents, approved the small board in a 5–1 victory in November 1916.[41] At the time, Detroit's white clubwomen in general, and Laura Osborn in particular, were credited with the victory. The DFWC reported that the support of clubwomen for reform and later their election of board members "accounted for a large share of the victories."[42] In the first election after the school board reform measure was passed Osborn was elected as a board member, and she served until her death in 1949. The Twentieth Century Club endorsed her candidacy because they believed that the education and character of children were best understood by mothers. Osborn was also endorsed by the Woman's Historical Club, Women Taxpayers League, North Woodward Woman's Club, and the Congressional Union. In addition, Osborn had been a teacher before having children, and since there were many female teachers, most thought she would be able to work well with them.[43]

There were many teachers among the African American clubwomen as well, and it is thus not surprising that they focused their efforts on educational reform as well. Black women's desire for racial uplift was oftentimes channeled through educational reform. For example, Fannie Richards, an African American Detroit clubwoman and teacher, was instrumental in the effort to desegregate Detroit's public schools, and she persuaded the Detroit School Board to initiate one of the earliest kindergartens in 1872.[44]

Richards and three other black Detroit teachers, Meta Pelham, J. Cook, and Etta Edna Lee, were born in the free black community of Fredericksburg, Virginia. The Richards family migrated to Detroit in the 1850s, and Fannie Richards received her education at the Teacher Training Institute. She became the first Detroit black teacher in 1865 and originally taught in a segregated school. She was active in both educational and club work. Richards helped found the Michigan Federation of Colored Women's Clubs in 1898. The *Detroit News Tribune* published an article about her retirement on June 20, 1915, and the *Detroit News* printed her obituary on the front page in 1922. There is a school named after her in Detroit, and her portrait hangs in the Detroit Public Library.[45]

Not only was Richards a pioneer but she and her fellow black clubwomen used their clubs to further enhance their educational and uplift agendas. In the early part of the twentieth century, black clubwomen believed that real reform began with children and thus advocated programs for education and child care.[46] For example, the Detroit Study Club, whose members included many of the earliest black public schoolteachers, held lectures and raised money for underprivileged students.

Thus both black and white clubwomen championed the cause of improving education in Detroit. They also sought to improve children's health and to keep families intact. Along with playgrounds, they pioneered lunch programs. In 1911 the Jewish Women's Club started a one-cent lunch project, which was the forerunner of later DFWC-sponsored nutritional projects. Clubwomen recruited important contributors, in particular automobile manufacturer John F. Dodge. By 1921, when the Board of Education took over the program, it was serving milk and graham crackers daily to approximately 6,500 children.[47] Clubwomen also wanted to keep widowed or deserted mothers with their children, so in 1912 Detroiter Ruby (Mrs. Herman J.) Zahn founded the Political and Civic League and immediately set out to secure a Mothers' Compensation Bill, which was passed in 1913 by the state legislature.

While the emotional, physical, and educational health of children was a high priority for all clubwomen, businessmen's concern about municipal corruption and the undue influence of "lower" social groups led them to initiate a movement for charter reform in Detroit. Thirty percent of Detroit's aldermen were saloon keepers and the partisan nature of the elections had led to corruption. This involved a reorganization of the municipal government whereby the power shifted from the neighborhoods to a centralized city hall. Among the chief proponents of such reform was the Detroit Citizens League. Organized by Henry Leland in 1912, the league supported Prohibition and clean government. Leland also believed that immigrants were potentially dangerous and needed to be controlled. He stated that the purpose of the league was "Increasing the activity of the better class of men in politics."[48]

The city's largest newspaper, the *Detroit News*, agreed with the Detroit Citizens League and others on the need for charter reform.[49] The new charter included a provision for a strong mayor who would appoint or dismiss department heads and submit a budget. He would administer the city along with the city clerk and the treasurer. The charter reform commission abolished the twenty-one-member, ward-based City Council and replaced it with a nine-member, at-large council. Elections would be nonpartisan and held in odd-numbered years. The city clerk scheduled a special election for charter approval on June 25, 1918.[50]

Detroit's white and most likely black clubwomen supported the Detroit Citizens League's plan to reduce the forty-two-man Common Council to a nine-man, at-large one. The Common Council's alternative plan was to reduce the size of the council to only one alderman per ward, which would result in a twenty-one-man council. The Legislative Department of the DFWC reported that the measure sponsored by the Common Council "could only more firmly fix the ward politics which are so generally deplored." The report went on to praise the Detroit Citizens League's proposal. In the report, DFWC Legislative Department chairperson Marjory Miller Whittemore noted that although clubwomen could not vote in the election, they should exert an indirect influence by urging all the men they knew to vote for the nine-man City Council.[51]

Detroit clubwomen had good reasons to endorse the city charter in 1918. Just as they had worked for a smaller, less corrupt school board, they now supported the proposed charter's plan to eliminate ward politics with the smaller, nonpartisan, nine-man City Council. Like the members of the Detroit Citizens League, clubwomen abhorred municipal corruption and especially bemoaned the waste of taxpayer dollars, which clubwomen believed betrayed the public's trust. Although there is some evidence that middle-class women believed that ethnic neighborhoods did not vote "wisely" and that Detroit white clubwomen shared these fears, describing ward politics as "generally deplored," the Detroit charter reform was about more than class and ethnic differences.[52] The wasteful aldermanic council had left a legacy of disgust with the municipal government, and large numbers of workers from various ethnic backgrounds voted for charter reform.[53] There are no extant sources on this issue for black women's clubs, but the reform was overwhelmingly supported by all groups. Most Detroit clubwomen supported the 1918 charter reform because it promised to curb corruption and graft. They were gratified when Detroit voters approved the new city charter by a vote of 32,690 to 4,587 (87.7 percent).[54] It was approved in every ward and every precinct.[55]

The Detroit Citizens League charter reform made profound changes in Detroit politics. In the move from partisanship, other pressure groups became important in sponsoring issues and candidates. Council candidates in a citywide election had to have money, press coverage, and endorsements. In the first election of the new council, eight of the nine elected were business or professional men. The last was a labor candidate who received the endorsement of the Citizens League. Between 1918 and 1933, sixteen of the twenty-four men elected to the council had a business or professional background. The league favorably rated four of the seven mayors during the same time period. In 1921, 1929, and 1933 the voters turned down the opportunity to return to the old system.[56]

While Detroit women were supporting charter reform in Detroit, they were also pursuing the franchise. Both MESA and DESA expanded their activities for state suffrage throughout this time period. A failed attempt to secure statewide suffrage in 1912 led to more campaigning. But not all Michigan women were in favor of women's suffrage. In 1913 the anti-suffragists organized the Michigan Association Opposed to Woman Suffrage (MAOWS). They were joined in their efforts by the liquor interests represented by the Royal Ark, which was comprised of Detroit's liquor dealers. This connection resulted in the women being erroneously accused of being funded by the liquor dealers. The MAOWS believed that voting was a man's responsibility and that extending the vote to women would harm the family and the home. MESA supporters agreed that the home was important, but they claimed that women needed the vote to protect it.[57] Consequently, while organized women agreed that the home was of paramount importance, they disagreed among themselves as to how best to protect that home.

By 1914, Michigan women could vote as mothers or guardians for school board members. Taxpaying women could vote on issues involving the direct spending of public money. However, they were not allowed to choose who would spend their money and had only a secondary role in how such money was spent.[58] Similarly qualified African American women were entitled to franchise privileges. They joined the suffrage battle and enumerated the reasons why women wanted the ballot: "Equal Suffrage is woman's desire to see in all walks of life, the honor, the virtue, the justice, the genuine human sympathy which she interprets as the foundation of any permanent social structure." African American women also hinted at their maternalist message when they stressed that the ballot was not intended for women to rule over men but rather so they could keep "his city home and his nation's home clean and wholesome."[59] Prominent African American clubwoman Mary McCoy was identified with women's suffrage, but there is no evidence that Detroit clubwomen reached across racial lines for a common cause in the suffrage campaign.[60] In this regard, the actions of Detroit women mirrored those of their sisters in the suffrage battle nationwide. In 1903 the National American Woman's Suffrage Association said that women's suffrage might be the "medium through which to retain supremacy of the white race over the African."[61] There is no mention of racial motivations in the clubwomen's records pertaining to suffrage, but there is also no mention that African American women might be useful as allies in this shared goal. Consequently in Detroit, as elsewhere, black and white women waged separate but parallel struggles for suffrage.

The U.S. entry into World War I caused Michigan women to focus more intensely on directly influencing public policy. Clara Arthur and other suffragists believed "war with expenditure of life and treasure holds back civilization and the full citizenship of women."[62] Women believed that they had a responsibility to make their political voices heard in such an important issue as war. The clubwomen of Detroit supported the U.S. war effort with their extensive volunteer work, but they noted the irony of working for democracy abroad while still striving for it at home. Marjory Miller Whittemore criticized Detroit congressmen Charles Nichols and Frank Doremus, who supported the war but opposed women's suffrage. She wrote that they "probably saw nothing inconsistent when they cast their vote in favor of this nation joining the great conflict in [*sic*] behalf of democracy. We can only sadly wish that while championing democracy abroad, the country might have created a real democracy at home."[63] Michigan clubwoman Ella H. Aldinger protested with other Michigan women outside the White House with a sign using Woodrow Wilson's war message about people's right to have a voice in their government.[64] Detroit clubwomen Kathleen McGraw Hendrie, Marjory Miller Whittemore, Betsey Graves (Mrs. Paul) Reneau, Geraldine Sheehan, Lillian Snedicor, Lillian Ascough, and Phoebe Munnecke also picketed the White House. Whittemore and Reneau were among the women jailed for their efforts.[65] Detroit clubwomen emphasized the connection between their war work and the franchise. In a DFWC Board of Directors' resolution they explained that women needed enfranchisement "not only as a just privilege, but as an opportunity to serve the nation with the fullest patriotism at all times, but, especially during the present supreme test."[66]

In November 1918, the state women's suffrage referendum was slated to come before Michigan voters. Once more, organized women in MESA and DESA worked hard for its passage. The campaign was directed by Detroit clubwoman Ida (Mrs. Arthur) Peppers of the DFWC. The Board of Directors of the DFWC issued a resolution pledging their support for "full patriotism" in the upcoming election.[67] Laura (Mrs. A. B.) Cramer's October report of the Legislative Department stressed that clubwomen "must lend every energy for the next few weeks in getting every clubwoman in Detroit interested to the extent of seeing every voter favoring suffrage casts his vote."[68] The lessons of past campaigns were well learned and clubwomen stayed at the polls to watch for irregularities. Although an outbreak of influenza limited the number of poll watchers to only about one thousand, there was less fraud and women's suffrage was passed by 34,506 votes (out of 400,000 votes cast).[69] The 1918 success was due to four factors: an earlier adoption of Michigan Prohibition removed the risk that enfranchised women would vote the state dry; politicians both nationally and statewide had become amenable to woman suffrage; women participated greatly in war work; and MESA persistently promoted woman suffrage.[70]

At the national level, Michigan clubwomen continued to work for suffrage. The Michigan State Federation of Women's Clubs (MFWC) had officially endorsed suffrage in October 1910. In 1918, the DFWC, which now had 6,500 members, sent countless telegrams to senators and the president endorsing suffrage. Senators William Allen Smith and Charles E. Townsend of Michigan were on record as supporting the Susan B. Anthony or Nineteenth Amendment by May 1918.[71] In addition, clubwomen sent letters requesting suffrage support to key senators like George Moses of New Hampshire, William Borah of Idaho, and Edward Gay of Louisiana so that the Nineteenth Amendment might be passed in that congressional session.[72] The Board of Directors of the DFWC adopted a resolution supporting the Susan B. Anthony Amendment and forwarded it to U.S. congressmen Frank Doremus, Charles Nichols, and Patrick Kelly.[73] The overall success of the drive for suffrage for Michigan women could be seen in Governor Albert E. Sleeper's reaction to the congressional passage of the Nineteenth Amendment. On June 5, 1919, the governor wired the State Department in Washington asking that a certified copy of the amendment be sent to Michigan at once. Sleeper wanted the state legislature to vote before the adjournment of its special session. There had been a concurrent resolution passed unanimously by Michigan representatives urging their federal counterparts to support the amendment. There was hope that Michigan might be the first state to ratify the Nineteenth Amendment.[74] Instead, Michigan was the third state to ratify on June 10, 1919.[75]

If we compare the agendas of both black and white federated organizations, we see that white clubwomen were interested in understanding each other's work and unifying their efforts. Black clubwomen were also trying to unify, but they were focused on improving their communities first and foremost. White women's clubs organized first and then took up a civic agenda, while African American women organized to facilitate their civic agenda. This difference can be attributed to two factors: the twenty-five-year lag time between the creation of the white and black federated organizations and the increasing racism in 1920s Detroit. When African American women federated in 1921, they had witnessed the civic success of organized white women even without the franchise. But black clubwomen were facing urgent social problems. The great influx of African Americans into Detroit after World War I heightened existing racial tensions. Both male and female African Americans responded to the deteriorating racial environment in Detroit with calls for equal education, housing, and employment. As Kevin Boyle notes in *Arc of Justice,* African Americans emerged from the Jim Crow South determined to prevent a racially segregated North.[76]

While they had different social agendas, the members of the women's clubs of both races consisted of well-educated, middle- to upper-class women. In her sociological study of the DFWC, Gladys Nauss demonstrated that white clubwomen often had professional training or expertise in a related field. Some were members of professional societies.[77] Many clubwomen were college educated, and they all sought culture and self-expression in their clubs. These women had the resources and free time for club work.[78] Club work could be very time-consuming, and clubwomen were often able to afford domestic help and thus could pursue activities outside the home. Active club member Edith (Mrs. William) Alvord's personal calendar revealed that she devoted four or five days a week to club activities.[79] Club-related activities included attending meetings and lectures that might not be sponsored by the club; members were thus responsible for many of the club-related expenses.[80]

Nauss examined where the DFWC past presidents lived. She concluded that although in 1895 all the club presidents lived within three miles of city hall, as those areas became less reputable, the membership moved to the more upscale outlying areas.[81] In 1922 the DFWC's publication *The Club Woman* pictured twelve of the club's officers and departmental chairs with their own automobiles. At that time, many women were unable to drive and most were unable to afford their own cars. These clubwomen drove a variety of vehicles, but none drove the working-class Model T.[82] In 1926 there were 37 women who comprised the officers, executive committee, and chairs of departments. Of those 37, 29 lived within the same four grids of the fire department map. This means that a large number (78 percent) of the club leaders came from the same neighborhoods. Eleven of the 37 (30 percent) came from the same grid.[83]

African American clubwomen were also among the best-educated and relatively wealthy members of their communities. While in the pre-migration period there were only ten black public schoolteachers in Detroit, half of them were also club members. Clubwomen Delia and Meta Pelham were both from an early elite black family of Detroit. The *Detroit Advocate* said the Pelhams were "among our most cultured and highly respected ladies in the black community."[84]

Victoria Wolcott's extensive research on African American women during this time period has revealed how black clubwomen embraced the notion of bourgeois respectability, which promised uplift for the race but relied on class exclusion within the race.[85] The motto of the NACW, "Lifting as We Climb," denotes racial sameness but connotes social difference.[86] For example, the New Era Study Club was established in 1926 by African American women who wanted the intellectual and cultural stimulation of their school days; many of the members had husbands who were college friends.[87] They described themselves as homemakers, but there was at least one professional member—Miss Grace Murphy, an attorney. They had book reviews, debates, and panel discussions, but they were eager for civic responsibility and the betterment of their community. Since neither the New Era Study Club nor other black women's clubs in Detroit had a clubhouse, their meetings had to take place in private homes with suitable accommodations. In addition, club meetings demanded stylish dress. Wolcott thus concludes that the fashion and domicile needs of clubwomen served as a barrier to those in lesser circumstances.[88] She quotes Detroit Urban League director John Dancy, who described the Women's City Council as women who "seemed to be of a high grade."[89] Thus, in the early twentieth century, clubwomen of both races had privileged class backgrounds and time to devote to club activities.

In spite of these similarities, there were key differences in the lifestyles and motivations of black and white clubwomen. Educated black women were raised with a strong commitment to racial uplift. Black families with resources to educate their daughters inculcated "socially responsible individualism" in them. As the daughters grew to adulthood, they understood that high achievement was not simply an individual crusade but must always be attached to community uplift. Black women oftentimes went to schools that had roots in missionary work.[90] For example, both Sarah Dudley Pettey and Mary McLeod Bethune attended the Scotia Seminary where the founder declared his students would be "motivated by a zeal to serve others."[91] Educated black women always understood their privileged status had a social obligation.[92]

Black women's motivation to serve their communities appeared to be similar to that of some white women, particularly clubwomen.

However, there was a crucial difference: educated black women were engaged in waged work whereas white clubwomen seldom were. Between 1890 and 1954 most black women, even professional ones, needed an income. Professional black women were often expected to do their own cooking and domestic work. When they were in school, they had chores at home to do as well. Consequently, while there appear to be striking similarities between the class statuses of the black and white clubwomen, there were decisive differences as well. Black clubwomen were almost always interested in community service while many white clubwomen were not. Furthermore, white clubwomen failed to comprehend the economic and social challenges of women in waged work, and the gulf between black and white clubwomen only widened.[93]

For myriad reasons there is scant evidence of cross-race cooperation between the women's clubs in Detroit. In 1917, the NACW advised members to seek cooperation with white women's clubs. It emphasized that white women were also campaigning for the civic and moral good of the country.[94] In Detroit, African American women were members of white women's clubs, and two African American clubs belonged to the DFWC. African American clubwoman Mary McCoy had been a charter member of the Twentieth Century Club. Meta Pelham, who was active in the Michigan State Association of Colored Women, was also in the DFWC.[95] In addition, the African American clubs (the Detroit Study Club and the Entre Nous Club) were admitted to the DFWC. Although the Detroit Study Club was admitted in 1900, there was some controversy as to whether the General Federation of Women's Clubs (GFWC) would allow it and thus possibly refuse the DFWC's application for national membership. The DFWC replied that the newspaper accounts were wrong and that it had not been officially rejected by the GFWC. The evidence shows that the DFWC was correct in its assertion that it had not been rejected, and the GFWC admitted the Entre Nous Club in 1922 as well.[96]

Both black and white clubwomen had similar concerns, and there were a few instances in which African American clubwomen sought white clubwomen's support. The Twentieth Century Club hosted Forrester Washington of the League of Urban Conditions among Negroes (later the Detroit Urban League) to address their club. Washington appealed to the clubwomen for their support regarding incarcerated African American girls who were held indefinitely in detention homes. Washington wanted the Twentieth Century Club to request the court appoint a paid investigator for these cases. Club members pledged their support.[97] The issue of lynching was crucial for African Americans, and in this case black clubwomen sought and received assistance from the white clubwomen of the DFWC. The Detroit Study Club wanted the DFWC to join them with signatures endorsing the Dyer Anti-Lynching Bill.[98] Although there is some evidence that white Detroit clubwomen occasionally found common cause with African American clubwomen and there was some cross-race cooperation, it was rare and irregular.

The rare instances of white and black club cooperation in Detroit were more likely to occur before large numbers of African Americans migrated to Detroit. Before the influx of blacks to Detroit there had been some connections between the white and black communities. For example, the Detroit Study Club, which was admitted to the DFWC in 1900, was founded by members of Detroit's old black community. However, during the suffrage campaign, white and black women did not work together, and much of clubwomen's political experience began at that time. Thus there was no consistent pattern of cross-racial cooperation in the crucial years before the franchise. Deborah Gray White explains that when black women worked with white clubwomen, they had to compromise. They could not be candid with white women.[99] Cooperation made for cautious relationships as black women were careful not to overstep racial boundaries that were invisible but enforced.

These barriers became visible during the 1920s when large numbers of African Americans migrated to Detroit and racial lines hardened. In 1921 the *Detroit News* reported that while the Ku Klux Klan membership was not great, its ranks were increasing steadily.[100] In the pre-migration period, Detroit had more fluid racial relationships, but these usually did not involve the activities of clubwomen.[101] Moreover, cross-race cooperation was tangential to the programs of the Detroit clubwomen.

Since the suffrage battle was waged separately, it is no surprise that when Detroit women got the right to vote that policy endured. The

Michigan Equal Suffrage League and Wayne County Equal Suffrage League evolved, respectively, into the Michigan League of Women Voters (LWV) and the Detroit League of Women Voters. The LWV remained nonpartisan and had an open membership.[102] Its activities were to coordinate women's efforts on legislation, but it was primarily a white women's organization.[103]

In the 1920s, therefore, Detroit clubwomen, both black and white, had the vote and were prepared to use it alongside their club organizations. By this time the DFWC included 107 clubs and 15,000 members. The federation's main task was to represent the interests of the city and its residents. The standing committees of the DFWC had changed from mostly informative and cultural (Programs, Free Lectures, Music, Entertainment, Membership, Legislative, and Industrial) to the predominantly public service–oriented committees such as Public Welfare, American Citizenship, and Applied Education and Fine Arts along with a Child Welfare Department and a Civic Department.[104] Member clubs sent their representatives to serve on the DFWC's various committees. In addition, activist Detroit women maintained specific clubs that devoted all their activities to promoting specific public policy, such as the Progressive Civic League led by Ruby Zahn.[105]

The Detroit Study Club added political discussions to their agenda and led the way for African American women to join together in the Detroit Association of Colored Women's Clubs, which encouraged member clubs to take on more political work. In addition there were black women's clubs that were decidedly political. Under the leadership of Elizabeth Gulley, African American clubwomen in Detroit organized the Women's Political League in 1923. It was independent from men's organizations, and clubwomen conducted their own investigations into candidates' voting records and sent letters with their endorsements to female members of the black community.[106] Two prominent African American clubwomen, Lillian Johnson and Veronica Lucas, were also officers of the Women's Political League.[107] Regardless of race, the clubwomen of Detroit were organized, middle-class, educated women who, when enfranchised, considered themselves full citizens entitled to full participation in the political affairs of Detroit, which were becoming increasingly complex.

The phenomenal rise of the automobile industry and the increased industrial production of World War I turned Detroit into an industrial giant. By the early 1920s, Detroit was the third largest producer of manufactured goods in the nation, after New York and Chicago. Its population had grown threefold since 1900, and almost half of that population was foreign born. By 1920 the city's population of almost a million included foreign immigrants, southern blacks, and those leaving the lumber and copper work of Michigan's Upper Peninsula.[108] When foreign immigration came to halt with the start of World War I, the Ford Motor Company and other businesses sent recruiters south to hire black workers to come north.[109] *The Detroiter* (a weekly publication of the Detroit Board of Commerce) used the statistics from the 1930 census to report that from 1900 to 1930, the African American population grew from 4,110 to 120,000.[110] Eighty-one percent of Detroit's blacks were from the South. Thus by 1920, Detroit was vastly more urbanized, industrialized, class stratified, and racially diversified than it had been only twenty years earlier. The city's industrial and urban realities created new challenges for the city.

Many of the new demands being placed on the city did not simply reflect the additional numbers of inhabitants but also a new interpretation of the responsibility a city had to its citizens. Before suffrage, Detroit's white clubwomen had had some influence in this progressive interpretation through their campaigns for healthy recreation, public baths, and school board reform. In all these instances, they had to convince the city fathers these projects or reforms were financially advantageous. Supervised play, they had argued, meant less juvenile delinquency; personal hygiene meant healthier workers; and school board reform meant less money wasted. Clubwomen had to launch massive educational efforts, using statistics and the advice of trained experts. They fought uphill battles because their ideas about the welfare of Detroit's residents ran counter to those of powerful men. As Chicago activist Anna Nicholes asserted, the municipal government "must make the city work for human betterment."[111] Throughout the 1920s, Detroit clubwomen took this message to heart.

The Detroit Chamber of Commerce's *Detroiter* described the many needs of the city in its January 1920 issue. The unprecedented growth of Detroit led to increased demands for city services. Among these needs were new schools and playgrounds, a new main library, a museum of art, and a new prison. *The Detroiter* believed the water supply was presently adequate but if the city's growth continued unabated, a new larger filtration plant would be needed. The city needed better garbage removal. Additional street paving and an extended street railway system were both necessary. The city's geographic and demographic increase meant that the fire and police departments required branch stations. A one-thousand-bed municipal hospital needed to be built. Immense bond issues had to be sold so that these demands could be met. In addition, Detroit would have to employ a large number of people to construct and service the many needs of the city.[112]

This rapidly changing and increasing need for municipal services provided the backdrop for the continuing political activities of Detroit clubwomen. They had learned much from their pre-suffrage political activism, but the pattern of black and white clubwomen working separately continued throughout the 1920s. Michigan men had been only recently converted to women's suffrage and their pejorative attitudes about women's political abilities had not disappeared. Clubwomen believed that an urbanized and industrialized Detroit needed social and industrial reform. They understood from their campaigns for playgrounds and public baths that their vision of civic betterment was often at odds with that of men. Many therefore chose to remain within their clubs where they had been politically effective and where they could pool their organizational and networking skills. By 1920 they were fully franchised and set out to test the political waters of this new status. They used their voting rights not exclusively but as a supplement to their other political pressure tactics. Detroit clubwomen approached the 1920s convinced of the necessity of their civic work but mindful of the potential challenges ahead of them.

2

The Club Work of Enfranchised Women

"Vote, Women Vote"

Lillian Johnson, quoted in Victoria Wolcott, *Remaking Respectability*

By the early 1920s many Detroit clubwomen had established patterns for their enfranchised political activities, which would continue for the rest of the decade. They used their newly acquired voting rights in combination with other political tools they had developed pre-franchise. Throughout the 1920s organized clubwomen promoted a civic agenda and tried to overcome the constraints that hindered their political effectiveness. They formulated strategies for political work that involved not only the study of contemporary political, social, and economic issues but the dissemination of information for public education. They pursued projects to educate voters and to encourage them to get involved in the political process. This agenda offended few, cost little, and suited clubwomen's philosophy that an informed polity would make sound judgments. They were most effective when they employed their franchise in great numbers, could demonstrate that their ideas and programs would benefit the community, and maintained a unity of purpose. However, even though black and white clubwomen often embraced similar agendas, they rarely crossed racial lines. At the same time, both black and white clubwomen presumed they spoke for larger groups of women. Black clubwomen assumed their education and status put them in a position to represent all black women. White clubwomen had similar ideas but believed they spoke for all races and classes of women. By 1920 Detroit clubwomen had carved out a place for themselves in Detroit politics but strove to enlarge their political space throughout the rest of the decade.

Politically active women created coalitions with organizations led by men when the two groups had common cause, and clubwomen supported male candidates who shared their philosophy and enacted legislation they supported. But white clubwomen's views diverged from those of the men of their class from time to time, causing clubwomen to pursue their own agenda. For example, they tried to make Detroit politics more accessible to the public through an unofficial pre-primary convention and a state law for permanent voting registration. They specialized in networking among themselves and grassroots activism. Their organizational ability was respected, and white clubwomen's counsel was often sought by city officials. But clubwomen continued to be perceived as auxiliary members of the body politic rather than full-fledged citizens. Clubwomen thus employed a variety of strategies to maximize their political strength.

Detroit clubwomen, both black and white, faced the post-suffrage era with cautious optimism. When women in Michigan were on the verge of the franchise, the DFWC had organized a Legislative Committee within the federation to study national, state, and city legislation. This committee focused on child labor laws, compulsory education, and the ratification of Prohibition as well as women's suffrage. The DFWC believed that both industrial reform and social improvements were necessary for American society to avoid being "hopelessly defeated in the competition of peace." Therefore clubwomen would support legislators who saw the value of community life and the necessity of protecting men, women, and children from industrial economic and social evils. Women had learned from the war that a country's most valuable assets were its people, not simply property. They now sought social welfare legislation that would eliminate the need for organized charity so that future generations would have less social conflict.[1] Charity alone was futile; real reform would happen only when the causes of poverty were addressed.[2] African American clubwoman Elizabeth Gulley claimed that charity would not be necessary if black women worked to ensure that children received quality education. Black clubwomen focused less on charity and more on programs pertaining to health, education, and day care.[3]

Detroit clubwomen were responding to the massive industrial growth of Detroit during World War I. They saw the social dislocation that accompanied it and looked to political institutions to provide solutions.[4] As they looked to the state, white clubwomen professing to represent all women rarely addressed the problems of the black community. African American women understood that the programs and policies advocated by white women usually did not include them or their community so they established programs in their own communities. In this manner, they were pursuing the policy of the NACW as it combined club work with that of civil rights.[5]

The franchise was another weapon Detroit clubwomen used to pursue their civic interests. In this regard they were part of a larger women's movement of civic involvement that attempted to integrate women's political culture into the previously all-male political process.[6]

At the same time, both political parties made a show of welcoming women, but disparaging remarks from those quarters told women they would probably only be apprentice members there. Belle Moskowitz, advisor to Al Smith, said, "The major political parties are still man-made and man-controlled. Few of their leaders can work with women on a basis of equality."[7] New York women faced obstacles to political power similar to those of Detroit women. When New York women got the right to vote and hold office, they were rarely elected. The vote had not altered traditional gendered ideas and they remained outside the circles of policymaking in the parties. In Detroit as in New York, "Society still expected men to lead and women to serve."[8]

The political environment in which they were enfranchised opened new but limited possibilities for municipal activity. In Detroit, white clubwomen had successfully appealed to their local and state governments before the franchise to secure public baths, playgrounds, and school board reform. It stood to reason that they would continue doing political work within their organizations. Also, while most clubwomen were interested in general civic betterment, they were, like many Progressives, uncertain whether this could be accomplished in partisan politics.[9] This was especially true in Detroit, where the pre-1918 city charter politics had abused the public trust. The noted exception to this skepticism about partisan politics was the *National Association Notes,* the official organ of the NACW. This periodical combined club and political work in printing articles promoting the Republican Party written by Detroit and Michigan women, among others.[10]

Regardless of whether clubwomen joined a political party, they were convinced that they should make full use of the franchise. Edith Alvord said, "Voting is evidence of peace-time patriotism."[11] In the first primary to include women in 1919, the *Detroit Times* reported that women were as numerous as men at the polls.[12] The paper also noted that Detroit women's clubs had been studying the upcoming election since Michigan women received the vote in November 1918. The women showed their interest by voting in proportionally larger numbers than men. Women made up only 25 percent of the registered voters but cast 40 percent of the vote in the March primary.[13]

Black club leaders Elizabeth Gulley and Lillian B. Johnson claimed that in Detroit African American women were so politically active that it was much easier to get these women registered to vote than it was to get black men to vote. Gulley and Johnson gave no explanation of or evidence for this statement, although it was in a paragraph regarding the Women's Political League founded by Gulley, which maintained its independence from men's organizations and endorsed its own slate of officers. The club was very active in get-out-the-vote campaigns in the black community in Detroit.[14] There were also a large number of African American women who were officers and executive board members of the NAACP; out of a possible fifteen executive board members, six were women.[15] Still, these women's efforts here appear to be only one part of a much larger effort regarding the use of the franchise for both men and women in the black community.

White women in Detroit exhibited an independent streak in terms of how they voted. The *Michigan Citizen*, the Democratic mouthpiece, claimed that Michigan women were not content to simply "vote as the husband does" and that they made intelligent inquiries about taxes, services, and so forth.[16] For example, Ella H. Aldinger accepted an appointment as a delegate to the Ingham County Republican Convention even though her husband was a Democrat.[17] The *Detroit News* continued to be impressed by the number of women who voted and said the tremendous registration has "shown conclusively that the new woman voter is taking her duties most seriously and is determined to do her best by the city and state."[18]

There is some debate among scholars as to whether Michigan's women voters reflected what was happening in other states. Since states did not separate voting by gender (except Illinois from 1913 to 1921), it is impossible to determine exactly how many women voted. Some evidence suggests that black women voted in larger numbers than white women but in equal percentages as black men.[19] However, recent scholarship by Loraine Schuyler concludes that in the 1920s in the American South the proportional increase in voters exceeded the percentage increase in population; thus southern white women's votes account for this difference. Schuyler claims that white women's efforts to increase voter participation explain this trend.[20] Throughout the country, the 1920s saw low voter turnout due to a decrease in party affiliation, the presence of immigrants, and the voter realignment of 1896. Although the number of women who voted varied from region to region, women who were civically active were more likely to vote than those who were not.[21]

Civically active Detroit clubwomen were acutely aware that now that they had the franchise they were embarking on a new relationship to government that required them to be conscientious and diligent. When Lillian Smith Mathews spoke in 1922 of "Woman as a Working Power," she stressed the connection between public policy and the home as well as the fact that politically active women must take part in the social and economic life of their communities. The DFWC further believed that good citizenship was a result of the exercise of the franchise.[22]

As was typical of many clubwomen, Mathews combined club work with other passions. She was a tireless worker for women's suffrage and later a valued member of the LWV. She was the chairperson of the Detroit Committee for the county LWV and president of the DFWC from 1922 to 1924. She also maintained a partisan interest and was the vice chairman of the Wayne County Republican Club.[23] In this way she combined her club work with party politics to maximize her political influence. Many clubwomen did the same, although some preferred to remain in their clubs solely to engage in political work.

Elizabeth Gulley was another clubwoman who combined partisan politics with her club work. She was a member of the National League of Republican Colored Women and traveled to their conventions around the country.[24] However, she was not content to simply do political work within the Republican context, so she founded the African American Women's Political League in 1924. Its leadership consisted of prominent black women like Veronica Lucas (founder of the Detroit Association of [Colored] Women's Clubs) and Lillian Johnson (member of the Detroit Study Club and executive secretary of the NAACP). In 1924, on behalf of the Women's Political League, Gulley wrote to Lucia Grimes to offer her support for Grimes's candidacy for the state legislature. Gulley told Grimes that as chair of the Michigan State Association of Colored Women's Clubs, she would "be glad to help you in any way possible."[25]

Gulley explained that black clubwomen were also "learning the power of the ballot." She added that clubwomen had responded by demanding the state oversee charities and they focused club attention on education. Consequently, black women altered their club programs in light of this new political tool.[26] In a speech to the Detroit Study Club in 1923, Lillian Johnson outlined the needs of women and how they could be achieved with the ballot. She chastised women for not pulling together to help elect women to anything other than school boards or prison commissions. She also stressed that it was a crucial time for women because, with unity, they could make politics "an instrument of service to the community and not just a man's game."[27]

Lillian Bateman Johnson was a pre-migration Detroiter who, though employed by the *Detroit Independent* as a bookkeeper, was an extremely active clubwoman: she was a founder of the Detroit Study Club, worked at polling stations during elections, was secretary of the NAACP, and was an active member of the Second Baptist Church.[28] She spoke of unity in her speech to the Detroit Study Club, but most white clubwomen did not share her views, even though the club was part of the primarily white DFWC. Other black clubs, such as the Progressive Mother's Club, applied for admission in the DFWC but were never admitted.

Cross-racial cooperation was often problematic for African American women, many of whom distrusted white people with good reason.[29] Still, they were in a bind. The black activist and settlement worker Victoria Earle Matthews believed African American women were best represented by black women, although she agreed with many of her race that they needed white women as allies. Black women understood that white women were partly responsible for racial oppression, which reinforced white hegemony. Furthermore, many of the policies white women championed were tacitly, if not explicitly, for whites only.[30] Thus black and white women's clubs pursued separate civic agendas while both black and white women joined political parties individually and worked together within the framework of the party.

The records of both black and white women's clubs testify to their separate but similar agendas. The DFWC considered itself a nonracial organization (it had admitted the black Detroit Study Club in 1900), and it does seem likely from the information available that black clubwomen reached out to white clubwomen for support on issues such as vice and lynching. However, the lack of cooperation resulted from white clubwomen's preference to interact with black women in small groups and of a higher social class. Before the exponential population growth of African Americans in the 1920s, white clubwomen had some interaction with black clubwomen because a few African Americans belonged to white clubs. Black activist Fannie Barrier Williams said she experienced trouble with interracial work and "soon discovered that it was much easier for progressive white women to be considerate to one colored woman whom they chanced to know and like than to be just and generous to colored young women as a race."[31] The early black clubwomen came from a community that was much smaller than the black community of the 1920s. Although many en gaged in waged work, it was white-collar work; thus these working women were of a higher class than the uneducated southern migrants and hence more "acceptable." For example, the black upscale Entre Nous Club was admitted to the DWFC in 1922. As migrants from different races and classes poured into Detroit, racial distinctions took on a new importance. Even though black clubwomen were of a higher class than the migrants, their race became the more important factor to white clubwomen in the 1920s.

In 1926 the mayor of Detroit formed the Committee on Race Relations after a riot occurred (in which one person was wounded and another was killed) when a black family moved into an all-white neighborhood. The Rev. Reinhold Niebuhr served as chairman, and

The Executive Board of the Detroit Federation of Women's Clubs in the 1920s. Arthur J. Lacy Papers, 1891–1975, Box 9, Bentley Library, University of Michigan.

Bishop William T. Vernon of the African Methodist Episcopal Church was vice chair. The committee included business leaders and lawyers of both races, and the only two female members were clubwomen: Pearl (Mrs. Charles M.) Novak came from the DFWC and Mrs. C. S. Smith was a member of several African American women's clubs. Although the committee was composed of prominent members of both the white and black communities, the committee's 1926 report is laced with inherent racism. First, the report indicated that many whites believed separation of the races was conducive to better relations between them. Second, the report made a crucial distinction between "old" black Detroiters and new migrants: while most educated blacks maintained their property and "[kept up their] personal appearance and demeanor," crime was rising because of the "incomplete adjustment of the recent southern immigrant." Third, the report referred to southern blacks as "retarded" because of their lack of education but speculated that this situation would improve over time. Fourth, the committee recommended that the Young Women's Christian Association (YWCA) open a vocational school for black women to learn domestic science, household arts, and home nursing. Finally, the report stated that many southern migrants were dependent upon the Department of Public Welfare because "many of this class take dependency for granted." Thus many whites in Detroit believed that there were "good" African Americans ("old" black Detroiters) and "bad" ones (southern migrants).[32]

The DFWC faced a dilemma. Its philosophy dictated that it represent all women of the city. The report of the Legislative Department in October 1923 (about five months after the black Progressive Club failed to be admitted to the DFWC) declared that the DFWC was a "non-racial, non-political, non-sectarian organization, whose goal is to educate, study, investigate and disseminate the negatives and positives of all laws being legislated."[33] However, many members of the DFWC promoted middle-class values and segregationist policies, though not explicitly as doing so would have undermined their claim to inclusion and their justification for leadership. The continued affiliation of the Detroit Study Club within the DFWC and the acceptance of the Entre Nous Club indicated a willingness to associate with higher-class Detroiters. As the decade wore on, race supplanted class as a unifying factor, and no additional black women's clubs were admitted to the DFWC.

Civic effectiveness through club unity, rather than racial cooperation, was stressed in the early years of full franchise at the local level. Dora MacDonough, chairwoman of the Civics Department of the DFWC, reported in January 1921 that officeholders understood that the DFWC had ten thousand members (and thus potential votes), although even politically active clubwomen seldom voted as a bloc.[34] Lillian Johnson urged her fellow members of the Detroit Study Club, "Vote! Women vote! Running this government of ours is a joint job for both men and women. Now that we women have our full civic and political rights, it is just as much our duty to see that the right people are elected to office."[35] Although women did band together at times to defeat politicians, the expectation of universal bloc voting proved false.[36] Instead of relying on all women to vote the same, Dora MacDonough believed that if Detroit clubwomen dedicated themselves to civic betterment, officeholders would take notice.[37]

The Detroit LWV members also recognized that with the franchise, women had enhanced power to change public policy. Women's civic work could be more effective if they were unified within their clubs. Majorie Elaine Porter, club editor for the *Detroit News,* wrote that "[Clubwomen's] vision of women united, working with concerted effort toward the same goal of betterment of self, home, community, nation and the world, promises advancement and accomplishment."[38] Porter wrote of unity, but she reported on white women's clubs only. If unity existed, it would be among the white leadership. Ida Peppers, president of the Detroit LWV in 1922, said that the LWV existed for "uniting the country's woman power into a new force for the humanizing of government."[39]

The LWV purported to have an open membership policy, and in 1925 Katherine Keefe (Mrs. William) Warren directed the formation of a black women's group of voters for the LWV in Detroit.[40] There was no further mention if Warren had been successful. But for Peppers, "uniting the country's woman power" certainly meant under the leadership of white women.[41]

The Detroit LWV wanted to bring politics to the Detroit neighborhoods so they reorganized to allow for greater participation. Throughout the 1920s the LWV displayed two hallmarks of women's traditional political behavior when they combined educational work with grassroots organization. In January 1924, the increasing population and geographical size of metropolitan Detroit caused the Detroit LWV to expand their organization to include all of Wayne County. The Wayne County LWV began a campaign to encourage more informed voting among women. The LWV understood that women were new to politics and inexperienced, which could cause them to make poor voting choices and lead to the defeat of important legislation. All women were entitled to membership in the Wayne County LWV.[42]

Although the LWV had expanded to reach the suburbs, it realized that its strength lay in an organization that was responsive to the local level. A year later, the Wayne County LWV reorganized to allow more grassroots participation. The larger districts were divided into precincts, and the precincts were subdivided into blocks. Each block had an LWV captain who lived in the block and was responsible for the members who lived in that neighborhood.[43] When the LWV held meetings, they were in the community and run by a local board of directors.

The LWV's failure to include most black neighborhoods as part of their new suburban expansion prompted black women to organize similar programs during the 1920s.[44] Elizabeth Gulley encouraged African American clubwomen to use their franchise and lobby the state to pass legislation to address community problems and not simply resort to charity as a remedy.[45] For example, the members of the New Era Study Club, which originated as a study and fellowship club for African American women in 1926, felt that their work should address the needs of the community and that the club should not be so insular. They "eagerly accepted the responsibilities of citizenship, namely working for the betterment of the community, therefore, New Era."[46] The Las Cheres Amies Club of teachers' college students also devoted itself to civic problems, such as the education of young black children.[47] Even the Detroit Sorosis Literary Art Club devoted a meeting to the subject of "Women Voters and the Political Issues of the Day."[48] The Detroit Study Club's yearbooks are filled with meetings devoted to subjects like capital punishment, the Johnson immigration bill, juvenile court, civics, and social philanthropy.[49]

Beulah Alexander (Mrs. James) Young recognized the importance of grassroots organization and founded the black Political Leaders Assembly, whose main goals were a better community, a better government, and 100 percent registration and voting among the black community.[50] Later she was appointed by Mayor Frank Murphy to serve on the Mayor's Women's Committee as well as Governor Fred Green's state Women's Committee. She established the *Detroit People's News* and published it from 1924 to 1930. She was a tireless worker for her community and upon her arrival in Detroit she was determined to influence the politics of the city.[51]

The Political Leaders Assembly included men and women but women held the most prominent executive positions. Young was president; Eva Jackson was first vice president; Eleanor Saunders was second vice president; and Mary Rhodes was chairperson of the Executive Committee. The assembly emulated the organization of the Second Baptist Church, which served a large congregation but addressed the needs of individual families.[52] The Political Leaders Assembly was divided into neighborhoods; each neighborhood had an assembly president and assembly members. On the first and third Mondays of every month, the neighborhood groups met and discussed local issues. These meetings were for serious political work only. On the second Monday, the assembly presidents and recording secretaries convened with the president and officers of the general body at the offices of the *Detroit People's News*. Led by Young, they discussed psychology, Americanization, good public behavior, social ethics, home economics, parliamentary law, good political leadership, and other community issues. On the fourth Monday, a general mass meeting was held. Special speakers were invited, assembly presidents presented their block reports, and there was an open forum in which members could ask questions and voice concerns. In this way Young attached a grassroots organization to a larger body for more political clout.[53]

With energetic crusaders like Young, the mobilization efforts of women's organizations tended to have a favorable impact on female voter turnout.[54] Women's clubs were especially good at educating the public and networking among themselves. Detroit clubwomen often spent several weeks studying one particular issue. Early in the decade, the Board of Directors of the DFWC carried a motion that "sufficient printed material be provided for information regarding all legislation the Federation is supporting; that winter all clubs be urged to study these bills so that all will be well-informed."[55]

Clubwomen believed that as voting citizens, they needed to constantly study political issues; this was a legitimate part of club work. Their informative programs rarely challenged entrenched political or economic interests and therefore were quite successful. In addition, clubwomen discovered interesting and innovative programs from other cities and states and adapted them for their own use. Among these would be the permanent voting registration reform that the LWV secured in the late 1920s.

Well-informed clubwomen became community leaders who understood that civic education was crucial to their political credibility. As a result, the Wayne County LWV established "citizenship schools" for women. During these seminars women studied many of the most important issues of the day and heard speakers who discussed such issues as the child labor amendment, women's relation to the three branches of the government, how taxes fund the government, international relations, and the process of nominations and elections. These seminars, which were several days long, also addressed such controversial issues as faith versus reason. They also had a variety of representatives from the areas of commerce, labor, religion, and women's interests speak before the clubs. Lastly, they discussed international peace.[56]

In election years, white clubwomen sponsored "candidates' days" to educate women voters and to ensure that women's issues were addressed by candidates. Candidates were allotted a specific amount of time (usually five to ten minutes) to address the women. Many women's clubs, including the Wayne County LWV, Northwestern Women's Club, Women Citizens' League, and DFWC, held candidates' days throughout the 1920s. White clubwomen sometimes cosponsored candidates' days with the Detroit Citizens League and other men's organizations, although on such occasions the candidates were not always prepared to discuss women's issues.[57] In August 1920, at a meeting prior to the municipal primaries, candidates spoke to women who were interested in good government. The candidates discussed important issues but knew little about women's concerns such as mothers' pensions, equal guardianship, and the eight-hour working day. Politically minded Detroit women made it their business to see that these issues were addressed.[58]

Like white clubwomen, black clubwomen believed that as voters, they needed to be politically informed. They, too, invited speakers to their clubs for political education. They understood that political education was their best defense against being politically marginalized. Throughout the country and in Detroit, both black and white clubwomen brought attention to issues of concern to them and other women, signaling a shift in campaign appeals from an emotional to a factual one. When candidates spoke, women demanded a question-and-answer session afterward.

The importance of these meetings to the candidates themselves varied. In 1923 candidates spoke to Wayne County Woman's Republican Club, the Woman's Citizen League, the Progressive Civic League, and the LWV. In the early 1920s, fearing the new political power of women, candidates were eager to capture the female vote.[59]

Although candidates sought female votes, there was a decline in voting rates in general during the 1920s. The LWV joined other clubwomen who mounted a response to the falling vote totals with get-out-the-vote (GOTV) campaigns and voting reforms, which included both primaries for candidate selection and permanent registration. They sought these reforms because they wanted to open up the choices in the electoral system, stimulate civic interest, and make voting easier. Although these reforms were supported by men and the community as a whole, in Detroit, they were primarily initiated by women.

In 1920 the DFWC joined with the LWV, Woman's Republican Club, Women's Democratic Club, WCTU, YWCA, and Eastern Star to conduct a house-to-house canvas of wards and voting districts in a drive to register women.[60] Only 54.7 percent of the total eligible voting population of Wayne County voted in the 1920 election. The LWV took voting seriously and labeled those who did not "traitors." The league feared a low voter turnout meant the "rule of the indifferent many, by the selfish few" and encouraged every woman to help get out the vote. They understood that when women exercised their franchise it was a powerful political weapon.[61]

Although clubwomen understood the power of the ballot, falling voter participation continued to be a problem. The women were the primary motivators to counter this trend throughout the decade. The *Detroit News* noted that before women were given the franchise, no one had heard of a get-out-the-vote drive. Prior to the 1924 presidential election, the Wayne County LWV engaged other clubs like the DFWC, American Association of University Professors (AAUP), YWCA, American Legion Auxiliary, Detroit Board of Education, Detroit Federation of Churches, and Boy Scouts in a general campaign to help get out the vote. Each organization had a representative on a general committee with Dorothea (Mrs. Harry) Steffens of the Wayne County LWV as chairman. Automobile caravans traveled throughout the city with signs telling people to vote. The Board of Education instructed children to urge their parents to vote, and church bulletins included election calendars. Five thousand Boy Scouts went door-to-door with campaign literature encouraging people to vote. Within the clubs themselves, all those who voted would stand at the meeting after the election; the goal was to have 100 percent of all club members standing.[62]

GOTV campaigns took place nationwide. Some claim they stemmed from a fear that upper- and middle-class voters were abstaining while radicals were voting. Working-class organizations were not prominent in the GOTV campaigns.[63] But in Detroit the picture was more complex, and there is no evidence that Detroit clubwomen held these fears about radicals. However, there was racial anxiety. In 1923 the *Detroit Free Press* reported that large numbers of blacks were voting, thereby introducing an "underworld" element in Detroit politics. The article was subtitled, "Voters Flock to Registration Office to Offset Massing of Negroes." It described an unsubstantiated claim that scores of black women and men had registered with false addresses and that the "better class" of citizens, both black and white, did not want this. It also equated the franchise for black Detroiters with a criminal element. The article ended by erroneously saying that there had been no election irregularities until recently.[64]

The GOTV programs were directed toward white citizens; black citizens had to conduct their own voter encouragement programs. The African American Second Baptist Church urged its members to vote. In an article titled "Special to Members," Rev. R. L. Bradby urged his congregants to "give equal opportunity and advancement of the community in which you live."[65] The African American Women's Political League met throughout the entire year and actively promoted voter registration. They made house visits and even provided transportation to city hall for registration.[66]

Historian Liette Gidlow has argued that white clubwomen joined businessmen to promote their own dominance in the political system. Gidlow disagreed that clubwomen were altruistic and class neutral; she noted that the GOTV campaigns were not conducted evenly throughout the city.[67] Gidlow's accusations are not entirely applicable to Detroit. Although there is no evidence in club records that white clubwomen excluded black neighborhoods from their GOTV campaigns, African American women had to make their own GOTV arrangements and did not mention working with white women. However, many programs that clubwomen initiated, such as permanent registration, were prompted in part to help ease the registration burden on the poor and on factory workers. They always claimed that when more people voted the government would be more representative, and they never spoke of racial qualifiers.

Greater voter participation in Detroit was hampered by a variety of factors. Among these was the lack of primary elections for city positions. In 1923, the Legislative Council of Michigan Women reported that the convention system of nominating candidates was controlled entirely by the political bosses.[68] This closed system led to voter indifference. The white women in the Highland Park Women's Club sought to address this apathy with their plan for a pre-primary convention. Laura Cramer, chairman of the Citizenship Committee of the Highland Park Women's Club, sponsored this plan. Inspired by the idea of the old town meeting, she planned to invite every organization in Highland Park, including church organizations, women's clubs, commercial organizations, trade unions, noonday luncheon clubs, and fraternal organizations. The purpose of the ensuing meeting would be to discuss the apathy surrounding Highland Park politics.

The meeting was a reaction to the previous election in which so few candidates were nominated that there were no primary elections. The president of the Highland Park Women's Club, Mrs. J. J. Livingstone, said, "Everyone is veering off from politics through fear of being called a politician, and by doing so, is playing directly into the hands of the politicians who have everything their own way!!" Livingstone emphasized that the town meeting was not an affair of the women's club but rather one of the whole city. The Highland Park Women's Club took the initiative because no one else did. No matter the outcome, there was a feeling among the women that raising the issue contributed to raising the civic conscience of Highland Park residents.[69]

At the town meeting in December 1925, a resolution was unanimously adopted to call a town pre-primary convention in January 1926 and to have the Highland Park clubwomen assume this responsibility. During the interim, the attending clubs and organizations went back to their own groups and discussed who would be the best choices for public office; they would present those names at the convention. The town meeting was attended by prominent people representing professional and social groups and presided over by Livingstone. In an effort to alleviate the feared prejudice toward a political meeting initiated and led by women, she felt obligated to state that the women were not going to "do anything emotional or anything to embarrass you."[70] Cramer, the first speaker, stated that the intent of the plan was not to promote any one individual, class, or group but to provide a greater quantity and quality of people for public office. She claimed that it was difficult to encourage voting when people felt that their vote did not matter. Edith Alvord, chairman of the Citizenship Committee of the DFWC, spoke and acknowledged that there was a nationwide trend toward apathy in politics; she challenged the Highland Park community to lead the way in arresting that trend. Mayor Gittins also spoke in support of the primary, and the women's initiative for a pre-primary plan was adopted.[71]

The *Detroit News* headlines proclaimed the first of the two Highland Park pre-primary conventions in January 1926 as making civic history. At the first convention, the names of fifty-one eligible, desirable nominees for mayor and the city commission were put forth. Those who nominated the candidates had one week to send their reports to George Bohm, chairman of the Committee on Candidates, for consideration. After this process, a second meeting would be held to select several of the ablest. The response from the various civic, fraternal, religious, and other organized groups was better than expected. The *News* reported that the first town meeting held none of the "steam roller" tactics associated with partisan conventions. Furthermore, the usual bickering was diminished by a community spirit. The *News* claimed that the meeting was the result of the efforts of intelligent men and women without personal agendas and with only the community well-being in mind. Livingstone was unanimously chosen as chairman of the second convention and former Michigan representative Fred E. Dunn as secretary.[72]

The second convention took place a week later and was short and efficiently run. George Bohm reported that six nominees had withdrawn their names. Of the remainder, only fourteen sponsors had issued reports for their candidates. The reports were read and the meeting was adjourned. Some people arrived late after the speedy adjournment and claimed it had been a "crooked" meeting. Livingstone replied that the purpose of the convention was simply to read the issued reports and adjourn. There were no endorsements and if persons arrived late, unable to submit a report, it was unfortunate. Livingstone stressed that all the rules had been laid out and were followed to keep the convention as fair as possible.[73]

The object of the pre-primary convention had been to arouse voter interest and have a slate of qualified nominees from which the voters could choose. Livingstone claimed that because some of Highland Park's best citizens had been nominated, the new system had been a great success. In addition, the opening of grassroots nominations through various clubs provided added interest.[74] Clubwomen were successful in this instance because the pre-primary convention faced little organized opposition and the *Detroit News* provided consistent favorable reporting on the convention.

Most clubwomen did not follow Cramer's lead into electoral politics (although she was nominated to the city commission, she was not elected), but Detroit clubwomen continued to try to stimulate interest in elections. One of the most successful reforms advocated by white clubwomen that benefited all citizens was permanent voter registration. Clubwomen joined forces with other civic groups, scholarly and administrative experts, and male legislators to successfully institute permanent voter registration in Michigan. This reform was needed in Detroit and other large municipalities because Michigan law required complete re-registration every presidential election in communities of over five thousand citizens. Voters could only register at city hall, which was convenient for people who worked downtown but burdensome for women, factory workers, and those who lived in the outlying areas. By the late 1920s, citizens could not vote because of registration difficulties. In 1927 there were 456,937 registered voters in Detroit, reflecting an increase of 28,206 new voters and 22,092 address changes in a ten-day period in October 1927.[75] The last registration day for the 1928 election saw 21,000 citizens lined up to register at city hall. The Election Commission had 130 clerks on hand and practically the entire city hall was given over to the work of registration, but the situation remained impossible. The unprecedented growth of the city increased the population and meant that people had to wait for hours to register. Some were even turned away.[76]

Voter registration reform was necessary and other civic-minded organizations assisted the MLWV in this campaign throughout the decade, although there is no evidence that African American clubs were among them. Throughout the decade, the Detroit Citizens League worked with the Wayne and Michigan LWV regarding permanent registration.[77] In addition, the LWV worked with scholarly and administrative experts on permanent registration. In December 1928, Governor Fred Green allowed the LWV to have a hearing with the Commission for the Revision of Election Laws. The commission saw the benefits and asked the LWV to draft a bill.[78]

In 1928 Michigan joined sixteen other states in passing a permanent voter registration bill, which stipulated that a voter need only register once in a lifetime rather than every four years. This would be not only more convenient for the voter but also ultimately less expensive for the city. The original changeover to the permanent system was costly at the outset but cheaper to maintain over time.[79]

The Permanent Registration Bill, as drafted by Senator Claude Stevens, passed with only three minor compromises. It was not mandatory in rural (defined as less than five thousand residents) districts, had no literacy test, and allowed registration on election day if the voter had been absent from the city on the last registration day. The Michigan state legislators gave the MLWV full credit for the bill's passage.[80] The *Detroit News* reported that the MLWV had realized its political opportunity and offered a constructive piece of legislation. The *News* believed that it was a fine example of civic spirit.[81]

The LWV was not only the major promoter of permanent registration but was also instrumental in the installation and operation of the law. They educated voters by making speeches, showing exhibits, and sponsoring newspaper and radio publicity. They also answered an unfavorable press by defending permanent registration against attacks. The league enlisted people and organizations in an effort to get 100 percent registration in the original list. They also ensured that the system was properly administered by closely cooperating with the chief registration officials. They remained available for consultation and demonstrated their significant knowledge of the law.[82]

Clubwomen had valuable allies in their sponsorship of permanent voter registration. The Detroit Citizens League was a consistent supporter, along with the *Detroit News*, political science experts, and even the governor himself. In this way, clubwomen maximized their political efficiency to achieve voting reform.

Clubwomen's constant study of civic affairs coupled with their club responsibilities and visibility in the community went a long way toward dispelling the notion that women's clubs were simply pastimes for women with leisure. While admitting that might have been the case fifty years earlier, the *Detroit News* said, "But since then, the woman's club has taken root in community life, and its product, the trained clubwoman, is more than justifying its existence by public service."[83]

The women's club connection to the community was well understood because one of its chief functions was to train women for service to the community. The same *News* article stated that Pearl Novak, Edith Alvord, and Ethel L. Thomas (respectively, executive secretary of the International Institute for the YWCA, treasurer of the Highland Park Board of Education, and lunch room conductor for the Detroit Schools) were all past presidents of the DFWC. It explained that the clubs acquaint women with the needs of the community, give them contact with the public, and help them develop self-confidence. The article noted that the knowledge and ideals of women's clubs were consequently applied in a practical way. The days were long past when a woman's responsibility was strictly within the home. While Alvord agreed that club training helped educate her for her position on the Highland Park School Board, she cautioned against the idea that some of these community positions were therefore best served by women. She stressed that the best community service was possible through the collaboration of men and women. Novak explained in an interview that her experience as president of the DFWC was a "second college education" and that it was the mission of the women's clubs to stimulate interest in the community. Novak claimed that clubs stress not only information but action as well.[84]

African American women did not join their clubs first and later decide to serve as leaders in their communities. Their club work was always tied to an agenda of community uplift. Some of the members of Detroit's black women's clubs were also engaged in professional work. These women had been raised with a high degree of community consciousness, which meant that their achievements would be measured by their service to the black community. For example, Beulah Whitby graduated from Oberlin College in 1920 and came to Detroit two years later. She joined the YWCA and met southern female migrants arriving in Detroit. She helped these black newcomers find housing and jobs. She later joined the Women's Division of the Detroit Police Department and by 1931 became a social worker for the Department of Public Welfare.[85]

According to reports in the *Detroit News*, by the mid-1920s the number of women who were exercising their right to vote was increasing.[86] But club leaders feared these reports were sometimes overstated. Nonpartisanship, no traditional female voting history, and the criticism some women received for voting from family and friends contributed to this problem. The club editor for the *Detroit News*, Marjorie Elaine Porter, reported in 1926 that clubwomen were not attending candidates' days in large numbers. Attendance at candidates' days reflected the campaigns they represented; and tightly contested campaigns drew larger crowds.[87] The evidence about clubwomen's attendance at candidates' days is difficult to quantify. In their letters and papers, Edith Alvord, Dorothea Steffens, and Mrs. Harry Woodhouse all admitted that they would have preferred larger attendance at candidates' days without further explanation.

Detroit clubwomen who were politically active wanted to enhance their new position as enfranchised voters and therefore cooperated with male organizations.[88] Women were wary, though, about how men's groups might receive them. There was already a movement to bring white women, whose husbands supported the Detroit Citizens League's values, together to discuss civic matters. Mildred Lane Simpson was one such member. She stated that women would not be dictated to as members now in what had been male-dominated organizations. In a letter to the executive secretary of the Detroit Citizens League, Pliny Marsh, Simpson insisted that a woman be included on the executive board. Simpson claimed that women would shun men's organizations if they were not allowed to have leadership positions in previously all-male organizations. She ended her letter by saying that women would lose confidence in the Detroit Citizens League if membership and council seats were not offered to them.[89] Marsh replied that the bylaws of the league would be amended appropriately to increase the size of the executive board so women could take new places. He added that every effort would be made to give "public evidence" that the league advocated cooperation between men and women in civic matters.[90]

Male organizations were cooperative, but cautious, about their association with women's clubs. Members of the Detroit Citizens League often gave lectures to white women's clubs, especially the DFWC. The Detroit Citizens League worked with many women's groups like the LWV, WCTU, YWCA, Eastern Star, and Women's Republican and Democratic clubs in an effort to influence clubwomen.[91] But when the Woman's First Campaign League wanted to maintain their political work under the name Women Citizens' League, the Detroit Citizens League objected. Marsh, the attorney for the Detroit Citizens League, argued that people would associate the name Women Citizens' League with the Detroit Citizens League. Marsh claimed that since the Detroit Citizens League had had that name for many years, the women should be the ones to change the name of their organization.[92]

The Women Citizens' League board considered Marsh's request

and refused. Marsh had suggested the women adopt the name Good Government League. The women directors knew that an earlier organization by that name had endured some unfavorable publicity and they "smiled at the proposal." The women held that there was a significant enough difference between the Detroit Citizens League and the Women Citizens' League to prevent misunderstanding. The organization was therefore incorporated under state law as Women Citizens' League.[93]

Clubwomen understood the importance of political education and continued to emphasize it. Their educational programs demonstrate the political sophistication of clubwomen in both world and national politics. For example, the MLWV understood that excessive war reparations could lead to armed conflict so they supported the Conference of Nations' attempt to settle such economic problems.[94] In 1928 the Wayne County LWV conducted a three-day citizenship class that focused on the experiences of women in party caucuses, conventions, and direct primaries. They investigated the nomination process and more particularly the role of women in that process. Clubwomen understood the importance of the nomination process and wanted their voices heard.[95]

In their effort to educate voters, the Wayne County LWV pioneered new ways to communicate with them. In 1924 the LWV began to publish a weekly question-and-answer column in the *Detroit Sunday News*. Voters would send questions to the league and the *Sunday News* would publish the answers.[96] By 1930, the National LWV teamed up with the National Broadcasting Company (NBC) to provide a "Voter's Service" to disseminate information on issues likely to predominate in the current election. In May 1930, the program addressed the new tariff (Hawley-Smoot) and specifically the new duties relating to agriculture, industry, and foreign trade. They engaged speakers from Congress, industry, and the Foreign Policy Association.[97] In this way, women's organizations reached out to a larger audience with civic education.

Throughout the 1920s Detroit's politically minded clubwomen, black and white, strove to maximize their political strength through the use of the franchise. Much of this strength came from their organizational and networking ability. Detroit clubwomen worked toward greater political inclusion of the public with voting reforms and informational meetings. In addition, both black and white clubs constantly studied political issues, believing that informed voters were more effective. In a decade in which voter turnout declined nationally, clubwomen in white and black communities in Detroit and the suburbs fought this trend by stimulating election interest and initiating get-out-the-vote campaigns. White clubwomen occasionally joined white male organizations to pursue similar political agendas, but white clubwomen never united with African American women to do the same. White clubwomen continued to presume they were the most articulate spokespersons for all women, black and white. However, black women understood that white clubwomen advocated programs and policies that were overwhelmingly for white recipients only. Detroit's African American clubwomen continued a tradition of service via activism in their own communities. The historian of the Detroit Association of (Colored) Women's Clubs, Mrs. Senora D. Smith, explained, "It was difficult in those days. [My] people didn't have anyone to help them. We had to take care of our own. We just saw needs in our community and took care of them."[98] In spite of a huge contradiction between assumptions and reality, white clubwomen clung to their belief that they spoke for all women. It was this belief that led them to speak loudest when promoting policies for women and children.

3

Policies That Affect Women and Children

We believe in the glory of woman,
Her influence, her motherhood blest.

New Era Study Club Song, "Early History of the New Era Study Club"

Once women gained the franchise, they began voting in large numbers, which caused politicians and policymakers to take notice—they began to reach out to women for their perspective on issues that concerned the home.[1] Detroit clubwomen realized that they could be a powerful factor in the community in various ways. In light of all the changes that were occurring in Detroit in the early twentieth century, both socially and economically, clubwomen believed that mothers' love and education would be the best way to produce a healthier society.

Detroit clubwomen's activities reflected those undertaken by women throughout the country. In many American cities, clubwomen linked the private to the public through "scientific homemaking"; they believed that educated, organized housewives could help improve public health and make cities cleaner. Their position as mothers prompted them to campaign for playgrounds, building inspectors, and classroom supplies. They lobbied for community improvement, including projects such as libraries. As they were the primary champions of many of these projects, they established female influence in these public spaces.[2]

When women used motherhood as a wedge into civic activism, they advanced policies that were class oriented instead.[3] Certainly women reformers were committed to motherhood, but their ideas of motherhood and womanhood were in direct opposition to the realities in the lives of many black, immigrant, and working-class mothers. Women reformers were opposed to industrial homework because they believed it turned the home into a factory, but for many women, this type of work was the key to their family's survival.[4]

Because Detroit's white clubwomen did not understand working-class women, they also failed to reach out to African American women's clubs. The recent migration of southern blacks presented class and racial issues for white clubwomen, who increasingly reflected the racism of Detroit's white population. Even though all clubwomen, black and white, were interested in the political and economic status of women, mothers' pensions, the Sheppard-Towner Maternity and Infancy Act, and child labor legislation, they did not unite to affect public policy and thus their political influence was diminished. Most were divided on the issue of further equal rights for women, and they wavered on child labor.

During the 1920s race became a volatile issue in midwestern cities. The Great Migration brought enormous numbers of black southern migrants into industrial cities, which were already crowded with large numbers of foreign immigrants. Whites reported feeling "strange" when they encountered African Americans, who had been previously few and far between in these cities. Many whites believed that white Protestant culture was not merely the preferred way of life but far superior as well.[5] These people provided fertile ground for Ku Klux Klan (KKK) organizers, who enrolled tens of thousands of new members in the Midwest and West during the 1920s. In the mid-1920s Michigan had more members of the KKK than any southern state but still less than Indiana, Ohio, and Illinois.[6]

During the Great Migration southern whites also moved to Detroit in large numbers. In the KKK's mass initiation ceremony in June 1923, one thousand people joined. The Klan nearly elected a mayor in Detroit in 1924 and burned crosses in front of city hall and the Wayne County Courthouse.[7]

While whites joined the Klan for a variety of reasons, even non-KKK members began to erect racial barriers in employment and in their communities. Retail shops and restaurants refused to serve black customers. Real estate agents, bankers, and insurance agents worked together to keep black residents in certain areas of the cities. Neighborhoods prevented blacks from moving into their communities by establishing protective associations that forbade selling houses to African Americans. This hardening of racial barriers was not an organized conspiracy but a collection of formal and informal agreements that resulted in solid racial divisions within midwestern cities.[8]

Southern blacks migrated to acquire privileges that they understood to be theirs as Americans but that only whites enjoyed in the South.[9] Black ghettos became increasingly crowded in urban areas, and blacks competed with whites for housing and employment. Blacks' determination to make a better life for themselves was greeted with the equal determination of whites to deny them those opportunities. Throughout the Midwest in cities like Chicago, the new migrants threatened the racist social system of white superiority.[10]

Detroit's women's clubs were not immune to this racial discord. For example, in April 1923 the black Progressive Mother's Club of Detroit applied for and was refused membership in the DFWC. The objective of the Progressive Mother's Club was to better the homes of African American people of the city. They were advised to apply in the fall of 1923. However, there is no record of the club's acceptance by the DFWC or of why they were denied membership.[11] In 1916, when the DFWC had applied for membership in the GFWC, the DFWC risked rejection because it had allowed the black Detroit Study Club to join the DFWC, and in early 1922 the DFWC had risked expulsion from the GFWC when it accepted the Entre Nous Club, whose members were affluent black women from the West Side. Perhaps the increasingly deteriorating racial climate of the 1920s motivated the DFWC to reject the Progressive Mother's Club. Earlier, we can see from the Detroit Study Club's scrapbook that other clubs, such as the Jewish Woman's Club, the Twentieth Century Club, and the New Century Club, invited the Study Club to join their organizations.[12] Some members of the Detroit Study Club (Mary McCoy and Meta Pelham) were also members of white women's organizations.

The white Detroit Woman's Club became increasingly uneasy about interracial mingling in the 1920s; in their club minutes they expressed concern about and addressed the issue of black and white students sharing the same facilities. The club agreed that both parents and students would be more comfortable in separate schools, understanding that separate facilities would mean greater expense, but they felt that the increased costs would be minor compared to the expense of teaching foreign immigrant children. The club made an amendment to go on record as supporting racial segregation.[13] The Detroit Woman's Club wanted to use educational resources to racially separate children.

In an article published in *The Detroiter* in 1919, the Detroit Board of Commerce reflected the same racial attitudes apparent in the mayor's report later in the decade. The board enumerated the immense problems associated with the influx of large numbers of African Americans to Detroit, distinguishing between established black Detroiters, who were literate and mingled freely with whites in the center of the city, with the new migrants, who were illiterate and brought their "filth" with them into the "nicer" neighborhoods.[14] The "old" black Detroiters were not happy about the arrival of the southern migrants either, viewing blacks of lesser means as "vulgar." Forrester Washington wrote that the migrant "does not receive a warm welcome from the great majority of colored citizens of the better class."[15] Detroit's old black community also wanted to preserve their elite position.[16] Established black Detroiters (and many whites) viewed migrants, who were obviously of a lower class, as alien and to be avoided.

In their clubs, African American women focused on the connection between the home and the municipal government for political and social purposes. Black clubwomen believed that by establishing respectable, middle-class homes, blacks would be recognized as worthy members of that class and garner the respect they deserved, thereby contributing to racial uplift in general. Black clubwomen "stressed motherhood, cleanliness and home life as central to uplift."[17] In the *National Association Notes* Elizabeth Gulley wrote that black clubwomen must work to better the housing conditions in congested cities. She explained how overcrowding, especially in homes with male boarders, led to "the unmarried mother's problem." She advised clubwomen to work with local social agencies to remedy this situation. Gulley also believed that disruptions in the home had social consequences; families must be "awakened to the understanding of the problems revolving around the child-life because of neglect." It was clubwomen's responsibility to try to solve these problems in the home.[18]

Like white clubwomen, black clubwomen were in the elite class and failed to understand that poor black women's choices were controlled more by the economy than by any lack of morality. Thus black female low-wage earners made choices that were disapproved of by white and black reformers.[19] Black reformers, male and female, oftentimes were so committed to bourgeois values that it prevented them from understanding the exploitative nature of industrial capitalism.[20] They were distracted from such economic realities as they pursued the patriarchal family with bourgeois morality and its attendant female domesticity.

African American clubwomen in Detroit could not simply employ their strategy of Victorian female domesticity amid the growing, vicious racism in the city. The guiding theory of the NACW that the race would progress when its women did became less potent.[21] African American clubwomen needed to protect their homes not simply from an immoral environment but also from the physical violence that plagued them. While white clubwomen were understandably less worried about racial violence, both white and black women's organizations emphasized the connection between municipal policies and the home in an urban environment. In 1923 African American club leader Lillian Johnson addressed the Detroit Study Club about the concerns of all Detroit clubwomen; she said that they wanted cleaner streets, better sanitation in bakeries and meat shops, better milk inspection, adequate fire protection, cheaper food, better housing, protection for women and children in industry, better child labor laws, and better institutions for the incarcerated.[22]

As white clubwomen emphasized the importance of the home, they also valued the position of the homemaker. They requested that the secretary of commerce recognize homemakers on the 1930 census and thereafter. The DFWC resolved that "wife, mother or in place of one, [who] is caring for home and family be designated as Homemaker."[23] Clubwomen thought that women's role in the home was the great common denominator for all women, and they felt that they spoke for all homemakers.

Clubwomen's exaggerated assumptions about their capacity to speak for all women were reinforced by others in the community.

The *Detroit News* claimed that the role of clubwomen (probably white clubwomen) in the 1920s was to bring the "progressive" world to the home. The clubwoman was the link between the two.[24] Since women thought that their civic activity was the bridge between the two, they believed they had a responsibility to take part in the economic and social lives of their communities.[25]

Detroit clubwomen were concerned about issues pertaining not only to the home but also to the status of women. As franchised, politically active women, they felt they occupied an ideal position from which to speak for all women. But they did not understand the needs of all women and were not unified on the issue of equal rights. Once they had achieved their political franchise, some Detroit clubwomen pressed immediately to alter women's legal position.

In 1923, the president of the Women Citizens' League, Jennie Patton Beattie, and Detroit's state senators, George M. Condon and Donald A. Wallace, drew up a bill recognizing the legal equality between husbands and wives. Senator Condon said the woman's rights bill rested on two assumptions: that a husband and wife were equal partners and entitled to rule the house and share the responsibility for it, and that a woman marries to better, not hinder, her condition. The bill declared that a married woman should have all the rights of a single woman—to sue and be sued, to make contracts, to seek employment, and even to choose to establish her own domicile. Furthermore, both husband and wife were head of the household and both were entitled to the earnings of their minor children. Most Detroit clubwomen were concerned about the potential loss of protective labor legislation, so there was a special section saying it did not affect the employment of women in industry. The proposed Michigan law was an attempt to stop the legal disabilities of married women and provide the same rights, privileges, and immunities as men. Senator Condon pledged his complete support for these measures, both in the Judiciary Committee of which he was chairman and on the Senate floor, but the bill failed to pass in 1923.[26]

The Women's Bill of Rights had some high-profile supporters among white Detroit clubwomen, including Emma A. Fox and Harriet Robinson McGraw (Twentieth Century Club), Lillian Ascough (vice president, Michigan branch of the National Woman's Party), and

Lucia Grimes (president, State Legislative Council of Women).[27] Despite this support, the bill met a great deal of opposition among clubwomen in general. They feared the bill would not only remove the common law disabilities of married women but eventually remove protective legislation as well.[28]

The controversy surrounding women's rights reflected a similar division among activist women around the country. Nancy Cott's work reveals heated debates among former suffragists regarding the Equal Rights Amendment. Women like Alice Paul and the members of the National Woman's Party (NWP) advocated total legal equality for both sexes. Their ideology stemmed from a strain of liberal individualism and a desire to free women from a political classification that needed special state attention. The League of Women Voters, National Consumers' League, and the National Women's Trade Union League all feared their work for female protective legislation would be jeopardized by such legislation. While Paul insisted that the amendment was not aimed at destroying protective legislation for women, the wording had to be broad enough to accomplish its goal: equality between the sexes.[29]

Detroit clubwomen also feared that the removal of protective legislation would hurt working women. By 1920, Detroit was the third largest U.S. city for manufacturing. One-sixth of all Michigan wage earners were women, one-fifth of whom were married. A high percentage were gainfully employed until age forty-four (37 percent of female workers were between the ages of twenty and twenty-four, 18 percent were between twenty-five and forty-four). Consequently, when women had the greatest responsibility in the home, they were also employed. The increase in the number of women wage earners was not simply a temporary reaction to abnormal conditions.[30] The Detroit Study Club devoted an entire meeting to a debate about whether married women should be employed in industry. Meta Pelham and Lillian Johnson argued that married women should be in the workforce, and Kate Johnson and Delia Barrier argued against.[31] Regardless of the debates, the women were in the workforce to stay. Edith Alvord agreed, adding that women were important wage earners for their families; they did not simply work for "pin money."[32] The DFWC's annual report of the Civics Department for 1921 claims that

85 percent of working women were supporting others through their work.[33]

With more women in the workforce, Detroit clubwomen sponsored legislation to make the workplace more suitable for them. In 1919, the Political and Civic League (whose name changed shortly thereafter to Progressive Civic League) had worked to establish restrooms for women on each floor of a large office building. This effort was in response to the deaths of two young Detroit women who, in their haste to return to work, had fallen into an elevator shaft on their return from the restroom on another floor.[34] The Board of Directors of the DFWC sent letters to downtown department stores urging them to provide restrooms for their sales ladies.[35] The Political and Civic League also tried to establish lunchrooms for businesswomen in the downtown district. Clubwomen asked their Michigan senators to support the federal Hawes-Cooper Bill, which required merchants to provide chairs for female clerks. They subsequently monitored compliance with the bill because they felt the law had loopholes.[36]

While white clubwomen strove to make the workplace more suitable for women, they were aware that the problems of an industrialized, urbanized Detroit required both political and economic solutions. Still, white clubwomen were in a dilemma. They were seldom wage earners themselves and did not fully understand the needs of either working-class or professional women. To cite just one example, Theresa Doland, an attorney, was hired by the Women Citizens' League (of which she was a member) in April 1919 to draft the articles of incorporation for the league. (The league had passed a resolution supporting women's rights to do any work for which they were qualified.)[37] When Doland charged a fee for her services, a fundamental difference between clubwomen and working women became apparent. She sent the bill for her services to the league, but the league never paid it. She later brought suit against them for this debt. She was distressed by the league's unprofessional behavior and complained that the clubwomen had no sense of responsibility. Jennie Beattie, who supported equality between husbands and wives, ironically protested that oftentimes women gave their money and services gladly for the benefit of all. She and other members believed that as a member of the league, Doland should follow suit.[38]

Clubwomen's position on further equal rights for women rested on their own experiences and what they thought was best for middle-class families, not business-minded women. White clubwomen's advantaged status blinded them to the problems of working-class women. In an article in the 1923 *Club Woman* titled "Reform Begins at Home," white clubwomen were reminded that they were the employers of their servants. As such, they should adhere to the same standards regarding work hours, labor, and work conditions that they demanded of shops and industries.[39]

The Louisa St. Clair Chapter of the Daughters of the American Revolution (DAR) failed to understand the many responsibilities of working-class women. They sponsored a cottage industry in which immigrant women could sell their handiwork. An article praising the program appeared in the *Bulletin of Women's City Club*. It claimed that *after* doing their housework, these immigrant women would sew "far into the night." The article described the work as beneficial, not onerous, because it gave "their homesick minds something to think about not the newness of the U.S."[40]

Clubwomen were also perplexed by mothers as wage earners. In discussing the proposed new law prohibiting night work for women, the Women's City Club recognized that some women with children might prefer night work. Work at night allowed them to be at home with their children during the day (although clubwomen failed to address how working women would actually implement that type of schedule). In 1919 Michigan had prohibited night work for women under age eighteen, but this law did not apply to 95 percent of the working women in the state.[41] The proposed law would extend this prohibition to all women. As the City Club discussed this proposed law, they understood that this might present problems for some mothers, but they believed that no protective legislation for all women would do more harm. Consequently they supported the night work prohibition for women although this law was not passed.[42]

Another instance of clubwomen's insensitivity toward the socioeconomic realities of working-class women was their campaign to encourage women not to buy bread but to make it at home. Jessie (Mrs. Alexander) MacDonald, who claimed to have always baked her own bread and thus saved money, inspired a bread-making contest sponsored by the *Detroit News*.[43] As a privileged leader in local white club circles, she failed to understand the situation of less fortunate women and women who worked outside the home. In an article in the *Detroit News* she claimed that homemade bread was more wholesome for children and thus mothers who "have any regard" for their children's health should bake their own bread since it was "cleaner" and had no chemicals added.[44] Making bread, however, was not always possible for working women, whereas MacDonald's husband was a doctor and she admitted that bread making was her hobby. She conceded that apartment kitchens might make baking difficult but that it was still well worth the effort.

African American clubwomen who lived a comparatively privileged lifestyle were also wage earners, albeit in professional positions. Still, they had trouble understanding the economic choices of their working-class black sisters. Many black clubwomen who worked for wages did so as teachers, journalists, or attorneys. The meetings of the Detroit Study Club were thus held at night because women got into the "world's work during the day."[45] In 1923 when the Michigan State Association of Colored Women discussed the position of working women, they conceded that the labor of black women contributed to household budgets in a meaningful way.[46] They would have agreed with Edith Alvord that women were not simply working for "pin money." However, the association discouraged the practice of allowing men to board in the homes of African Americans, even though the rent derived from this practice helped households. African American clubwomen's emphasis on middle-class respectability became increasingly at odds with the practices of some working-class black women who, by necessity, had to carve out less "respectable" strategies for themselves and their families.[47]

Even if black and white clubwomen failed to understand working-class women, they generally agreed that women had the right to work and the right to equal pay. They oftentimes, but not always, believed that protective legislation for women was especially important. Edith Alvord addressed this dilemma in 1920 in an article in the *Club Woman* titled "Equal Opportunities for Women Wage Earners." She stated that the GFWC supported protective legislation for women but that the Women's Equal Opportunity League opposed it. Alvord pointed out that "the effective field for women's work is broadened by protective legislation." She understood that industry leaders would not voluntarily institute a limit on the number of hours in the workday, and the alternative only led to exhaustion. Alvord concluded that a laissez-faire policy toward women who worked in industry resulted in oppressive, exploitative conditions.[48]

This explains white clubwomen's opposition to the Condon bill. They sometimes sought policies for working women that were at odds with their actual needs. In this instance, the supporters of equal rights were at odds with many clubwomen. Women's political effectiveness was fragile, and strident differences over expanded women's rights caused this issue to remain problematic throughout the decade.

Black women were concerned about how certain policies affected working women but also about the racist nature of employment in Detroit. To address some of these issues, black women founded the Progressive Women's Civic Association in 1925: "These ladies are always on the alert to any problems pertaining to our race, and they aid in remedying them if possible." For example, they agitated successfully for jobs for African Americans at the Kroger supermarkets in the black section of the West Side.[49]

The ways in which white clubwomen addressed the importance of white working mothers' time with their children demonstrated their belief that the best caregiver for those children was their mother; they thus strove to keep mothers and children together. However, this same mentality did not apply to black working mothers, whom white clubwomen viewed as simply workers, not as women or mothers. For example, when the Detroit Urban League requested the endorsement of the DFWC for a day nursery for black children in 1928, the DFWC not only "heartily" supported this proposal but also pledged that the Child Welfare Division of the DFWC would donate chairs, tables, and financial aid to help meet this "important need."[50] In the eyes of white clubwomen, black women who stayed at home with their children exemplified "female loaferism." White maternalists constructed a cultural route for the equality of motherhood, but their racism prevented black mothers from even getting on that avenue.[51]

White clubwomen were ambivalent about working black mothers; they facilitated their work with support for day care but also championed mothers' compensation to keep all poor mothers at home with their children. They had strongly supported the passage of the Mothers' Compensation Law in Michigan in 1913. In January 1921 organized white women, meeting in Lansing, complained that the enforcement of the Mothers' Compensation Law was at the discretion of a judge who could deny relief. They wanted a new law to make it mandatory. The 150 women at the meeting represented more than 100,000 organized women and were united in their complaints about the law. An Oakland County judge even stated that it was unconstitutional, although the State Supreme Court affirmed its constitutionality. Ruby Zahn reminded judges that the people of Michigan supported provisions for the compensation of widowed mothers and that home life must be preserved. The *Detroit News* characterized Zahn as a tireless worker who would spend "as many as twenty hours a day to further some project." She worked not only for mothers' pensions but also for prison reform.[52] She declared, "We are going to get a more just and sympathetic interpretation and application of these laws or we are going to chase some of the judges in Michigan off the bench."[53] Zahn used the credible threat of women's votes to demand compliance with the Mothers' Compensation Law.

Other clubwomen spoke at the January 1921 meeting and bolstered their case for mandatory mothers' compensation by revealing their knowledge of the laws that applied to women and children. Furthermore, they understood how these laws were administered by courts and executive officers. Women wanted payments to be on a cost-of-living basis, not simply a flat rate. Zahn presented statistics demonstrating that a mother and child needed twelve dollars per week to live, which could include other sources of income such as wages, help from relatives, and assistance from charities. Zahn agreed that judges could decide whether a mother qualified for the compensation, but if she were qualified, he had to order payment.[54]

The battle over Mothers' Compensation in Michigan continued to be centered on the amount of payments and the discretion of probate judges. White clubwomen wanted a more generous stipend but ultimately supported the McArthur Bill, which stipulated not only a six-dollar maximum but also a four-dollar minimum. Weighing their chances for success, the women were forced to compromise further by accepting a two- to ten-dollar weekly stipend. They feared that if they forced a fight in the legislature, they might lose altogether.[55] In this instance, clubwomen focused on the crucial mandatory nature of the law rather than exact dollar amounts. The final bill allowed probate judges to fix any amount between two and ten dollars if there was only one child.

Afterward, the probate judges were seen as "burying" the Mothers' Pension Bill in the Judiciary Committee. The Progressive Civic League sent a letter to Representative Ralph Liddy, chairman of the Judiciary Committee, advising him that the people of Detroit supported mothers' pensions and asking him to release the bill. Zahn planned to see Representative Liddy in person to urge the same.[56] Finally, two years later, in January 1923, the clubwomen supported the Hense Amendment, which limited the absolute power of probate judges in administering the provisions of mothers' pensions.[57]

Mothers' pensions would only be awarded if a woman had had no support for two years due to the death of her husband or divorce from or desertion by him, if her husband was in a mental or tuberculosis institution, or if she was unmarried. The program rested on the assumption that the mother was the child's best guardian. If the mother had only one child who was fit to work, she was not eligible. Boarders were discouraged, but money from relatives was encouraged. The pensions were awarded according to need; the goal was to enable a mother to receive 65 percent of the income she would have had with an employed husband.[58] This system of awarding pensions tended to reinforce traditional gendered roles—mothers' pensions were designed to keep a family together until a better arrangement (meaning, permanent attachment to a male breadwinner) could be worked out. Pensions were possible because they were advocated as a cost-effective measure compared to institutionalization. The payments were kept at a minimum to highlight the savings, and they were promoted as preventing delinquency.[59] But even here, there were racial limitations to mothers' pensions as black women made up only about 3 percent of the recipients. Aid usually went to white, English-speaking widows, and there were different budgets for various nationalities.[60]

Ironically, maternalists understood that all women were vulnerable economically because they were dependent on men, but they supported a program that created dependency. They usually were in favor of protective legislation and child labor laws, but they seldom supported day care or maternity benefits, which could have afforded mothers the opportunity to work and thus not be dependent on the state. The prominent supporters of mothers' pensions, such as the GFWC and the National Congress of Mothers, certainly wanted to assist poor mothers and their children, but at the same time they promoted the social importance of motherhood. Motherhood, according to historian Sonya Michel, was the raison d'être for their political activities. Although the GFWC and the National Congress of Mothers gained political authority through their advocacy of mothers' pensions, their insistence that a mother's place was in the home meant that women who were working in the least-skilled and poorest-paying jobs found little common cause with upper-class clubwomen.[61]

White reformers' ideas about mothers' pensions also highlighted their racial and cultural ideas. Maternalist reformers believed mothers contributed to the state by raising good citizens; therefore, they should get aid. They hoped immigrant women would learn the "proper" way to raise their children. They wanted to impose their traditional gendered ideas on immigrant mothers and get modern medical information out to mothers. They used their concept of motherhood and attached public importance to that concept to Americanize immigrant children and alleviate the problem of cultural diversity. This meant that middle-class women attempted to teach ethnic women how to keep house and raise their children. They sponsored a series of intrusive home visits, during which social workers and nurses would evaluate child-raising methods and inform mothers about health and hygiene.[62]

The Michigan Mothers' Compensation Law allowed small stipends for qualified mothers but also carefully scrutinized how those payments were dispersed. In 1924, Clara Saunders of the Juvenile Court Detention Home described this process to a meeting of the Civic Department of the DFWC. She explained that 1,059 families had applied for pensions in 1923. The mothers who qualified were given a bank account, from which they could make house payments. They were required to keep receipts of all their expenses. There were unusual variations in the program; for example, Italian mothers received 10 percent less for food because it was thought they their diet required less, and tubercular families received 10 percent more because it was thought that these families needed better nutrition and larger quantities of food. The pension program was closely monitored, as administrators were constantly on the lookout for fraud, especially by immigrants. There were eight to ten fraudulent cases every month as unqualified foreigners tried to get aid. Consequently, careful investigations were carried out. Additionally, the pension officer dispensed discipline and advice about thrift.[63]

In the early 1920s while Detroit women were imposing their ideas about "proper" motherhood through pensions, the federal Sheppard-Towner Infancy and Maternity Protection Act was being debated in Congress. Detroit's white clubwomen supported this legislation, which would provide federal and state subsidies to clinics that educated mothers about health care for their babies in the hope that doing so would reduce the rate of infant mortality. Throughout the country white clubwomen used their organizational abilities and political clout to secure the act's passage.[64] In the effort to secure Sheppard-Towner matching funds, white clubwomen pioneered the pressure tactic of the personal interview with a legislator to get their votes. Earlier Ruby Zahn had practiced this technique with Representative Liddy over mothers' pensions. The clubwoman would sit privately with the legislator and make a personal plea for his vote. This differed from traditional lobbying by making the contact more personal. Recognizing this potential power, Edith Alvord advised civic-minded clubwomen to attend public hearings and have personal interviews with legislators.[65]

The 1921 report of the Legislative Department of the DFWC listed at least six Michigan congressmen who were in favor of Sheppard-Towner. Representatives John Esch, Edward L. Hamellin, and Frank E. Doremus were actively seeking its passage. Representative Esch informed the DFWC that Sheppard-Towner was favorably reported out of committee but opposition remained. Some congressmen wanted to shelve the act because they feared that it would promote birth control; others felt it would violate states' rights by putting state money under federal control. The clubwomen responded with a letter campaign to the Honorable Phillip Campbell, chairman of the Rules Committee, House of Representatives, demanding a date for a vote.[66]

When Sheppard-Towner was finally passed and signed into law on November 23, 1921, Michigan women lobbied to secure its passage in Michigan as well. (The federal law provided funds, but each state had to pass enabling legislation.) Governor Alex Groesbeck respected this effort and signed Sheppard-Towner into law because the Michigan legislature was not in session. Still, the Michigan legislature had to approve the appropriations and there was opposition to Sheppard-Towner funding. The Wayne County Medical Society, for example, urged the legislature not to pass the Sheppard-Towner appropriations. Once more, the white clubwomen took action. Dr. Blanche M. Haines, director of the Michigan Bureau of Child Hygiene and Public Nursing, spoke to a meeting of the DFWC and emphasized that Sheppard-Towner provided education to mothers and infant clinics for the poor. DFWC women were quite vocal about their indignation against the Wayne County Medical Society, believing that with the federal matching funds there would be an opportunity to make a real difference for needy mothers.[67] Prior to the acceptance of Sheppard-Towner, Michigan had spent only $29,000 per year through various state bureaus on infant and maternal health, but with federal matching funds, this amount would double ($30,000 in 1923, by 1929, $65,000).[68]

By March 1923 the Sheppard-Towner appropriations bill passed the senate in Lansing but was held up in the House Ways and Means Committee. Blanche Haines once more turned to women's organizations for their support. She wanted representatives of women's clubs to confer with Representative Farrier, chairman of the Ways and Means Committee, to get the bill reported out. There were strong political forces to kill the bill, but personal conferences with members of the committee and increasing public pressure secured the passage of the appropriations bill.[69] Ultimately, the civic-minded women prevailed and Michigan voted funds for Sheppard-Towner. Dr. Richard Olin, commissioner of the Michigan Department of Health, wrote to the DFWC members to thank and congratulate them. He said, "There is not the slightest doubt but that the affirmative vote in both the Senate and House was due entirely to the unremitting efforts of the organized women of the state."[70]

Women's groups met in Lansing the following July to discuss Sheppard-Towner's passage and implementation in Michigan. Among those present were representatives of the MFWC, LWV, WCTU Congress of Mothers and Parent Teacher Association, Ladies of the Maccabees, Woman's Benefit Association of the Maccabees, and the Michigan Agricultural College Extension Division. These representatives drafted organizational plans for cooperating with the State Health Committee to coordinate and disseminate information. Dr. Haines wanted this committee to be composed of members from women's organizations to gather information like a state census of the children in the state. She wanted to enlist clubwomen's help in getting the information out about Sheppard-Towner to needy mothers.[71] Clubwomen successfully combined their political clout, organizational abilities, and respect for women's issues to achieve the passage of the Sheppard-Towner act and its appropriations in Michigan.

The clubwomen helped secure Michigan funding for Sheppard-Towner in 1923, but the funding had to be renewed every two years. Sheppard-Towner appropriations were extended in Michigan in 1925, 1927, and 1929. By 1929, Michigan was appropriating $65,000 for Sheppard-Towner funds.[72] But in June 1929 the federal legislation was due to end. White clubwomen mobilized to support the (unsuccessful) Newton Bill, which would have continued maternity and infancy health work.

Michigan clubwomen believed that the Sheppard-Towner bill and its results had proven beneficial to mothers and babies. In an article written for the *Michigan Woman,* Dr. Lillian Smith, director of the State Bureau of Child Hygiene, described the many Sheppard-Towner successes over the decade: twenty-one thousand children had been examined by doctors and nurses at infant and preschool clinics; lessons on child and infant care for adolescent girls (Little Mother's League) had been established in all counties; and classes in prenatal, infant, and child care had been offered to and attended by women. Dr. Smith also mentioned that infant mortality had dropped in Michigan since the passage of Sheppard-Towner: in the five years prior to the act's passage, the mortality rate was 88 out of 1,000 births; in the five years after the passage of the act, that rate decreased to 76 out of 1,000; and in 1927, the rate further decreased to 67 out of 1,000. Maternal mortality dropped as well: before the act, 7 out of 1,000 mothers died in or soon after childbirth; after the act's passage, that number declined to 6 out of 1,000. Smith estimated that without Sheppard-Towner, there would have been 415 more maternal deaths and 5,680 more infant deaths.[73]

The Sheppard-Towner legislation reflected the views of white clubwomen regarding the proper role of women. The act also promoted certain cultural ideas as white maternalists tried to modify the behavior of immigrant mothers regarding how their children should be fed and how their homes should be maintained.[74] Progressive Era activist Sophonisba Breckinridge said that Sheppard-Towner was simply an extension of women's traditional roles in the family and neighborhood. Women assisted in childbirth, helped with newborns, and nurtured children. Sheppard-Towner was simply raising those responsibilities to a national level.[75] Not everyone viewed the legislation this way; some saw the delegation of federal funds as a form of communism. The *Dearborn Independent* reported that the leadership of women's organizations had fallen into the hands of radicals; a congressional committee even investigated this claim.[76] Thus, while clubwomen celebrated the success of Sheppard-Towner legislation in Michigan, the seeds of its demise had already been planted.

In addition to being concerned about mothers and infants, clubwomen wanted more societal protections for children. The federal child labor laws of 1916 and 1919 had both been ruled unconstitutional by 1922. As a result, there was a national effort to pass an amendment in the 1920s that would have given Congress the power to regulate and limit labor for those under eighteen. In her November 1923 report the chairman of the Legislative Department of the DFWC wrote that the federation was against child labor.[77] Mary Church Terrell, president of the NACW, advised the members to support the Child Labor Amendment. Terrell claimed that this was "humane and beneficent legislation" of vital interest to all women. She appealed to women in states (like Michigan) where the legislation had been rejected by one house to write to their representatives in support of it.[78] However, in Detroit, the membership campaign for the National Child Labor Committee was disappointing. This committee had worked to get federal and state laws forbidding child labor. In the 1920s they focused on getting approval for a national child labor amendment.

Although a good number of Detroit women's clubs gave generous gifts to the committee, few clubwomen were willing to engage in an all-out effort to prevent child labor. Although the DFWC was the first Michigan organization to join the National Child Labor Committee, they did so without active participation. DFWC president Pearl Novak noted that clubwomen were good at helping needy children but not as good at passing preventive measures.[79]

The members of the DFWC were lukewarm in their support of the Child Labor Amendment in part because they were uncertain as to what the federal government's role should be in labor legislation. Gertrude (Mrs. Arthur) Wallace, chairman of the Legislative Committee of the DFWC, explained to the *Detroit News* that the DFWC supported child labor legislation but wondered whether this particular issue was best remedied by adding another amendment to the Constitution or by allowing each state to determine for itself whether to enact such legislation. Wallace said that women were being accused of being motivated by sentimentality and adopting policies without knowledge of their ramifications. The DFWC planned to debate this issue to explore all the possible effects of child labor legislation. At an upcoming meeting, this debate would be conducted with members representing both sides of the issue. The DFWC worried that the proposed national prohibition of child labor under the age of eighteen would have a profound effect on the Detroit school system.[80]

Although the DFWC members were halfhearted in their support of the Child Labor Amendment, the MLWV turned to civic action in support of it. The MLWV joined the nationwide effort to exert pressure on U.S. senators and congressmen for the most comprehensive bill and frustrated efforts to weaken it. They addressed various organizations and spoke about the benefits of the law. They closely monitored political candidates as to whether they supported the amendment. Michigan legislators were ambiguous in their opposition to child labor. In April 1924 Michigan senators Woodbridge Ferris and James Couzens voted for the amendment in the Education and Labor Committee, but neither of them voted for it in a June Senate vote. In the House, only seven of the twelve Michigan congressmen voted for passage.[81]

The passage of the Child Labor Amendment proved problematic for Michigan clubwomen for several reasons. Mary (Mrs. Craig) Miller of the State Legislative Council of Michigan claimed that the Booth Syndicate controlled the powerful newspapers in the state. This syndicate followed the lead of the National Manufacturers Association in issuing editorials against the amendment. In Michigan, these editorials especially targeted the farmers. Although the MLWV sent counter-circulars in favor of the amendment, they lost the media war.[82]

The issue of child labor also raised sensitive issues about the home. In Michigan some state senators opposed the amendment because they felt it would destroy parental authority and responsibility. This, in turn, would make children more rebellious and give tyrannical, centralized authority to Congress.[83] Not all Michigan women were taken by arguments of tyrannical federal power. In a report on the 1925 legislature, Ella Aldinger of the State Legislative Council noted sarcastically that while the fish of Michigan were fed and protected, a federal amendment for the protection of children was considered communist propaganda.[84] With media opposition reflecting the interests of Michigan's big business and clubwomen's ambiguous support, there was little state support for a national child labor amendment. The campaign by clubwomen to prohibit child labor demonstrates the limits of women's political work. Clubwomen were often passionate supporters but not in an organized, large-scale manner.

As Detroit rapidly industrialized and urbanized, Detroit clubwomen addressed the resulting social dislocations. White Detroit clubwomen were confident that their views were good for all women. African American clubwomen were equally confident that they knew what was best for black women and the uplift of the race.

The passage of the Nineteenth Amendment led some women to press for greater equality and others to hold back. Clubwomen of both races acknowledged a woman's right to work but often failed to understand the choices of their working sisters.

While Detroit's white clubwomen advocated both mothers' pensions and the Sheppard-Towner Maternity and Infancy Act, their support for pensions was usually tempered. Mothers' pensions were administered by the state, which meant that women might become dependent on the state. The Sheppard-Towner program, however, was wholeheartedly supported by Detroit clubwomen because it directly benefited women and children without engendering dependency. Clubwomen had mixed views regarding child labor legislation, and those who supported it faced powerful enemies in big business.

Although black and white clubwomen did not join forces on issues regarding women and children, they were aware that the family in the modern urban environment faced common hazards. They would turn their attention to these issues throughout the decade.

4

Protecting the Home against Enemies

If there is one thing that clubwomen the country over stand
for more than another, it is the American home.

Detroit News, March 4, 1922

In the 1920s the city of Detroit, with its burgeoning population and proximity to Canada, faced grave issues of crime and punishment. The city's rapid industrialization and urbanization created new "temptations" and at the same time caused it to outgrow the communal and institutional restraints under which it had functioned. Detroit clubwomen wanted to protect their homes and families from the evils associated with this urban environment. Some of the earliest women's organizations such as the WCTU promoted moral reform by capitalizing on the popular notion that women had a special moral nature and using that notion to gain access to public space. Organizations like the WCTU then moved beyond Prohibition and into other areas of social and political concern.[1] Contemporary female activists like Anna Shaw and Frances Willard argued that women's moral nature and domesticity naturally propelled them into civic activism to represent those interests. Women had transformed their roles as moral guardians in the home to moral guardians in the public realm.[2] In doing so, they were expanding their potential public power. As Nancy Cott has noted, "the language of moral reform evoked women's power: power to avenge, power to control and reform."[3]

Detroit clubwomen took their position as guardians of virtue seriously and tried to create a more moral environment. They also believed in crime prevention and rehabilitation and therefore championed a Women's Division of the Police Department, which would assign female petty offenders to social agencies rather than the penal system. Their support for court and prison reform, along with their opposition to capital punishment, completed their commitment to their judicial ideas. White clubwomen had successfully campaigned for a woman police officer in Detroit in 1919, Josephine Davis. Exemplifying the same motives as clubwomen in New York City, they tried to balance both "the welfare of the individuals involved and the city's need for social order and fiscal responsibility."[4] In the debate over Prohibition reform in 1930, some believed "women found that the application of their traditional moral sources of strength through the agency of a women's organization still empowered them more politically than any other approach."[5] Using their clubs for political work attracted powerful allies such as the *Detroit News* in the anti-gambling crusade but also powerful enemies such as the Detroit Citizens League in the Recorder's Court election of 1923.[6]

Once again, even though both black and white clubwomen wanted to protect their homes from the evils of an urban environment, they failed to work together. Black women strove to create a more moral environment by the adoption of white bourgeois values. In this manner, they were pursuing a strategy that combined general uplift of the race through the emulation of white middle-class behavior and values. The NACW's motto, "Lifting as We Climb," exemplifies this strategy. For example, in Atlanta the Neighborhood Union led by Lugenia Burns Hope wanted to not only eradicate vice from black neighborhoods but also punish Sabbath breaking.[7] In Detroit, mothers' clubs were established where southern migrants received instruction in food preparation and proper attire for outside the home. "Old" black Detroiters helped migrants not only find a house but also find a church.[8] African American clubwomen were especially sensitive to the issue of vice because their agenda of uplift through middle-class respectability demanded it. The NACW continued to stress moral purity throughout the 1920s, in spite of contemporary changes in women's sexuality even though this policy threatened to make the organization an anachronism. Deborah Gray White concludes that the 1920s "crippled" the NACW.[9]

In addition, as other scholars note, the acceptance of white cultural norms simply reinforced them and the racism that was an integral part of such pervading attitudes. The racial and sexual ideologies of white values helped maintain white power and thereby inadvertently contributed to the racial oppression black women were ostensibly opposing.[10] As the adoption of bourgeois values reinforced racism, it shifted the foundation of difference from race to class. Elite blacks thought an emphasis on class similarity with middle-class whites would temper anti-black racism. Even as an African American intellectual like W. H. Ferris championed black rights to citizenship, he believed black poverty stemmed from immorality and pathology.[11]

But the explanation for black poverty was more complex than this, and the economy, not moral depravity, was the largest contributing factor to black working women's behavior. As elite African American women promoted Victorian morality, which dictated evening curfews, they failed to understand that black women could often be out at night because of their work schedules. This behavior in the eyes of black clubwomen was suspect because it was not what a Victorian woman should be doing.[12] The efforts of African American clubwomen to emphasize similar moral programs as white women's clubs failed to gain them allies and furthermore may have diverted resources and energies from the fundamental causes, both economic and social, of black wage-earning behavior.

Although Detroit's white clubwomen did not collaborate with similarly minded black women, they did work with valuable (white) male allies in their fight against gambling; still, they had only limited success. Ethel (Mrs. George) Walters likened the addiction of gambling to that of alcohol. Referring to "dope sheets," she said, "The hold that they seem to get on the men who follow them is only comparable to the vicious influence of drink or drugs; it is 'dope' indeed, poison of the worst kind, which seem [*sic*] to get into the veins of the men who play the races and are the dupes of the bookmakers."[13] Lillian Mathews, president of the DFWC, said, "If there is one thing that clubwomen the country over stand for more than another, it is the American home. Anything which threatens or attacks it, we are ready to fight to the last ditch, and we look upon the race track evil as one of the enemies of the home which we as clubwomen must pledge ourselves to fight to the limit."[14] Clubwomen therefore advocated strong anti-gambling legislation.

African American clubwomen also opposed gambling, but its unique position within the black community made it far more difficult to eradicate. The numbers games that were run by the storefront or Spiritualist churches were popular with newly urbanized migrants. Although many black clubwomen disapproved of these institutions and their practices, the money generated there circulated within the black community, sometimes in helpful ways. For example, Reverend William Peck, the husband of the African American founder of the Housewives' League, needed the assistance of a numbers banker for a construction project. Therefore, the gambling money generated in Detroit's black community provided cash for the community in ways that white employment and philanthropy could not. African American clubwomen's opposition to these practices was increasingly at odds with developments within their own community.[15]

By 1922, Detroit's anti-gambling laws were proving difficult to enforce. The problem drew the attention of the MLWV, which joined the Detroit fight for stronger enforceable legislation.[16] Ministers joined clubwomen and law enforcement agencies in supporting candidates for the 1922 elections who opposed gambling and supported stronger legislation. By September there were a total of 107 Wayne County candidates (for all offices) who pledged to support anti-gambling legislation.[17] Shortly afterward, Dr. James W. Inches, the police commissioner, and Mayor James Couzens endorsed an ordinance to impose heavy fines and jail sentences on gamblers. There was a similar law in Highland Park that Couzens and Inches viewed as successful.[18]

Detroit clubwomen supported the municipal ordinance against gambling but believed state legislative action was also needed. Creating front-page news three days in a row in the *Detroit News*, white clubwomen made their opposition to racetrack betting clear. The Board of Directors of the DFWC met in March 1923 to issue a unanimous resolution to Governor Alex J. Groesbeck and the Michigan state legislature. The resolution stated that the rise of gambling in Detroit made innocent women and children its victims. It praised the *Detroit News* for its stand against gambling and the publication of racing odds and finally pledged its endorsement of all anti-gambling legislation. Detroit clubwomen went to Lansing to show their support for the Voorheis-Bahorski Anti-Handbook Bill. To the legislators, Ethel Walters recounted the true story of a young expectant bride who had been left destitute because her gambling-addicted husband had been sent to jail.[19] The Voorheis-Bahorski Bill was passed on April 20, 1923. It was hoped that Detroit's proximity to the track in Windsor would not simply take the racetrack gamblers across the river.[20]

Michigan clubwomen were joined in the anti-gambling effort by not only prominent members of the clergy but also newspapers like the *Detroit News*. The *News* gave white clubwomen's anti-gambling activities more publicity than their other activities, including front-page headlines. This extra publicity was helpful, perhaps crucial, in this instance. Still women could not count on this kind of support for all their campaigns.

Although the Voorheis-Bahorski anti-gambling law passed, the Michigan Supreme Court overturned it on a technicality. In 1925, a revision of the law, the Bahorski Anti-Gambling Bill, was passed with a unanimous vote in the state house and senate.[21] However, enforcement of that legislation was only half-hearted. Throughout the decade, a lax attitude on the part of Detroit's law enforcement was evident. Police Commissioner William Rutledge deflected criticism by saying that the legislation allowed for injunctions and legal technicalities. Consequently, his hands were tied.[22]

The creation of a Women's Division of the Police Department would, many Detroit clubwomen believed, result in crime prevention and criminal rehabilitation. They were confident that women who ran afoul of the law did so only because they lacked the proper supervision, which would include care and nurturing in middle-class values. For example, when a woman was arrested the Women's Division would send her to a social welfare agency. If the woman was brought before the court, the Women's Division had the same policewoman accompany her throughout the process. The Women's Division also worked closely with the recreation commission to set behavior standards for dance halls and amusement parks. As part of their anti-crime initiative, the Political and Civic League invited Josephine Davis to their meeting to describe the purpose of the proposed Women's Division in 1920. She explained that policewomen were valuable because they could warn young girls of the dangers of the city and help women and girls who had run afoul of the law by attending their trials, houses of correction, and hospitals. Policewomen could also be employed to keep minors away from gambling and tobacco. They could cooperate closely with travelers' aid and protective leagues. Davis suggested Detroit adopt a special Women's Department with an experienced, trained woman at the head. She further suggested that the division include both uniformed and non-uniformed women officers. These officers should be on the same footing as their male counterparts with all the same rights and responsibilities.[23]

The Women's Division of the Detroit Police Department was organized in January 1921 along the lines proposed by Davis, although the division was not headed by her. Instead, after a nationwide search, Police Commissioner Inches appointed Virginia May Murray of New York City to undertake this task. While there was some criticism of a non-Detroit choice, the decision was generally greeted with enthusiasm.[24] Murray was and remained the head of the Travelers' Aid Society of New York. She spent the first six months of 1921 organizing the Women's Bureau of the Detroit Police Department and thereafter divided her time equally with her New York responsibilities.[25]

Murray's ideas about the purpose of the Women's Bureau were similar to those of Davis. In an interview with the *Detroit News* she explained the bureau would offer protection and guidance for all Detroit women but especially young women. She declared that there would be cooperation among the Police Department, social welfare organizations, and the Recreation Commission. In fact, Murray's policewomen would enforce the commission's standards at dance halls and other places of amusement. However, although female officers would have the title "policewoman," they would not carry weapons or wear uniforms. Murray preferred to think of them as "municipal welfare workers" who supervised women and girls who needed attention. This could include attending court with them or accompanying them to reform or social agencies. Murray concluded, "With the organization of the Women's Division, the day when a woman or a girl is brought into court, fined, sentenced or freed and then lost sight of, is past."[26]

Murray's position on these issues echoed the feelings of many Detroit clubwomen about crime prevention and rehabilitation but also revealed how their ideas were rooted in notions about class and gender. Those who were concerned about women's criminal behavior used their own ideas about proper middle-class female conduct as a guide in dealing with this issue.[27] For example, Murray believed women who ran afoul of the law should be thought of first as human beings who suffered from broken homes or having had unwise parents, not as "fallen" or "wayward." She believed that each case was unique and that each woman or girl should be treated as an individual. But because most of the girls who needed the attention of the Women's Bureau came from "disadvantaged" homes and because Murray believed a crucial component of her police work was educational, she believed that parents should be taught how to raise children properly. In addition, Murray advocated a program, which was supported by Detroit's white clubwomen, for farm colonies for troubled girls. Murray's work in New York led her to conclude that many delinquent women were in fact mentally deficient and should therefore be trained in a separate facility. In a farm colony, the girls would develop skills or trades so they could function in society. This would benefit society as well as the individual. Murray's plan to have plainclothes policewomen patrol dangerous areas for young girls and investigate troubled girls completed her design for crime prevention and rehabilitation.[28]

Crime prevention among women and girls was an issue for African American clubwomen as well. Black elites thought working-class parents were creating "bad" homes or, as Murray would say, "disadvantaged" ones.[29] Elites were especially worried about the behavior of young women in unsupervised dance halls.[30] The sexually implicit and explicit lyrics of black blues singers made middle-class black women cringe as such singers raised the specter of black women's sexuality.[31] Consequently, Detroit's African American clubwomen also supported Murray and her work. They believed that her plans were so important that they held an open meeting for all interested people when Murray spoke before the Detroit Study Club. Murray was thus able to disseminate her philosophy to a wider audience.[32]

It is not clear whether the preventive services of the Women's Division extended to Detroit's black community. The African American Women's City Council supervised school grounds to protect younger girls, and a men's organization called the Young Negroes Progressive Association did the same at dance halls.[33] But Murray's lecture before the black Detroit Study Club raises the possibility that the programs of the Women's Division would extend to both the white and black communities.

The white community of Detroit most certainly benefited from the city's new police services. White clubwomen's opinion as to the effectiveness of the Women's Division was so valued (and perhaps influential) that it was sought out by Commissioner James Inches as he decided whether to make the division permanent. In a letter dated June 24, 1921, from Inches to Pearl Novak, president of the DFWC, he requested that the DFWC appoint a committee to thoroughly examine the Women's Division and report whether its results justified making the division permanent.[34] In October 1921, the Committee to Investigate the Work of the Women's Division of the Police Department, composed of Clara J. (Mrs. James) Downey, Lillian Mathews, and Edna H. (Mrs. Herbert) Prescott, issued a ringing endorsement. The women praised Dr. Inches as being sympathetic toward and thus cooperative with the Women's Bureau. They also felt Murray was a wonderful superintendent, whose preventive work was well done. The committee reported that of the two thousand girls who came to the attention of the Women's Division, only 3 percent were committed to penal institutions. They felt the bureau's work was indicative of the most progressive and effective ways of "social betterment." In addition, they believed Detroit was preeminent among U.S. cities for its work. Consequently, the committee recommended that Dr. Inches make the Women's Division a permanent part of the Police Department. The Detroit clubwomen endorsed the Women's Division because they felt that work with women and girls was best carried out by women. Their report requested that the division always be headed by a woman and that future matrons be qualified to teach vocational training. Lastly, they requested that women who retired from the position of matron be awarded pensions.[35]

The DFWC report of the Committee to Investigate the Work of the Women's Division was a front-page story in the *Detroit News* in October 1921. The paper gave a detailed account of the conditions prior to the creation of the Women's Division and described how it had alleviated those circumstances. Overall, the article was favorable toward the findings of the DFWC regarding the Women's Division. The *News* once more showed its support for a DFWC position by giving it front-page coverage.[36]

Detroit's white clubwomen strongly supported both the Women's Division and the choice of Virginia May Murray as its head. When Daniel W. Smith, candidate for mayor, appeared before the Detroit LWV in November 1921, he was heckled by the women for his criticism of Murray. According to the *Detroit News,* "The attack was so spirited and successful, that before the chairman had restored order, Mr. Smith admitted the city administration was justified in hiring Miss Murray."[37] Smith conceded the point, but as he tried to move the debate away from the Women's Division and Murray, the female audience insisted that more be said. Although the discussion eventually moved to Prohibition and the transportation problems in Detroit, the women of the DLWV had forced a complete airing of the candidate's views on the Women's Division. Clubwomen's unwillingness to end the debate until the issues had been thoroughly discussed and their insistence that the candidates speak specifically and not in glossed-over generalities demonstrated one way in which they were attempting to influence Detroit politics. It also demonstrated their political influence as their resolve, in fact, forced Smith to change his views.[38]

In 1922 the DFWC voted to endorse an amendment to the city charter establishing the Women's Division of the Police Department with a woman at the head. They sent their recommendation to Mayor Couzens and the president of the Common Council, John C. Lodge, in March 1922.[39] The DFWC's amendment to the city charter required a municipal vote, as it would reorganize the Detroit Police Department. On March 7, 1923, the amendment passed; thereafter, the police commissioner would appoint four deputy commissioners: for police knowledge, administration, public safety, and to head the Women's Division (the latter could be headed only by a woman).[40] The *Detroit News* praised the effort of the DFWC when they stated that this amendment was due "to the efforts of the Civic Department of the Federation and was taken to ensure the permanence of the Women's Division."[41]

In spite of the success of the Women's Division and the activities of civic-minded men and women to reduce vice, by mid-1926 Detroit was declared "the blackest, vilest city in the United States so far as vice is concerned." It estimated that there had been a 300 percent increase in prostitution since 1916.[42] At the request of the Detroit Citizens Committee, but financed by the Rockefeller Foundation, George E. Worthington of the American Social Hygiene Association had conducted an investigation of Detroit during the first half of 1926. Worthington concluded that because of the city's rapid growth and industrial prosperity, the laxity of the local police, and the widespread belief that toleration existed, prostitutes from all over the country were flocking to Detroit.[43] Some of these factors were beyond the scope of women's political activities, but prostitution grew in Detroit while it declined in other cities because there was no well-organized anti-prostitution drive in Detroit.[44]

Clubwomen championed anti-vice laws, but they were unsuccessful in stemming the tide of prostitution. Mayor Couzens sent a letter to DFWC president Novak, seeking the help of white clubwomen in routing out illicit massage parlors. James Inches believed massage parlors were sites of immoral activity, but he was unable to obtain sufficient evidence.[45] The DFWC Legislative Department worked with welfare workers, lawyers, judges, doctors, and Judge Henry Hulbert to get a law passed that would make men just as guilty as women in prostitution. The governor was willing to get the bill into the Criminal Code, but there was not enough legislative support.[46]

Since clubwomen, both black and white, were unable to convince male legislators of the urgent need to change the laws regarding prostitution, in Detroit, prostitutes were merely fined, not jailed. Prostitution flourished within one mile of Cadillac Square, the main business district, and even in the vicinity of Detroit's large schools. As a result, there were numerous cases of venereal disease, and men even made indecent proposals to respectable women.[47] Therefore, in spite of the efforts of many to curb crime and vice in Detroit, the problem of prostitution only worsened during the decade.

African American clubwomen in Detroit and elsewhere were just as concerned as white clubwomen about the proliferation of vice and crime in large cities. The *National Association Notes* explained that vice was on the rise and would have deleterious effects on young people. The *Notes* advised its readers, "Women, fight it, march if need be to the City Hall, conduct a campaign, a YWCA and with all the energies of our souls let us stop the advance of this evil."[48] Elizabeth Gulley saw the congested housing conditions as a primary reason for the rising crime rate. She encouraged all women to work against the spread of crime.[49]

African American clubwomen wanted to prevent black female migrants from "falling" into prostitution to support themselves. The Women's City Council often met young black women arriving in Detroit at the train station to take them to safe housing. The first of these safe homes in Detroit was established in 1904 by African American clubwomen of the Second Baptist Church, called the Christian Industrial Home.[50] By the 1920s the Big Sister Auxiliary, also of the Second Baptist Church, established a second home.[51] While these accommodations were intended to help female migrants, they also showed a tacit acceptance of the myth of black women's promiscuity by elite black clubwomen.[52] However, the influx of migrants facing exclusion in the industrial workforce due to their race and gender encouraged the growth of "buffet flats." Buffet flats were usually private homes where a number of illicit practices took place, including drinking, gambling, and prostitution.[53]

Despite the proliferation of buffet flats, black clubwomen were unable to enlist white clubwomen in their anti-vice campaign. In 1920 Clara Downey reported to the DFWC that an African American group wanted to cooperate with the DFWC in ridding a particular neighborhood of buffet flats. There is no further mention that sought-after cooperation ever took place.[54]

There is evidence that white clubwomen expected the black community to clean up vice in their own neighborhoods. The Civic Department of the white Detroit Sorosis Club reported that there was growing vice among the "colored people of the East Side" and it was the work of the "better classes to clean this up."[55] This reflects a similar conclusion by Judge Jean Norris of New York City's Women's Court. Norris said, "Rich colored people . . . should establish homes and respectable houses where a girl may get wholesome food without a large amount of money."[56] The Civic Department meant, as Judge Norris did, strictly members of the African American community. Although Lillian Johnson had earlier claimed that the Detroit Study Club's association with the DFWC and its "advanced clubwomen was very beneficial to our members, furnishing a wider outlook for us,"[57] white clubwomen apparently did not feel strongly enough about the issue to engage in cross-racial cooperation.

Another issue about which black clubwomen were vitally interested was lynching. On this issue, they sought interracial assistance from white women's organizations.[58] Mary Church Terrell, president of the NACW, stressed the importance of an anti-lynching bill when she said, "for there is nothing now pending which affects the colored people of the country more deeply, directly and vitally than does this bill."[59] In Detroit, African American clubwomen appealed to the DFWC to send a petition to Congress supporting the Dyer Anti-Lynching Bill. The club agreed, and the petition was sent to the club office so the Board of Directors could get signatures.[60]

In spite of this effort, the anti-lynching bill failed. White clubwomen also failed to raise the age in the Age of Consent Law in Michigan. The Michigan Age of Consent Law said that a woman had to be over the age of sixteen to have consensual sex. In an article in the *Club Woman*, LaVerne Lane Betts explained that between January 1, 1920, and January 1, 1921, there were four hundred cases of offenses against girls under age sixteen that came before Judge Henry Hulbert of the Juvenile Court. Of these, twenty-nine were warrants for statutory rape, of which only fifteen went to trial, and only ten convictions were secured. Judge Hulbert explained to Betts that the average juryman would not convict on statutory rape and send a man to prison for five to ten years if the girl was mature or was delinquent. Consequently, white clubwomen felt that the public must be educated and public opinion should be changed. Judge Hulbert further stated that men were always worried about property crimes and sent offenders to jail. Although all twenty-nine cases were aggravated and constituted a threat against the community, more men considered sexual offenses against those under sixteen as merely a nuisance. Judge Hulbert suggested to Betts that the use of female jurors might help, but the law was not changed.[61]

Detroit clubwomen were interested in changing laws, but they were also aware that women would need different judicial services than men. The DFWC's Juvenile Court Committee had worked to create the position of female probation officer in Detroit. In November 1909, Judge Hulbert had appointed Ada Freeman to this position.[62]

Now, in 1920, the Recorder's Court, under the leadership of Judge Harry B. Keiden and Judge William Heston, organized the Women's Court Division. This division handled two hundred cases a month involving women who had been charged with larceny, drunkenness, or disturbing the peace. In addition, the division evaluated each offender's mental and physical health, as well as her home and family life. Recorder's Court judge Pliny Marsh believed that the Women's Division was valuable and should continue; he also believed that a separate prison facility was needed to separate women with venereal disease from the rest of the women in prison.[63]

Regarding the Women's Court Division, Pliny Marsh and clubwomen were in agreement. Marsh was a member of the Detroit Citizens League, an organization with which clubwomen often cooperated. But Detroit women chose candidates for the Recorder's Court who reflected their agenda, and these candidates were sometimes at odds with those endorsed by the Detroit Citizens League. According to the *Detroit News*, white clubwomen's perspective was a "battle for humanity and social vision on the bench."[64] Women's "social vision" wasn't always shared by the Detroit Citizens League. The Recorder's Court election of 1923 was a chance for these women to elect representatives who shared their philosophy. The big issue in the election was the control of the "bloc," meaning Judges Harry Keiden, Thomas Cotter, Pliny Marsh, and William Heston. Although Marsh and Heston supported the separate Women's Court, these men were not friendly to labor or the poor. They had the endorsement of the Detroit Citizens League, the Michigan Manufacturers Association, the *Detroit News*, the *Detroit Free Press*, and big business in general.[65]

Heston had incurred the wrath of civic-minded women because he had opposed the creation of the Women's Division of the Detroit Police Department. Clara Downey of the DFWC Civic Department had urged club members to attend Judge Heston's court to show their support for the Women's Division of the Detroit Police Department and their opposition to his position.[66] When clubwomen did just that, Heston was apparently rude to them. Furthermore, the *Detroit Free Press* wrote that the women only went to the Detroit Municipal Court to hear the salacious details of the Marie Smith case over which Heston was presiding.[67]

The DFWC's *Club Woman* reprinted the account of the incident by the *Detroit Labor News*. The *Labor News* report included a series of incidents at the Municipal Court including the one surrounding the sensational Smith case. The *Club Woman*'s reprint provoked a letter from William Lovett of the Detroit Citizens League protesting the reprint. Lovett described the *Detroit Labor News* as representative of a small political faction that wanted to overturn the court system. Lovett wrote that clubwomen should not publish pieces from such publications because they threatened the ability of the "civic forces of this community to stand together." He further insulted the clubwomen by implying they were naïve about the *Detroit Labor News* when he claimed they might not be fully "informed as to the attitude, intention and purposes of the publication from which this article has been taken."[68]

Alvord defended the club's reprint of the *Detroit Labor News* article, and she countered Lovett's accusation about a fracture in "civic forces" when she reminded him that Heston was rude to the same prominent clubwomen "whom you turn to in a crisis of municipal affairs." Alvord admitted she did not regularly read the *Detroit Labor News* but that the *Detroit Free Press* and the *Detroit Saturday Night* showed their contempt for clubwomen's activities, which did more "to create divisions in the ranks of citizens both men and women who have the best interest of the city at heart." Alvord was a member of the Detroit Citizens League and later an executive board member. She emphasized that the success of the Women's Bureau was of paramount importance to clubwomen and they were furious that any judge would belittle the bureau or the club's sponsorship of it. Alvord stated that the *Detroit Labor News* was the only Detroit paper that defended the clubwomen, whatever their motives. Therefore, the club published the article.[69]

This controversy raises several interesting points about the political atmosphere in which Detroit clubwomen operated. Lovett's letter makes assumptions about clubwomen that were insulting and erroneous. He assumes clubwomen put class solidarity above their civic vision and therefore, once informed, would assume the *Detroit Labor News* agenda was wrong. Alvord's response suggests that she believed clubwomen had the "best interest of the city at heart" and that laboring people were doing the same. Lovett hints that clubwomen might be naïve, but it is he who failed to recognize that the agenda of laboring people regarding the Municipal Court might have been the same as that of clubwomen. In this regard, it was Lovett who was naïve.

This "intrusion" of Detroit's white clubwomen into the courts confirms research on women's involvement in anti-obscenity reform, which has found that men resented women's presence in court cases. For example, in Minneapolis, reforming women organized the Women's Cooperative Alliance to review court cases in which women were the victims to prevent male offenders from being acquitted. But the presence of women in the courtroom challenged this male space; in addition they were, as they intended, affecting the outcome of some trials. Furthermore, many men felt it was wrong for women to even hear the proceedings: women who persisted in observing court hearings "endured unpleasant challenges to their dignity and character."[70]

Detroit clubwomen encountered similar indignities when they observed the proceedings in the courtroom of Judge Heston, whom they viewed as incompetent and dogmatic. The Detroit Citizens League endorsed judges (like Heston) who believed crime was deterred by punishing the criminal, not rehabilitating him.[71] Detroit's clubwomen disagreed and aligned themselves with Reinhold Niebuhr, a Detroit pastor, who said that "undisciplined and chaotic souls emancipated from the traditions which guided their fathers and incapable of forming new and equally potent cultural and moral restraint" needed social concern, not just punishment.[72] In the 1923 Recorder's Court election, Emma Fox, whom the *Detroit News* called the "dean of Detroit clubwomen," Pearl Novak, past president of the DFWC, Ida Peppers, president of the LWV, and Edith Alvord all campaigned for candidates Frank Murphy and Edward Jeffries, who supported their vision of justice in Detroit, which included maintaining psychiatric and probation departments, positions not shared by Judges Heston and Marsh.[73]

Although there is no any direct evidence regarding whom Detroit's African American clubwomen supported in the 1923 Recorder's Court election, in general, the black community had a low opinion of Heston. In a letter to Detroit merchants asking for their advertising, the black *New Era* newspaper's editor, Charles Campbell, claimed Heston should receive a "fair hearing." Campbell wanted to demonstrate to merchants how unbiased his newspaper was to promote the newspaper's advertising business. The black community was offended and responded by boycotting the paper.[74] As stated earlier, Detroit's big businessmen supported Heston. The *Detroit Free Press* reported that scores of black men and women fraudulently registered to vote so that they could vote for Edward Jeffries, Christopher Stein, and Frank Murphy. The paper then claimed that the "better class" of citizens did not support these candidates.[75] Consequently, there is evidence that the black community was opposed to the "bloc."

All of the candidates for Recorder's Court, both members of the bloc and the others, gave speeches at white clubwomen's meetings to explain their views.[76] The candidate whose views aligned most closely with those of the clubwomen was Frank Murphy. Murphy was neither a machine nor a business-interest politician. He endorsed many reforms such as psychiatric and probation departments and public defenders, and he opposed the death penalty.[77] Ruby Zahn, president of the Progressive Civic League, called Murphy "that splendid young man," and prominent Detroit clubwomen, in their effort to defeat Heston, had urged Murphy to run.[78]

The Recorder's Court bloc was defeated in 1923. Although Keiden and Cotter were reelected, Heston and Marsh were removed from the court. Frank Murphy received the most votes.[79] Politically active white clubwomen campaigned hard against the bloc and helped elect candidates like Murphy who shared their vision of the way the city's justice system should work. They had to battle against two media giants, the *Detroit News* and the *Detroit Free Press,* and the Detroit Citizens League. The candidates sponsored by the Detroit Citizens League were in favor of strict draconian punishment that "fit" the crime, while the candidates sponsored by the clubwomen believed offenders should be punished but also that they could be rehabilitated and returned to society. The day after the election, the secretary of the Detroit Citizens League wrote, "The old Detroit is disappearing and a new Detroit is arising. What it will be, nobody knows."[80]

The shake-up at the Recorder's Court reflected an acceptance of clubwomen's ideas about crime and punishment. These included psychiatric and environmental evaluations of first-time offenders and prisons as modern rehabilitators. These ideas were embraced by the voters of Detroit who defeated the antediluvian bloc candidates.

In keeping with their beliefs about crime prevention and rehabilitation, Detroit's white clubwomen opposed capital punishment. In 1846, Michigan had been the first state to abolish capital punishment, but in Detroit during the 1920s, the growing population and increased crime rate raised the issue again. When legislation arose to reinstate the death penalty, clubwomen worked against it. Dr. Mary Thompson Stevens, the only female commissioner of the Detroit House of Correction, claimed that capital punishment did not keep the crime rate down.[81] The Progressive Civic League was especially intent on defeating the death penalty bill being proposed in Michigan. In an effort to educate the public, they launched an intensive campaign, sending letters to one hundred newspapers in the state and handing out two hundred thousand circulars. They believed that while a small percentage of Michigan residents favored capital punishment, the majority did not. The Progressive Civic League thought most people believed it was backward, and they wanted to mobilize those who opposed it.[82]

In 1923, Harriet McGraw, a politically active member of the Twentieth Century Club, founded an association opposed to capital punishment that put pressure on legislators.[83] When the issue was raised in 1925 white clubwomen of Detroit were a factor in its defeat. They went in large numbers to Lansing to hear the debate, make their presence known, and listen to the roll call vote. Known as the McEachron Capital Punishment Bill, it lost 46–54. Believing this was an issue that resonated with women, the LWV's publication, *Michigan Woman,* declared that all women could rejoice.[84]

Two years later, in 1927, when a crime wave swept through Detroit, some white clubwomen began to have a change of heart about capital punishment. Throughout the decade there were twenty-five to thirty thousand gangsters in addition to the bootleggers in the city. In 1927 the *Detroit News, Free Press,* and *Saturday Night* all reported "a terrifying succession of holdups, daylight robberies, shootings and murderous raids by gunmen." There was a renewed call for the return of capital punishment.[85] At that time, Dorothea Steffens, president of the Wayne County LWV, said that while she was always opposed to capital punishment, she admitted the crime wave in Detroit had driven her to question her earlier views. She did not immediately approve of capital punishment but also did not rule it out. Katherine

Warren, president of the Catholic Study Group, also began thinking about capital punishment differently. Warren was especially disturbed by criminals' lack of respect for human life. She felt that perhaps a greater fear of the law might help prevent crime.[86]

Despite the wavering by Steffens and Warren, clubwomen generally opposed capital punishment. The Michigan legislature was unable to pass a capital punishment bill in 1927, but in 1929 the issue was raised yet again. According to the *Detroit News*, "Women pleaded for a sane, scientific, humanitarian attitude toward the criminal and the opposing men with the fervor of a deep-seated belief in the justice of their stand, demanded the rope or electric chair for those who kill."[87] At its Board of Directors meeting in April 1929, the MFWC went on record as opposing capital punishment.[88] Despite the clubwomen's protests, the capital punishment bill was passed. While the *News* article showed the emotional commitment the opposing sides had in the issue, it also noted that interest in capital punishment had died down in Michigan. The debate over the 1927 bill lasted eight hours and was conducted before packed galleries. In 1929, the debate was still heavily attended but lasted only three hours. The bill was vetoed by Governor Fred Green because he believed that it was too harsh and inflexible and because it did not provide for a referendum. Consequently, the decade-long battle waged by clubwomen kept capital punishment out of Michigan in the 1920s.

White clubwomen also pursued prison reform.[89] While the Progressive Civic League led the crusade for better prison conditions, Detroit clubwomen as a whole investigated prison conditions, campaigned for the construction of prisons that met the unique needs of women, and promoted more modern incarceration arrangements.[90]

Clubwomen supported modern prison reform and made their own investigations into prison conditions. Women like Zahn of the Progressive Civic League brought prison abuse to the attention of the public. In early 1921, Zahn was alerted to alleged floggings at the Jackson State Prison.[91] She wrote to John A. Russell, president of the Detroit Board of Control, and asked probing questions about the floggings and fiscal mismanagement. Russell replied by appointing a committee to investigate the situation.[92]

Zahn and the Progressive Civic League distributed twenty thousand flyers titled "Brutal Floggings at Jackson Prison" in Detroit as part of a campaign to draw the public's attention to what was happening in prisons. Clubwomen were among the recipients of this flyer. It showed Dr. Robert McGregor, the prison physician, holding the pulse of a man who, although still alive, had just been flogged 181 times. The text of the flyer indicated that three inmates at the Ionia State Asylum had been recently flogged. The last sentence of the flyer urged clubs and organizations to send telegrams to Governor Alex Groesbeck protesting this behavior.[93] The Progressive Civic League requested that the governor dismiss Warden Harry L. Hulbert, Dr. McGregor, and the Board of Control at Jackson State Prison. By 1921, Michigan had a prison anti-flogging law.[94]

The Progressive Civic League also investigated the women's facilities at the county jail in 1922. They found the jail officers efficient and kindly, and the prison was spotlessly clean although conditions were spartan. Zahn successfully lobbied for mattresses, sanitary tables, upholstered benches, and better lighting for the women inmates, as well as a female physician. Lastly, they demanded the auditors paint, install linoleum floors, provide lockers for clothes, and provide a better diet for the inmates. Five months later prominent Detroit clubwomen who had themselves contributed an electric stove, aluminum utensils, and a new Victrola toured the prison and found the improvements satisfactory.[95]

By the summer of 1926, the county jail was again in need of refurbishment and repair. The mattresses, secured several years earlier by the Progressive Civic League, were in need of repair. There were few sanitary toilets and one leaked so badly it soaked through the floor. The league again sent their list of requirements to the prison auditors, who slowly complied. The league also donated $3,500 for repainting where necessary. New linoleum was laid, clothes lockers were added, and the mattresses and beds were renovated. The league also contributed waste paper baskets, bread boxes, soap, curtains, and bedspreads. A privacy screen was added to the health room along with an instrument cabinet. The league also donated kitchen equipment. Flowers, candy, and fruit were regularly supplied by sympathetic organizations. Attempts by the league to provide the women inmates with such items as sugar for coffee, dried fruits and vegetables, and additional milk for drug addicts met with some success. The league secured a social worker to buy necessary supplies for the Women's Division.[96]

In 1926, Mrs. Kenneth G. Smith, chairman of Institutional Relations of the MFWC, undertook a survey of Michigan jails. She visited fifty-four institutions, fifty of which were county jails and four of which were in Detroit. She concluded that Michigan jails as a whole were relatively good but that the county jail system was outdated. The *Club Woman* suggested a more modern system of farm colonies or cottages where prisoners were better protected against disease and had an opportunity to have some vocational training.[97] The MFWC supported a bill in which the governor would appoint a commission to investigate prison conditions. Smith, Laura Cramer, and Estelle Jamieson entertained the members of the Senate Committee on Penal Institutions at a luncheon to encourage the passage of the bill. The bill passed the Senate but was defeated in the House.[98]

Although the bill failed, white clubwomen began a successful campaign for a women's reformatory. The appropriation bill for such a reformatory passed the Senate but not the House because so many legislators had gone home. Esther Smith Hunter, president of the MFWC and wife of the chairman of the Senate Rules Committee, issued a frantic appeal to the governor, who summoned the legislators to return and the bill passed.[99]

While clubwomen were especially concerned about women's prisons, they also felt women possessed particular insights that would make them good prison administrators. Dr. Mary Thompson Stevens was the first woman to oversee a prison in Michigan. She was appointed acting superintendent of the Detroit House of Correction pending the appointment of a permanent one. Dr. Stevens replaced Dr. Bernhardt Jacob after an investigation disclosed horrific conditions at the prison.[100]

Dr. Stevens invited white clubwomen to the prison and gave them a tour of the facility. She pointed out various improvements that were a result of women's ideas.[101] When Dr. Stevens resigned from the House of Correction Board, the DFWC requested that she be replaced by another woman. Oftentimes, clubwomen wanted nonpartisan women placed on institutional boards.[102] This demonstrates two of clubwomen's most important contributions to public office. One was their unique vantage point as women, and the other was their tendency toward nonpartisanship when attempting to address social problems that they wanted government to resolve.

In addition to seeking alternative forms of incarceration, Detroit's white clubwomen were also interested in alternatives to imprisonment such as probation. In 1920, Detroit reorganized its probation system. Earlier, offenders had been placed on probation but with little follow-up evaluation. A new system equipped with a psychiatric clinic attempted to bring efficiency to the probation system. Offenders underwent psychiatric exams and extensive interviews, which provided a detailed history of the offender's behavior. Using this information, it would be determined whether an offender was mentally, morally, and physically capable of not committing a crime.[103]

White clubwomen also promoted more modern prison management. In February 1919, Jessie MacDonald, president of the Woman's First Campaign League, had investigated the conditions at the Michigan Industrial Home for Girls in Adrian. She was appalled that it was not run with twentieth-century, enlightened ideas but was "an institution which rivals Dickens notorious Dotheboys Hall in its callous indifference to the rights of childhood." MacDonald felt the rules of the institution made the girls sullen and downcast. They were not allowed to talk to each other and laughter was discouraged. She blamed this deplorable state of affairs on the fact that enlightened women were not consulted about how the school should be run.[104]

As a result of MacDonald's investigation, the superintendent, cottage managers, and institutional staff were discharged or quit. The new superintendent of the home was Detroit clubwoman Delphine Dodge Ashbaugh, who employed college graduates and training school graduates, administrators who specialized in disciplinary problems, and dietitians, just to name a few. The *Detroit News* reported that the new regime was impressive and embodied motherly instincts. Most of the staff were willing to work for less than their usual pay. For the very wealthy Ashbaugh, salary was of no consideration.[105]

As superintendent of the home, Ashbaugh lobbied the state legislature to quadruple the previous appropriation given to the school. She also allowed the girls to converse with each other and to make friends, a reversal of a previous policy. The *News* concluded that Ashbaugh's leadership was more than satisfactory and that her idealism, along with that of her staff, promised a better future for the girls at Adrian.[106] Her work at the home reflected that of many clubwomen who thought an improved home with motherly influence, even in an institution, would produce a better person for society.

All of the advocated facilities and programs described above were most likely racially segregated. This is difficult to decisively conclude because Michigan law prohibited discrimination in public facilities.[107] Still, it appears the practice in prisons deviated from the law. In general, white clubwomen believed that prisons should be segregated, but black clubwomen most certainly did not. African American clubwomen had consistently stood against Jim Crow rules, and blacks as a whole were loath to see the southern segregated system replicated in the North. However, white clubwomen were outraged when African Americans (or anyone else, for that matter) failed to receive due process. For example, when Forrester Washington claimed that the city needed to employ someone to investigate cases where the courts referred girls to homes that were unsuitable or where girls were otherwise suffering, the members of the Twentieth Century Club agreed and pledged to help get the paid investigator that Washington needed.[108]

Although Detroit's white clubwomen explicitly or tacitly accepted racially segregated incarceration facilities, they still believed that minor, younger offenders should be kept from hardened criminals. They therefore also campaigned for lenience in sentencing for wayward minors between the ages of seventeen and twenty-one. They knew that in New York if boys or girls were in places of ill repute or associated with undesirable persons, they could be charged with being wayward minors. They then went before a juvenile court and avoided contact with older criminals.[109] Detroit's clubwomen believed a similar policy should be put into place in Michigan, particularly Detroit. To put young offenders in prison with men and women who were hardened criminals would lead to further trouble, not rehabilitation, the clubwomen argued. In the spring of 1927, the Wayward Minor Bill was passed in Michigan.[110]

White clubwomen also hoped that by reforming Prohibition, this could also reduce crime. When Prohibition first became law, clubwomen believed that it would help protect the home, but by the end of the decade some Detroit women admitted that the Eighteenth Amendment proved impossible to enforce and had failed in its purpose. Although clubwomen in general viewed saloons as evil, they believed the speakeasies that had opened in response to Prohibition were even worse and needed to be closed. They thought this would happen if Prohibition were repealed. In addition, clubwomen believed that Prohibition had corrupted public officials and encouraged law breaking.

In December 1929 in response to what they saw as the evils of Prohibition, Detroit women founded a Michigan branch of the Women's Organization for National Prohibition Reform (WONPR).[111] Mrs. James Holden, chairman of the Finance Committee of this new branch, challenged every woman who complained about the evils of Prohibition to take a stand against it. She said that women who only complain and do not act contribute to the problem. She added that it was the duty of every woman, especially mothers, to work to repeal Prohibition.[112]

By 1931 Michigan had enrolled forty-five thousand members in WONPR, second only to New York. The women who joined WONPR were severely criticized by some, but their influence and cause were significant enough that Michigan's two U.S. senators, James Couzens and Arthur Vandenberg, and six representatives (out of thirteen) were considering repeal of the Eighteenth Amendment.[113]

Thanks to the Michigan WONPR, Michigan was the first state to ratify the Twenty-First Amendment on April 10, 1933.[114] As soon as Congress proposed the amendment in February 1933, Congress took steps to provide a ratification convention as soon as possible in Michigan. The resulting delegates included five WONPR members, and the convention met in April 1933. The delegates elected Mary Eldridge Alger president; she was the first woman to preside in the Legislative Chamber of Michigan. The convention, with ninety-nine delegates for repeal and only one opposed, voted overwhelmingly to repeal the Eighteenth Amendment.[115] Prohibition repeal fell solidly in the tradition of American women's reform politics because it emphasized the home, was basically nonpartisan, and reflected women's political culture and style.[116] In addition, Prohibition reform had widespread acceptance among male legislators and the public at large.

Detroit clubwomen experienced limited success in protecting the home against crime. Because so many of their efforts were directed at prevention, their success is difficult to quantify. Since they believed in criminal rehabilitation, Detroit clubwomen used their franchise right to elect judges who exemplified their judicial ideas even when this policy put them at odds with powerful foes like the Detroit Citizens League and the *Detroit News*. They insisted that women's needs in the judicial system required separate facilities. African American clubwomen also wanted to protect their homes and communities from crime. In this regard they clung to a class-driven moral code and they failed to recognize other alternatives. Their adherence to traditional bourgeois values and Victorian sexuality put them at odds with the community they hoped to serve. Clubwomen's battle, both black and white, to protect the American home involved them deeply in the issues of crime and punishment. However, the modern urban environment posed additional hazards to the American home and family, which clubwomen vowed to protect.

5

Home as Part of the Urban Environment

The water supply and our garbage pails remind us that
something is managed for us, not by us.

Clara Arthur, quoted in Alice Tarbell Crathern, *In Detroit Courage Was the Fashion*

Detroit clubwomen understood that a large, urban, industrial city presented many health and safety hazards. They expressed concern about clean food and water, as well as proper sanitation. They campaigned against urban hazards like air pollution and excessive automobile traffic. Clubwomen believed these issues could not be separated from their traditional concerns about home and family. In addition, they believed that the hazards of the modern city caused all residents of the city to be mutually dependent on each other. Anna Nicholes, a Chicago clubwoman and secretary of the Civil Service Commission, wrote in 1913 that within a city there was "a common dependency from which there is no escape."[1]

During the 1920s, Detroit clubwomen understood that the home and the city were inextricably linked and therefore believed that the problems of the city involved them as well. Although most used their women's clubs as an organizational base, they capitalized on their strengths and cooperated with other racially similar and like-minded groups.

Women's political culture, standing at the juncture between the public and the private spheres, brought issues previously associated with private life into the realm of public life.[2] Clubwomen challenged old notions of not only who participated in public life but also the issues a public person advocated. Thus, throughout the 1920s, the clubwomen of Detroit focused their public activities on creating a cleaner and therefore healthier city, which they believed would directly impact the home in a positive way. They also felt that the responsibility for maintaining healthy conditions in neighborhoods belonged to women.[3] But these were not Detroit's only problems. Water, sewage, and transportation were hotly contested throughout the decade. Clubwomen chose to remain knowledgeable and informed about these issues but not to become policy advocates. Urban infrastructure problems raised sensitive questions about public and private responsibility and oftentimes incurred the powerful opposition of Detroit's business community.

Detroit clubwomen wanted to protect people who lived in what they saw as a dangerous urban environment. They were especially concerned about the temptations such an environment held for children. As the remarkable growth of Detroit's population and automobile industry outpaced its laws and roads, Detroit clubwomen found themselves at the forefront of the safety campaigns to address this and other issues.

African American clubwomen were also concerned about how Detroit's urban environment affected the family and emphasized the important role women had in protecting the home. The *National Association Notes* asked, "How can she make the home atmosphere helpful, if she does not reach out to an understanding of conditions which encompass their social and civic environments?"[4] The *National Association Notes* was urging women to acknowledge the importance of the home-municipal relationship. The African-American Detroit Study Club even devoted three consecutive meetings to studying how to affect municipal reforms. They felt that if they understood how city services operated, they would be in a better position to reform them, if necessary. They also sponsored lectures with the city's administrative officials to better understand city departments such as public works, public health, and fire.[5]

The black clubwomen of Detroit embraced their homes as places of bourgeois respectability but did not always understand the less organized homes of their newly migrant sisters. White clubwomen also failed to comprehend that poor people often, by necessity, had to endure multiple lodgers and crowded conditions.

Another area in which civic-minded clubwomen directed their attention was children's recreational facilities. For children in crowded neighborhoods, playing in the street was often their only option.

Clubwomen believed the children of migrants in particular, both foreign and southern, would benefit from supervised play. For example, white clubwomen successfully campaigned for supervised playgrounds in Detroit because they felt that this was the best way to head off juvenile crime. By 1926, their efforts were rewarded when Detroit boasted 124 playgrounds and 15 municipal swimming pools.[6]

Although Detroit had a fair number of recreational facilities, they were segregated, even though this was in violation of the law, which outlawed discrimination in public places.[7] The 1926 report of the Mayor's Committee on Race Relations stated that while the Recreation Department wanted to uphold the legal rights of all, keeping the races separate was preferred, especially since "mixed bathing unfortunately becomes an occasion of unpleasant incidents." The report suggested, for example, that blacks and whites could have separate use times at the YMCA and that residents of the black community should have their own facilities.[8]

Detroit clubwomen were also alarmed by the immoral potential of motion pictures. All Detroit clubwomen subscribed to notions of middle-class Victorian morals and believed they were protecting children as they sought to enforce these morals through movie censorship. At a general meeting of white clubwomen and others in January 1921, Dr. Pierson of the Council of Churches introduced a plan to censor movies in the city of Detroit. With the motion picture industry the fourth largest in the country, parents, teachers, civic leaders, and social workers wanted an efficient plan of censorship against im moral, obscene, and vicious pictures. Detroit's clubwomen thus sent Mayor Couzens a petition outlining their concerns and recommending a course of action.[9]

Pierson's plan called for a three-person Board of Motion Picture Censors, including a policeman, a clubwoman (probably white), and possibly a social worker. The official censor at that time was Lieutenant Baker of the Detroit Police Department; he would serve as censor on the proposed board. The clubwoman's slot would be filled by a representative nominated by the DFWC because it was regarded as representing all the women's clubs of the city. The third member of the board was to be nominated by the president of the Social Worker's Club, William J. Norton, in conjunction with the executive secretary of the Michigan Motion Picture Exhibitors and the Detroit Council of Churches.[10] Although the plan had some support from the churches, it did not attract strong business support and did not come to fruition.

Clubwomen themselves did not agree on what was an objectionable film. While clubwomen believed that obscenity in movies was harmful to young people, they disagreed on exactly what was indecent. Furthermore, they never developed a unified, coherent plan to counter indecent motion pictures. Lastly, and perhaps most important, when clubwomen claimed to speak for all women, they were wrong. After gaining the franchise, non-clubwomen refused to allow clubwomen to speak for them.[11] Clubwomen reacted to this repudiation by rejecting the views of non-clubwomen. Prominent reformer Catheryne Cooke Gilman admitted that female reformers may "have developed techniques based upon conditions preceding the time when we had suffrage." Consequently, the crusade for movie censorship foundered in Detroit, as it did throughout the country, because clubwomen disagreed among themselves and they erroneously believed they spoke for all women.[12]

Regardless of the divisions among women regarding movie censorship, one of the issues that directly affected everyone was the high cost of living. This had troubled clubwomen both during and after World War I. Women especially felt the pinch: by 1915 women were buying 85 percent of the goods sold. In addition to the inflation of the war years, prices increased more than 30 percent between November 1918 and January 1920.[13]

In December 1919 Martha Ray, president of the DFWC, wrote to Mayor James Couzens to request a meeting of representatives of civic organizations and city departments to consider the means of reducing the high cost of living. She offered the DFWC clubhouse for the meeting.[14] Replying to Ray a month later, Mayor Couzens agreed with clubwomen's concerns and complained that Michigan was perhaps the only state that did not have a Fair Price Commission.[15] But while Ray and Couzens were corresponding, a committee of men in Michigan, concluding that this issue was a business one and not worthy of female input, had already begun to address the problem of high prices without the DFWC. As a consequence of the male meeting, a fair price commissioner, Judge William F. Connally, was appointed by the attorney general, Alex Groesbeck.[16]

Women's demands for "fair" prices really meant lower ones. The return of the Republican majority in Congress directed the blame for high prices onto the consumer herself, explaining the high prices were due to "wild spending."[17] It is not surprising that organized women would raise this issue and attempt to influence the problem of the high cost of living. However, since the issue involved business and management policies, it is also not surprising that the appointment of a fair price commissioner was made entirely without clubwomen's input.

Although clubwomen had little impact on the battle against high prices, they still worried about products they brought into their homes. Progressive Era thinkers believed that American consumers deserved some measure of government protection to "limit the dangers of an industrializing, urbanizing . . . 20th century America."[18] In 1919 the Civic Committee of the Twentieth Century Club exemplified this concern and suggested that since the Board of Health only had two investigators, club members would begin visiting cafeterias, candy stores, and bakeries to ensure that sanitary conditions existed. The Board of Health responded by saying they would appreciate the reports and help of club members.[19]

In January 1920, the Detroit Health Commissioner, Dr. Henry F. Vaughan, reported to the Political and Civic League that in 1919 the death rate was the lowest the city had ever known. He believed that restaurants in particular were much more sanitary than they had been had been a year earlier. This clean-up campaign was supported by the Political and Civic League, the Twentieth Century Club, and the DAR. Dr. Vaughan also attributed the low death rate to public health information, especially the sanitation lessons men learned in the army, which they brought home with them.[20]

However, Dr. Vaughan believed that meat inspection was totally inadequate because the government inspection only applied to meatpacking houses that did interstate business, which meant four of the forty-four establishments in Detroit. Dr. Vaughan estimated that 50 percent of Detroiters ate meat that had not been examined. He supported a plan whereby trained veterinarians would inspect the meat.[21] Lillian Johnson reflected clubwomen's concerns when, in an address to the Detroit Study Club, she reminded clubwomen that women expected their votes would result in better sanitation in bakeries and meat shops and better milk inspection.[22] In this way Johnson is representative of African American clubwomen who believed the private needs of the home became associated with public responsibility. Her emphasis on votes indicated women's new power to voice their concerns.

The DFWC shared the concern of the Detroit Study Club and Dr. Vaughan. The 1919–20 annual report of the Legislative Committee of the DFWC noted that the DFWC's investigation into food market conditions had improved them greatly.[23] The DFWC sponsored city ordinances so that bread would be wrapped, as well as a female food inspector who found approximately two thousand pure food and weight violations in Detroit in six months. The DFWC also joined the campaign to establish enforcement of legal weights and measures.[24] However, there was still no state meat inspection law in 1926 because the state legislature believed the issue had profound business implications beyond clubwomen's domestic concerns.

Detroit clubwomen's efforts to ensure cleaner handling of food was part of a larger clean-up effort. Commissioner of Public Works George Engel described Detroit as an overgrown village with a population that was increasing almost uncontrollably. He claimed the Department of Public Works could not keep the city clean and needed clubwomen's help. He wanted them to support an ordinance for regular collections of rubbish.[25] At that time, the city was planning to pass an ordinance to establish four, two-thousand-ton incinerators for burning garbage. This would render obsolete the transfer stations and reduce the number of leaking wagons. The Political and Civic League heartily endorsed the plan and Engel claimed their help was invaluable.[26]

In spite of the efforts and support of clubwomen to clean up Detroit in the early 1920s, the problems persisted and even worsened as the city's population continued to grow. By 1925 the Twentieth Century Club's Civic Committee joined with the Board of Commerce to eliminate the thriving rat population of Detroit. The *Detroit News* reported that the rats were leaving the congested sections of the city and migrating to the better residential areas. Since these areas had fewer alleys for shelter, the rats were going into homes. At a meeting of the Twentieth Century Club, attended by not only white clubwomen but representatives of the police and health departments, Board of Commerce, and food industries, it was decided that rats posed an economic and health problem. The extraordinary growth of the city had already increased the population of rats, which could spread a number of diseases.[27]

The extermination campaign had two parts. The first was to clean up the garbage in the streets, and the second was to set traps to prevent rats' entry into homes. Leaving rat poison around violated a city ordinance and was considered too dangerous. The Department of Health, joined by the Boy Scouts and the Police Department, cleaned alleys while the Board of Commerce blocked areas to prevent rats from entering. Detroit's white clubwomen participated by educating the public in a citywide campaign. The women used their clubs to spread the word about rat prevention and extermination to all women of the city. In this way, Detroit clubwomen reached out to other women, emphasizing their common concern about home cleanliness.[28]

White clubwomen were not alarmed by (or perhaps aware of) the dangers of the expanding rat population until the rats began migrating to the more affluent areas. Clubwomen's concern about this issue appears to have been triggered by the threat to their own homes and children. The rat issue claimed the attention of white clubwomen whereas the unhealthy conditions in black neighborhoods did not, even though white and black neighborhoods were connected because black women were employed as domestics and laundresses and commuted between the black and white sections of the city.[29] However, Detroit's white women did not appear to share the same anxiety as their counterparts in the South who feared black service women were "pathological agents of contamination."[30]

Although white clubwomen were concerned about the lack of city sanitation services in immigrant communities, they left no indication in their records that they were equally concerned about the deplorable conditions in black neighborhoods. In an article in the *Club Woman,* Grace G. Gray of the Americanization Committee of the DFWC admonished the city for its failure to provide sewers or city water for the immigrant residents living north of Seven Mile Road and for the overcrowded schools. Gray claimed this overcrowding forced half of the "mentally below" students to attend school for a half day.

In a warning about the social cost of unsupervised girls, Gray wrote, "The early life of girls fall prey to immorality and soon bring forth more of their kind."[31]

White clubwomen were certainly aware of the problems in black neighborhoods. In 1923 *The Detroiter* reported on the slums, overcrowding, and filth of Detroit's East Side,[32] and the 1926 report of the Mayor's Committee on Race Relations stated that certain areas on Eight Mile Road had poorly filtered water and no sewage disposal; the St. Antoine district was even "beyond help." The mayor's report on Negro housing conditions claimed that the situation was serious but if the black neighborhood got the appropriate services, they would stay where they were.[33] The poor living conditions in Detroit's black neighborhoods were thought by some, including Detroit's mayor, to have the "desirable effect of discouraging the influx from the South."[34] In her research on women's work with immigrants in New York City in the early part of the twentieth century, Cheryl Hicks explains how white reformers believed immigrants were ultimately capable of becoming modern and urbanized whereas African Americans, particularly southern migrants, were not and perhaps could not: they believed African Americans belonged in the South.[35]

White clubwomen in Detroit were concerned about the substandard conditions in the immigrant neighborhoods, although there is no evidence they brought their concerns to the attention of public officials. They initiated an Americanization Committee for immigrants but no similar program to help assimilate southern African Americans into Detroit. White clubwomen may have advocated city services for immigrant neighborhoods, but they did not want to see further immigration into Detroit. Therefore, they supported the severe restrictions of the National Origins Act. Gertrude Wallace, chair of the Legislative Department of the DFWC, urged club members to write to their congressmen and Michigan senators asking them to pass a highly restrictive immigration bill like the National Origins Act or Johnson Bill H.R. #6540. This bill proposed limiting further immigration to 2 percent of each nationality. Furthermore, it chose the 1890 census for the base numbers, thereby severely limiting the eligible numbers of eastern Europeans. White clubwomen believed foreigners already living in Detroit should be housed in ways that prevented public health problems. They should also be acculturated as soon as possible, if not the immigrants themselves then their offspring. However, they wished to prevent more migrants from coming to the city, whatever their race.[36]

African American women, on the other hand, could not ignore the problems in black neighborhoods because they lived in them. The old black elite were forced to have neighbors of a different class and feared their proximity to lower-class blacks would tarnish their own standing: "both white and native colored citizens believe the southern Negro is more criminal by nature than his northern brother; and it has created a general distrust against all Negroes."[37] When possible, some affluent African American residents moved out of their neighborhoods to white neighborhoods. Others moved to a West Side neighborhood; the women in this community formed the black Entre Nous Club. The club sponsored clean-up campaigns in this more upscale neighborhood to keep property values high and keep it middle class and respectable.[38] John Dancy of the Detroit Urban League described the West Side as a place "where Negroes have exhibited a progressive spirit and shown a desire for modern, attractive homes."[39]

One of the biggest health threats in increasingly urban Detroit was the smoke generated by industrial manufacturers. The pollution came from coal burned in industrial operations, large heating plants, stoves, and furnaces. The soot carried carbon, tarry products of distillation, sulfur acids, and ash.[40] Detroit had instituted an anti-smoke ordinance in 1917, but it had been difficult to enforce. Conditions during and after the world war where the only available fuel was a smoke-producing one led to leniency in enforcing this ordinance.

In 1923, Frank Burton, Detroit Commissioner of Building and Safety Engineering, asked white clubwomen for help. Underfunded and understaffed, his department needed assistance in reporting cases of smoke violations, and he wanted the clubwomen to undertake a campaign to make the public aware of the health risks associated with industrial smoke as well as the costly waste to those burning it.[41]

In spite of the efforts of clubwomen and other concerned Detroiters, the smoke ordinance continued to be difficult to enforce. In January 1925, the DFWC felt there should be more action on the issue and members were encouraged to write letters to the Board of

Commerce asking them to take this issue more seriously. The DFWC also sent a letter to Judge Cotter commending him for imposing severe fines on companies that violated the ordinance.[42]

Because industrialization was associated with progress, smoke abatement campaigners had to frame their arguments in terms of denouncing smoke, not industrialization.[43] The cleanliness of the home was important to clubwomen, but they were unable to persuade businessmen on those merits alone. Pre-suffrage political success had oftentimes depended upon connecting reform with financial savings, and the 1920s were no different. Consequently, the early campaign for smoke abatement failed until later in the decade when a cost advantage became clear.

After the cost advantage became apparent to Detroit's business leaders and an amendment was added to the City Charter that reorganized the Bureau of Smoke Inspection and Abatement into the Department of Building and Safety Engineering, the city's air quality significantly improved. This success was due in large part to technological advances such as smokeless combustion with gas and oil as well as alternative fuels. White clubwomen's advocacy was a contributing factor as well: "The women's organizations stood solidly behind the [Board of Commerce] all through its investigation and [a] great deal of credit for the passage of the amendment and creation of the department must be given to the women of Detroit who got out in large numbers to vote."[44]

The exceptional growth of the city of Detroit also brought problems in delivering clean water to and removing sewage from neighborhoods. Throughout the 1920s, the city grappled with the expense of providing clean water to its residents. For example, in 1925 the water commissioners requested a budget of $9 million more than that of the previous year to meet the city's increasing water needs. In addition, the water filtration plants could not always handle the volume of water needed.[45] By 1928, the city's growth also demanded more sewers; in April of that year, Detroiters approved a $30 million bond issue for the construction of public sewers.[46]

Detroit's clubwomen remained mostly silent on the issues of water and sewage in Detroit, although their concern about sewage disposal did prompt them in 1930 to claim in the *Michigan Woman* that a new sewage disposal plant was needed because Detroiters had been pouring the untreated sewage of one million people plus industrial waste into the water.[47] Part of the reason for clubwomen's silence might lie in the fact they knew they faced formidable opposition from Detroit's powerful business interests on these issues. Detroit's businessmen in general were concerned about the increasing cost of municipal activity to accommodate a growing population.[48] But the issues of water and sewage decidedly annoyed Detroit's businessmen and left little negotiating room for concerned clubwomen.

Clubwomen were also concerned about Detroit's massive transportation problems. Detroit's population growth between 1910 and 1930, as well as the phenomenal rise of the auto industry during and after World War I, resulted in a city plagued by too many automobiles and too few public transportation alternatives.[49] From 1920 to 1925, the number of registered automobiles in Wayne County increased by 150 percent. In 1925, one thousand more cars per week were registered; some estimates showed that there would be one million automobiles in Detroit by 1930.[50] As early as 1920, the *Detroit News* called the main street in Detroit, Woodward Avenue, "the highway of catastrophe" where "passenger cars struggle for a perilous hold."[51] The *News* reported that there was more traffic on North Woodward—which was only eighteen feet wide, with two-way traffic—than on any other road of its size in the country.[52]

The transportation problems of Detroit were pressing, complex, and of real interest to Detroit clubwomen. In addition to congested streets, Detroit had a woefully inadequate system of public transportation in the 1920s as a result of, among other things, disputes as to who would own it. In responding to these issues, Detroit clubwomen took the position of active, well-informed citizens but rarely advocated action as an organization. In other cities like Chicago, municipal ownership of public transportation systems was a sensitive issue because it meant that the city's power would be enhanced at the expense of private business.[53] Detroit clubwomen prudently avoided advocacy of a particular transportation plan because these issues involved entrenched business interests, and clubwomen were pragmatic about their political abilities.

One thing both clubwomen and businessmen were increasingly concerned about was traffic safety: a rising population and more automobiles on the roads caused an increase in traffic fatalities, especially to pedestrians.[54] To address these concerns, the Michigan Safety Congress (headed by Clara Downey of the DFWC) was held in 1929 under the auspices of the Michigan Department of Labor and the National Safety Council.[55]

The Michigan Safety Council failed to make progress in lowering traffic fatalities and as 1929 drew to a close, Mayor John C. Lodge reorganized the Safety and Traffic Committee into the Public Safety League in response to the alarming increase in street fatalities (up 13 percent from 1928) and because he and others believed that street safety must include a vast array of government, industry, business, and civic figures to be successful. The league consisted primarily of businessmen and city officials, but Jean (Mrs. Carl B.) Chamberlain, president of the DFWC, was also included on the executive committee. Among other activities, the league sent its representatives into neighborhoods and went door-to-door to educate residents, particularly the elderly and children, on pedestrian safety. With their vast networks among Detroit women, white clubwomen were a vital part of this safety campaign.[56] But as long as the automobile industry continued to prosper and pour additional automobiles onto the Detroit roads, the safety problem did not improve.

One proposed solution to the problem of unsafe, congested streets was a subway system. The bond proposal for a subway was slated for the April 1929 election. In 1922 Mayor Couzens had appointed a Rapid Transit Commission to create a comprehensive public transportation plan that would serve the whole metropolitan area, including both elevated and subway systems.[57]

The Detroit Woman's Club reminded its members to vote on the subway proposal in 1929, although the club did not support or oppose the subway.[58] This was typical of the attitude of several Detroit women's clubs: they advocated using the franchise but failed to endorse one or another transportation plan. As clubwomen they were not in agreement as to which was the best plan so it was prudent to remain on the sidelines.

The election resulted in a resounding defeat: only 28 percent voted for the subway plan because most voters feared the cost of constructing such a system would be exorbitant. The only voters who supported the measure lived in the downtown section or on the crowded Grand River and Warren avenues.[59] When the 1929 subway proposal was defeated, Detroit lost its opportunity for relieving its congested streets as other major cities had. By 1930, Detroit was mired in the Depression and the costly appropriation became prohibitive. Detroit had little choice but to rely on her surface streets.

Throughout the 1920s, Detroit clubwomen insisted that the home and the city were linked; thus as homemakers their input was crucial. Clubwomen wanted their advice to be informed and they held lectures and formed committees to study issues such as city services, public safety, and transportation. Concerns about supervised play and motion picture censorship stemmed from their responsibilities as mothers. As homemakers they were worried about public sanitation. However, they still did not reach out to African American women who were pursuing similar objectives. They also showed no concern for the deplorable conditions in black neighborhoods. Detroit women believed that, as citizens, they had a responsibility to contribute their input into the political process, but that input was racially limited.

Consequently, clubwomen in Detroit continued to increase their political power in the city. This power did not simply continue to expand in a linear fashion, however. While enjoying some political success, Detroit clubwomen were also increasingly aware of the limits of their enfranchised status.

6

The Limits of Enfranchised Citizens

Plan is not practical . . . it is just like a woman.

Detroit News, December 20, 1925

In the late 1920s Detroit clubwomen continued to pursue equal, enfranchised citizenship but increasingly realized the limitations of that citizenship. They were informed voters, but both political parties were hesitant about granting them leadership positions, much less running them as candidates. Clubwomen themselves were often not united with regard to certain policies, and some were even reluctant to use their clubs for political activity. They were plagued by negative stereotypes that cast them as silly and politically incompetent, and the persistent notion (of both men and women) that women belonged quite literally in the home cast suspicion on their political activities. Finally, as the decade wore on, the idea that women would constitute a voting bloc proved false; some women were not even using their franchise privileges. Clubs still sponsored candidates' days, but these were only sporadically attended by the candidates themselves. As the country became mired in the Great Depression, the political policies of Detroit clubwomen had achieved only moderate success. They were considered valuable—albeit unequal—partners in running the city's affairs, but enfranchised citizenship did not mean political equality.

Some persistent limits on equal political status were apparent following the franchise and remained so throughout the decade. Upon receipt of the franchise, some clubwomen did join political parties, but they were not in agreement as a whole as to whether they should join. They were, however, encouraged to do so by some leading clubwomen. At the MFWC's annual gathering in 1923 clubwomen were told, "The woman who wants to learn politics has got to learn it from men. We are going to urge every woman to go into politics, to join a party, because politics means good government."[1] As chair of the American Citizenship Committee for the GFWC, Edith Alvord reminded clubwomen that the government is ruled by the parties and that if women took the "non-partisan aloof attitude, we shall not get far politically." Women would not be a part of the "inner circle" unless they "wholeheartedly [got] into parties."[2] Ella Aldinger agreed but stressed that women should pursue political work in the parties while remaining members of their clubs. In 1922 she wrote, "We urge all women to join some political party but to bear in mind that the league [LWV] itself is not in politics."[3]

Detroit clubwomen joined the Democratic and Republican parties but did not confine their political work to within those parties. Party officials welcomed women with enthusiasm, but neither party wanted to share leadership positions with them. Other clubwomen who were concerned that party politics put the party before their principles confined their political work to their clubs. Some African American women were especially worried that party politics brought corruption and thought they could be more effective if they remained nonpartisan.[4] Fannie Barrier Williams, a nationally prominent black clubwoman, believed clubwomen should stand for the highest ideals and avoid partisan politics.[5] Dorothea Steffens, president of the Wayne County LWV, believed that because a woman tried to steer clear of a blind, partisan vote, she was an intelligent voter.[6]

Both the Republicans and Democrats gave the appearance of equality and courted the newly enfranchised women voters. The Michigan Democrats were the minority party during the 1920s and perhaps were that much more eager for women's votes. There was a feeling among Democrats that women could be a potent political factor because they had votes to swing elections.[7] The *Detroit Times* claimed in 1919 that the Democrats were even convinced that it was good politics to nominate a woman for superintendent of public instruction.[8]

The Republicans likewise were watching and made a show of welcoming women into their fold. In November 1919 the Grand Old Party (GOP) reorganized to "provide for full participation of women in the future affairs of the party" and into their national organizations. Their pledge was to include women as citizens with all the rights and responsibilities thereof. They claimed that the women's work was not auxiliary but on an equal basis with that of men.[9] Still, Michigan Republicans showed little evidence of putting women on "an equal basis as men." Men had exclusive control over Republican Party policy in Ingram County although women could participate as advisors.[10] While the Wayne County Woman's Republican Club had office seekers among them, like Lucia Grimes and Laura Cramer, there were no women listed as policymakers among the Detroit Republicans in September 1920.[11] Likewise, there were no women among Democratic policymakers, and women were treated more like apprentice members rather than full members. When women got the vote, the Democratic *Michigan Citizen* wrote of them, "Taken as a whole, their knowledge of party principles and accomplishments has been confined to the table utterances by the head of the family, and the more or less confused review of facts and fancies as have come from over the garden wall."[12] In the same issue of the *Michigan Citizen* another article was more flattering with regard to women's political abilities. It claimed that women were actually more analytical about party platforms and injected a spiritual and principled element into politics. Still, with all these fine attributes, "political knowledge and training is needed as ballast."[13]

There were serious institutional obstacles to women's equal participation in either party. Until the 1960s, real political power was not in the parties' formal structure but in informal networks that were male dominated. Women were readily appointed to committees because those committees brought them little power. Male committee members would meet privately, without their female members, to decide issues. Women were appointed to committees because they were considered "safe": they lacked a constituency and were beholden to the man who appointed them. Consequently, women had little choice in candidate selection, little involvement in patronage, and little access to political deal making.[14]

Partisan politics involved great patronage that men, who were considered "more conversant" in such things, did not want to share with women.[15] Women would thus be a small minority at conventions for many years to come even though they had earned the right to act as delegates.[16] Women's party work included campaign organizing and publicity. For example, women in the Democratic Party organized about sixty women's clubs between August and November 1924. Democratic women had been credited with educating non-Democratic women on how to vote and electing Woodbridge Ferris to the U.S. Senate in 1922. They helped organize all thirteen congressional districts in Michigan by going into each county and listing the names and addresses of all Democrats and independent women voters. Showing their aptitude for grassroots work, Michigan's women Democrats helped edit and distribute the county editions of the *Michigan Citizen,* which included special pages devoted to that particular county's needs.[17]

The major parties wanted women's assistance but not their voices in the running of the party. Both parties believed women's real usefulness lay in their organizational abilities and their flair for grassroots politics, including canvassing for registration and passing out literature.[18] Grace Stephens Jobe, corresponding secretary of the State Federation of Democratic Women's Clubs, claimed that Democratic women had shown a "knowledge of the practical end of the work," which the party deeply appreciated.[19] Both parties carefully supervised women's activities and discouraged organizations with another agenda. Consequently, "their public image was one of worker bees who gratefully made coffee not policy."[20]

African American women were also involved in party work in the 1920s. The Republican Party continued to be the party of choice for African Americans throughout Michigan. Hallie Q. Brown, director of Colored Women's Activities of the Republican National Committee, praised the "excellent work the women of my race have accomplished during the [1924 presidential] campaign" for Calvin Coolidge. She claimed that black Republican women had become an important factor in the party.[21] Black women were eager but in need of better political education, and some black women's club leaders believed a permanent women's organization would help in that regard.[22]

Like white women, black women battled sexism within the Republican Party, but they also had to deal with racism. They were barred from leadership positions as women, but as African Americans they may have been excluded altogether. At a meeting of the Detroit Study Club in 1928 on colored women in politics, Lillian Johnson claimed that Republican women's leader Mabel Willebrandt spoke of unity but implied unity under white leadership. In order to rid the party of black leaders, Willebrandt had conducted investigations into three African American Republicans, Ben Davis, Bob Church, and Walter Cohen. Johnson said Willebrandt was encouraged to do so by southern "lily whites."[23] This was apparently part of a strategy Republicans in the South practiced after women were enfranchised. The Republican Party was hoping to alter its minority status there by courting women's votes and used a "lily white" program to attract white female voters. They actually gained some votes in the South but, as this incident reveals, lost some support among Detroit's black women. Although few black Detroiters voted Democratic before 1932, some were questioning that approach.[24] As African Americans became angry at and disillusioned with Republican policies, they voted for Democrats, especially in local elections.[25]

The Republican Women's Study Club in Michigan considered all women political novices and therefore poor choices for elected office. In 1931 it issued a bulletin for Republican women that displayed a rather demeaning view of a woman's approach to politics. They claimed that women were not "learning the game as it is played." It went on to state that it was no wonder that the men "snicker" at women because club work or being a politician's widow did not make a woman qualified for public office. Since women continued to push for female candidates, they were only "petty and childish." The article ended by reminding them that three club members had husbands who were running for office and worthy of support.[26]

The Republican Woman's Study Club addressed the issue of women candidates in December 1931. The article not only questioned the wisdom of women candidates but ridiculed women who supported them. Apparently some clubwomen became angry when no women were nominated for the Detroit Common Council. The Republican Woman's Study Club claimed those angry women "think men folks real mean" and it was a "downright shame" that women were not nominated. Because the Republican Party dominated in Michigan throughout the 1920s, it apparently felt fewer concessions had to be made to their female party members. They were comfortable enough to even ridicule the advocacy of female candidates.[27]

Both political parties were cautious about nominating women for office. This caution was reflected in the nonpartisan writings about female office seekers. Speaking before the annual convention of the MFWC in 1923, Dr. Marion Leroy Burton, president of the University of Michigan, warned women to "count the cost" of public life. He explained political office was both financially and emotionally costly. He cautioned that it was a lonely life where high standards only brought obscurity. Dr. Burton may have been saying to women that the franchise was one thing but political office was best left to men.[28]

Female candidacy was rare and mostly unsuccessful. In 1919, the DFWC endorsed the candidacy of Lucia Voorheis Grimes and Cora A. Maybee for school inspectors. Laura Osborn, already a member of the school board, urged women to support other women, adding that her ideas were continually met by hostility from the male board members.[29] Osborn championed some controversial policies like the single-salary schedule for teachers. She also believed that the best equipped school buildings should be located in the poorest sections of the city. Her reasoning was that wealthier children had warm homes and meals whereas poorer children did not.[30] Maybee and Grimes came in third and fourth, respectively, in the primary. The four candidates who received the highest number of votes were on the election ballot. The *Detroit News* reported the election as one of "women vs. men in school issue." The top two vote getters, Edward D. Divine and Andrew P. Biddle, had been incumbents on the school board. The female candidates received far fewer votes than their male counterparts.[31] Only two positions were available and neither Maybee nor Grimes was successful in the general election.[32] Although Osborn was serving on the school board, when Grimes and Maybee were defeated, the *Detroit News* reported the defeat in gendered terms. They wrote that the "campaign of woman vs. man for the two school board places ended in victory for man."[33]

By mid-decade the situation had changed little in Detroit. In the October 1925 primary for City Council, none of the four female candidates made the top eighteen positions (Ida Peppers received 10,635 votes, Harriet R. McGraw received 8,374 votes, and Catherine Tattan received 3,648 votes) and therefore were not on the general election ballot.[34] The failure of Detroit women to gain elected office can, in some part, be attributed to the nature of their political experience. The central goal of the suffrage movement was the franchise, not officeholding.[35] For example, in Boston, suffragists had reached out to working-class women, but after women achieved the ballot, there was no cooperation between these groups to elect women. Gender was an important factor in pre-suffrage cohesion, but once that goal had been achieved, class became more important than gender.[36]

As the decade wore on, elective office remained unlikely for women. However, after women achieved the goal of suffrage, male politicians took note that the female franchise had changed politics as usual. Women held out the possibility of voting in large numbers and even running for office. In the early 1920s the passage of the Nineteenth Amendment raised fears among male politicians that a "women's bloc" would emerge and make political demands. In 1923, for example, candidates spoke to the Wayne County Woman's Republican Club, the Woman's Citizen League, the Progressive Civic League, and the LWV. The *Detroit News* claimed that candidates were eager to capture the female vote.[37] Politicians may also have feared that highly active club members might run for office against them.

One such candidate was Edith Vosburgh Alvord. Upon marriage and her move to Detroit, she joined the Detroit New Century Club and later became its president. Alvord was eventually the president of the DFWC and the MFWC. She was also the chairman of the Citizenship Department and the Press and Publicity Department of the GFWC. Alvord helped organize the Highland Park Woman's Club and the Salvation Army Auxiliary. She served for ten years not only on the Executive Committee of the Detroit Citizens League but on the Board of Education of Highland Park as well. Her tireless activity in the club and civic affairs of Detroit enabled her to acquire many contacts and admirers.[38]

Alvord had considered running for Congress in 1922 but decided not to. Republican Grant Hudson wrote to his potential opponent thanking her for refraining from running. He believed she would have done well because "you have many friends and admirers over the district." This letter may only represent good manners (and politics) on Hudson's part. In truth, female candidates, even those with significant name recognition, were seldom successful and any fear of their candidacy was short-lived.[39]

Even clubwomen who saw the merits of having women in elected office seemed to be hesitant about trying to get them there. In fact, the DFWC's Legislative Department urged clubwomen to work for "the placing of the best men in charge of city affairs." At their Twenty-Sixth Annual Meeting, the MFWC members were urged to support women on boards of institutions governing women. At the same time, Mrs. Burritt Hamilton, president of MFWC, urged women to go slowly in seeking office because she was worried that as officeholders women might not be qualified. Perhaps club leaders feared the extreme scrutiny a woman in office would receive or that women would have to be much more informed, diligent, and wise in their political actions than would men.[40]

Although elected office usually proved elusive for women, clubwomen continued to serve their community in appointed and, in a few cases, elected office. For example, in 1921 the chairman of the Wayne County Board of Supervisors, William P. Bradley, requested Minnie Stott Jeffries to preside over the board upon his retirement. The Board of Supervisors was the legislative branch of the Wayne County government. Jeffries was appointed to the Public Welfare Commission (formerly the Board of Poor Commissioners), where she served for eleven years.[41] The following spring, the *Detroit Citizen* reported that Jeffries was the only woman on the Public Welfare Commission and had been reappointed for another term. She was also president of the County Supervisors of the Poor and was elected for two years in succession. The article concluded that Jeffries's tireless work had been very helpful to the destitute.[42] Although women performed well in appointed offices, they were forced to depend on powerful men rather than on their own abilities to secure these positions independently.

While women like Jeffries were involved in highly visible political work, many women were not even using their franchise privileges. The chairperson of the Colored Women Voters of Michigan, Savonia Carson, thought women were voting in ever larger numbers, but she also believed that some women still viewed the ballot as useless and had little interest in politics.[43] While acknowledging that in some areas women voted at the same rate as men, attitudes, ethnicity, and class affected women's voting behavior. Lingering anti-suffrage ideas prevented some women from voting, and poor women and those of foreign extraction were less likely to vote. There is no way to determine exactly how many women voted; there are only figures for registered and actual voters and they cannot be separated by gender.[44]

The leaders of women's clubs often expressed disappointment with women's light turnout at the ballot box. In 1922, Jennie Patton Beattie, president of the Women Citizens' League, admonished league members that the legislature would be less likely to listen to women when they realized only 30 percent of them voted.[45] The LWV was concerned that after seventy-five years of agitating for the vote, women were ignoring their franchise responsibilities.[46] The *News* noted that only 32 percent of the registered women voted in the October 1926 election.[47]

African American women felt that voting was especially important for their race. Mary Church Terrell encouraged the members of the NACW to vote wisely and seek out women who did not vote to educate them about their duty to do so. Terrell believed the falling rate of voter participation was dangerous to the country. She stressed that it was important for all women to elect the best leaders, but "owing to the conditions which confront us as colored women all over the United States, it means more to us than it does to any of our sisters in the other racial groups."[48] The *Detroit Independent* echoed a similar thought when they published "Why the Negro Should Register and Vote" by a schoolgirl named Ida Mae Bell. She opposed the segregation in movie theaters and claimed this condition could be rectified if people used the power of the ballot.[49]

Clubwomen did vote more than women overall. A 1922 DFWC survey of twenty-one member clubs reported that 65 percent of their members were registered and voted.[50] But this evidence simply took clubwomen at their word. Some but not all Detroit clubwomen wanted to take advantage of their available political tools as they pursued their civic work in the city.

Traditional ideas about the home made the public uncomfortable with the visibility of women in public roles. During the 1920 presidential election in Detroit, many of the 250 women employed as registration clerks were asked who was taking care of the house in their absence. They constantly had to refute accusations that husbands were left at home to care for their children and make dinner.[51] Detroit women also had to counter stereotypes about what kind of politics was right for them. Some men believed that women were "naturally" suited for social welfare work. When that work intersected with the political realm, as it increasingly did, women's input was welcomed. Helen Russell, president of the MFWC, said, "When men cease to regard us as tepid philanthropists and receive us as fellow workers, we can sooner accomplish our aims and society will benefit."[52]

The equality that Russell advocated proved elusive in the 1920s. Women's enfranchised status was narrowly interpreted and did not include officeholding or leadership positions within the parties. This view was embraced by both men and women. White clubwoman Ethel Thomas explained that in managing a victorious campaign for Mabel Baldwin for the Royal Oak Council, "one of my greatest problems in gaining support for my candidate was to cope with the stubborn opposition and lethargy on the part of many women." She went on to say that they got women to vote by arriving at their homes on election day and escorting them to the polls.[53]

Similarly, white clubwoman Clara Downey declared she was "completely disillusioned" by women in politics. Downey claimed that women failed to work together and were ignorant of political issues. She believed women were simply in politics for their "own glorification and popularity." Downey's displeasure with the behavior of political women seems to be limited to women in party politics. She had worked for the Republican Party and believed that women who worked in party politics lost their commitment to the common good and replaced it with personal gratification. She concluded by saying, "To my mind Detroit women in politics are an absolute 'flop.'"[54]

Since some women were divided as to the role of women in politics, it is not surprising that they continued to be divided over the issue of equal rights for women. The issue of women's rights arose again in Michigan in 1925 when Frances Florer authored a bill that would give women full contractual privileges and protect them from the undue influence of their husbands. Having received the endorsement of Detroit's judge Ira W. Jayne, Florer sought but failed to receive the support of the DFWC. A law student herself, Florer was interested in raising the status of married women in Michigan. Florer stated that a married woman in Michigan could own a separate estate, contract for her services, and collect her own wages but was not considered "competent to enter into any engagement, transaction or contract the same . . . if unmarried." The 1925 Florer Bill attempted to end that disability for married women by granting them full contractual privileges. It would also protect married women who were coerced into signing notes with their husbands.[55]

While the DFWC supported the safeguarding of a wife's separate property and undue coercion from her husband, its Board of Directors did not endorse full contractual privileges. The board adopted a resolution (47–7) regarding women's rights that was a clarification of their ideas about equality and difference. It declared that the family was a social unit in which women had natural duties as wives and mothers. The law, the DFWC proposed, should reflect those differences. Consequently, absolute equality would be of no benefit, yet women were neither inferior nor superior to men.[56]

Lucia Grimes wrote to DFWC president Edna Prescott protesting this narrow view, claiming that if the board were against equal rights, then it must also be against women voting, women serving on juries, and equal guardianship. She went on to protest both the article in the *Detroit Free Press* denouncing the Florer Bill, signed by DFWC members Grace Krolik and Gertrude Wallace, and the fact that the DFWC sent the article to all the senators in Michigan. It was assumed the DFWC reacted vigorously against the bill because the board felt it was highly endorsed by the National Woman's Party (NWP). The NWP championed full equality for women and campaigned for the Equal Rights (ERA) or Lucretia Mott amendment. Most Detroit clubwomen believed in full citizenship, but they opposed the ERA because they feared it would disqualify women from protective labor legislation. The DFWC leadership wanted to divorce themselves from the Florer Bill and voice their disapproval. Grimes ended by claiming that the signed and distributed *Free Press* article killed the measure.[57] Ella Aldinger of the State Legislative Council of Women reported in the summer of 1925 that the bill had passed in the state House but failed in the Senate.[58] In this instance Michigan women in general and clubwomen in particular were in disagreement. Women's political effectiveness was fragile, and strident differences over expanded women's rights kept the issue problematic throughout the decade.

Volunteer and club work did not necessarily educate women as to the advantages of full contractual privileges. Throughout the 1920s, Senator George Condon repeatedly introduced a bill that would grant a married woman the right to contract. His efforts met with defeat because, according to Ella Aldinger, "Few men are willing to give the right to women after they are married to conduct their own business."[59] Finally, in 1929, the bill passed the legislature but was vetoed by Governor Fred Green. His veto offers some insight on the reasons why it was difficult to pass equal rights legislation in Michigan. The governor said, "In these days of installment buying and high pressure salesmen we need all the protection we can get not only for the wives but for the husbands as well." The governor believed that women were vulnerable to "high pressure salesmen" and susceptible to living beyond their means. The protection for husbands came in the form of preventing their wives from indulging in foolish consumerism. Green claimed that the number of women who might suffer without the bill would be very small compared to the number who would be adversely affected "if all protection were removed as in the proposed bill."[60] Consequently, women continued to suffer from disparaging stereotypes that portrayed them as spendthrifts and incompetent consumers.

In 1920s Detroit, most clubwomen battled those pejorative stereotypes with their political work. Although their political education was respected, in 1928 they still encountered marked hostility to any civic intrusion. The *Detroit News* reported that many clubwomen were discouraged by husbands who failed to take their club plans seriously. Their husbands greeted their ideas for civic projects condescendingly and said their "plan is not practical, that it is just like a woman." One politically active Detroit woman believed all men were hostile toward women's progress and if women wanted to accomplish anything, "they must have the courage to carry on without the men."[61]

Detroit women also had to counter negative stereotypes about being too silly, irrationally emotional, or entirely self-centered in order to be taken seriously in politics. In 1928, the *Detroit News* printed a full-page artistic rendering of women voters titled "Political Views." A stylish flapper at the center mused over a ballot box while all around the box other equally stylish women looked at candidates' positions, remarking, "Such eyes," "He's so adorable looking," "He has the most charming manners," and "What a wonderful physique." The message was quite clear that women (or least young women) voted based on superficial attributes, not issues.[62]

Although such characterizations were certainly unfair to civic-minded women, clubwomen did themselves a disservice at times by engaging in activities that reinforced stereotypes about women. For example, in 1928 the Wayne County LWV held a fashion show to educate the well-dressed woman voter on what to wear.[63] Janie Porter Barrett's 1925 report of the National Executive Board Meeting for the NACW described the appearance of the members as well as the issues: "They were well-dressed, stylish, conservative, well-groomed and well shod."[64] Marjorie Elaine Porter, club editor for the *Detroit News,* reported that at some lectures, Detroit's white clubwomen behaved like adoring schoolgirls before prominent celebrities instead of serious, intelligent women.[65]

Such incidents, however, were anomalies. Most clubwomen who attended political presentations were interested in informative, intellectual lectures. When male speakers simply complimented them or presented material in a simplistic manner, they were insulted. Mrs. J. Nelson Lewis, president of the DFWC, explained that men failed to believe that women could grasp intellectual concepts. They not only wasted the women's time but insulted them. While not all clubs had negative experiences with male speakers, many prominent ones did. Mrs. Harry V. Woodhouse believed that hundreds of votes could be lost as a result of the shallowness of a speaker's presentation.[66]

Those presentations often came during candidates' days, which were not always treated in Detroit with seriousness by male candidates. For example, in 1924 the *Detroit News* reported that many times male candidates addressed a particular club by the wrong name.[67] Another article, published later in the decade, noted that female candidates were courteous and accurate when they spoke to club members and distinguished themselves by speaking succinctly and forcefully. The *News* declared that the female candidates addressed their audience and finished their speeches before the men finished their "glad to be here" preliminaries.[68] Women candidates, who regarded clubwomen as astute voters, took their speaking obligations seriously and were well-prepared. Men were oftentimes neither serious nor prepared and this reflected their pejorative view of enfranchised clubwomen.

Male candidates in general viewed clubwomen as not politically astute enough for them to bother to give an intellectually rigorous presentation; they thought they could gain women's votes simply by showing up. Male candidates often ridiculed clubwomen's political intelligence and did not present serious-minded speeches; one candidate even manicured his nails while others spoke. These candidates were willing to speak but did not view women voters as a serious political audience.[69]

By 1929, underdog candidates were still appearing before women's clubs but others sent substitute spokesmen. For example, in April 1929, Governor Fred Green sent a spokesman to the DFWC to represent him,[70] and in the fall mayoralty election that year, neither candidate showed up. They both claimed they were exhausted from campaigning.[71] Candidates weighed their campaigning time carefully and if a slight to the women voters would not hurt their chances at the ballot box, they declined to speak at women's clubs or simply stayed away.

Candidates' casual attitude toward clubwomen's candidates' days are in marked contrast to the actions of their counterparts in the South, where they not only attended candidates' days ten years after women got the franchise but pledged support for women's issues, although they did complain about the endless questions from women. Like Detroit women, politically active southern women forced candidates to have a full airing of the issues. Nevertheless, southern candidates respected the voting strength of white women because southern women were slowly turning away from the Democratic Party to the Republicans. This happened in the 1928 presidential election when both Virginia and North Carolina went Republican. Southern candidates thus respected the power (or threat of power) of women's votes and courted female support throughout the decade.[72]

Southern politicians and those of Detroit encountered different political realities. Because of the disenfranchisement of African Americans in the southern states, the voting rolls there were substantially smaller. Between 1920 and 1930 only 20 percent of eligible voters participated in the South. Southern white women may have therefore had more political clout than white women in the North.[73]

While white clubwomen in Detroit struggled to attract participants for candidates' days, they also encountered problems getting their political message out. The newspapers continued to print their political activities on a separate women's page within a women's, society, or home section. The newspaper with the largest city circulation, the *Detroit News*, had both a women's page and a column called "The Club Man." These pages were devoted to reports of the various white clubs around the city. The activities of African American clubs were not reported.[74] However, the black newspapers filled this void by printing stories about black club members, but they also put the black women's club news on a separate society or church page.[75] Thus women's political activities were almost always printed in the context of strictly women's interests (society, home, or church). It was only on rare occasions (usually when the editorial staff agreed with a club's political position) that clubwomen's work, even if it pertained to important civic matters, ran on the general news pages. This policy simply reinforced the notion that women's political work had a narrow scope and was not pertinent to the wider political interests of the city. It was simply "women's work" and not to be taken seriously.

African American clubwomen not only struggled to gain political respect but had to counter racial stereotypes as well. Black clubwomen were aware that the large newspapers seldom printed positive stories about their race and therefore began writing for several of Detroit's black newspapers. In 1925 the Detroit Study Club's Lillian Johnson gave an address to club members on the importance of newspapers for the black community. She said that every racial group needed its own paper to keep in touch and express the needs of its community. Johnson noted that it was especially important for African Americans because they needed to be united against prejudice and seldom got a fair press otherwise.[76]

In 1925 clubwoman Meta E. Pelham, a reporter for the *Detroit Plaindealer,* encouraged African American women to join or help finance a black newspaper.[77] She claimed that there was always newspaper space for negative news about black Detroiters, but "the good things we do too often fail to bring to us the respect and consideration due us because they do not reach the public eye."[78] Several African American women took this message to heart. Isabelle Carter became the vice president of the *Detroit Independent*.[79] Clubwoman Margaret (Mrs. James) McCall wrote for the *Detroit Independent* during the 1920s, and in 1933 she and her husband joined the staff of the *Detroit Tribune*. Bettie Elizabeth Ellington was the vice president and managing editor of the *Tribune*, which was dedicated to breaking down barriers in employment that kept minorities from upward mobility. The paper published articles advocating for better jobs, equal wage scales, and promotions and more positions in fire and police departments for blacks, as well as African American teachers and jobs for blacks in city, county, and state governments.[80] Lastly, Beulah Young, who wrote for the *Detroit Independent*, later established the *Detroit People's News* in 1924 and published it until 1930.[81]

Beulah Alexander Young organized the Political Leaders Assembly, which helped elect Charles C. Diggs to the Michigan Senate. Burton Historical Collection, Detroit Public Library.

In spite of this effort, negative stories about blacks were printed even in the minority papers. African American clubwomen Geraldine Bledsoe and Nellie Watts believed that the racial situation in Detroit required a form of self-censorship in African American newspapers. In the 1930s they complained to the *Detroit Tribune* about its coverage of black crime. The women believed that since the paper was owned and edited in Detroit, it had an obligation to print the "progressive" news about the race and not sensationalize the negative news. The *Tribune* replied that the newspaper was a business and that sensational stories sold better than others.[82]

By 1930, with Detroit sinking into a deep economic depression, all clubwomen had additional concerns beyond negative media coverage. Their concerns were many: new construction had declined, business inventories had accumulated, new car sales were lagging, and the employment rate had decreased by 21.5 percent (the rate in factories had declined by 52 percent). Detroit had the highest rate of unemployment of any big city in the nation. In short, Detroit was the "hardest hit big city in the nation during the Hoover years."[83]

In response to the economic downturn, many women's clubs set about to study the causes of and cures for this problem. In December 1929, a committee of DFWC women appointed by Jean Chamberlain and known as the WMBC Relief Committee took over the relief work of radio station WMBC. The clubwomen oversaw the distribution of sixteen thousand dollars that had been collected by the radio station. The permanent treasurer of the WMBC Relief Committee, Berneice Collins, wrote to the DFWC and commended them for the help they gave in the face of terrible distress.[84]

The gravity of the economic situation demanded that Detroit clubwomen not only continue to study the problem but formulate more effective plans to alleviate it. At the Thirty-Sixth Annual Convention of the MFWC, the members endorsed a new resolution proposed by the state commissioner of labor and industry, Isabel Larwill, for old-age pensions. This whole project was undertaken as a commitment to provide, in a decent and humane way, for the elderly worker. Clubwomen would also study how old-age laws were administered in other states with an eye toward developing a similar program for Michigan.[85] Michigan clubwomen were committed to providing a modicum of security for working people.

In addition to the MFWC endorsement the MLWV was quite eager to support old-age pensions. It deviated from its usual policy of a two-year study period for any legislation when it voted in November 1930 to draft an emergency bill for the January 1931 legislature after hearing a lecture by William Leiserson, who was a professor at Antioch College and a former member of President Harding's Labor Conference. Professor Leiserson claimed that business had failed America because it should have been able to give all Americans an opportunity to make a living. He urged the league to draft a bill similar to the workmen's compensation bill but that would require employers to insure their workers against unemployment. He added that employers must consider their workers as carefully as they did their products. While some felt that the primary purpose of the league was education and voted against this resolution, most club members felt the situation demanded swift action and supported the resolution.[86]

In the fall of 1930, the DFWC sponsored a plan to create employment for five thousand men. President Hoover had suggested that people employ others to do repair and clean-up work; the DFWC announced a project to have members hire unemployed people to do odd jobs.[87] The first step in the plan was to enlist women from the 130 clubs in the city to determine how many housewives could use some help during the day washing windows, gardening, shoveling snow, and so forth. If twelve women each employed a man for four hours, this would be full-time work. The proposed wage would be $100–125 per month. The clubwomen did this in cooperation with the newly elected mayor, Frank Murphy; they also supported his subcommittee on creative employment to persuade employers to go ahead with all possible construction plans.[88] However, employing five thousand men would have required the participation of sixty thousand women. In the final analysis, the plan only produced twenty-seven jobs.

Another DFWC plan to provide direct relief for workers was equally unsuccessful. In January 1930, the league voted to give five hundred dollars to the International Institute to finance one half-time ethnic worker for ten months. The institute would then send the league monthly reports on his situation. When it came time to appropriate the money, the members voted to give only one hundred dollars. Even the DFWC had fallen on hard times. It also had to cease publishing the *Club Woman,* their magazine and main source of revenue, during the Depression.[89] In spite of all these hardships, both black and white Detroit clubwomen devised clever and successful ways to raise money and distribute it to those in need. While charity and welfare work had always occupied many women's clubs, the economic devastation of the Depression made this work far more common. At the December 1930 meeting of the white Detroit Review Club, the members paid to attend their annual Christmas party, then each member was given part of the proceeds to distribute to needy families. In addition to monetary gifts, the members gave clothes and Christmas food. Similarly, African American women raised more than two hundred dollars at a Christmas party and bought shoes and clothing for needy children with the proceeds.[90]

Female African American reformers in Detroit had been engaged in social welfare work long before the Depression. They often operated within Detroit's Second Baptist Church in clubs like the American Beauty Club, founded in 1922, which provided services for new members. By the 1930s, however, black reformers focused on black employment and civil rights. Employment and civil rights were added to African American clubwomen's agenda focusing on female respectability.[91]

The Housewives' League of Detroit demonstrated this combined emphasis well. Fannie (Mrs. William) Peck founded the club on June 10, 1930, to promote employment opportunities for the black community and to "stabilize the economic status of the Negro through direct spending."[92] This organization used black economic clout, what Darlene Clark Hine calls "economic nationalism," in their quest for greater racial economic independence. Respecting gender sensitivity, the women pledged to keep their activities to home, family, and community or areas that were commonly within female province, and pledged to patronize only Negro businesses and firms that employed Negroes. This boycott of white businesses was especially needed because by 1930 black men and women's employment opportunities were limited in the North. Black clubwomen's loyalty gave confidence to Negro businessmen and encouraged the next generation to strive for greater economic independence.[93] The success of the Housewives' League encouraged other African American women to found similar organizations in other cities; their motto was "Don't buy from where you can't work." In 1933 they joined together to form the National Housewives' League of America with Fannie Peck as the first president.[94]

As the economic depression worsened for all, Detroit was in political trouble as well. In July 1930 a campaign to recall Mayor Charles Bowles was under way. The public was dissatisfied with him because he had been unable to work effectively with the City Council, made appointments on partisan or personal bases, was suspected of having connections to organized crime, denied the press access to relevant records, refused to respond to questions, and had increased the fare on the Detroit Street Railway.[95]

Frank Murphy, who had been supported by Detroit's white clubwomen in the important Recorder's Court election of 1923, once more got their support in the mayoral election of September 1930. Murphy's relationship with clubwomen was certainly a politically compatible one. He endeared himself to the women's clubs by "presenting an image of sacrifice to public duty." More important, he embodied many of the same ideas about the proper role of government as clubwomen had: "good government was a social obligation for the education of youth, the peace, health and safety of the people and for the care of the poor and sick." He separated himself from earlier Detroit political leaders by advocating that government should be run efficiently, economically, and on a nonpartisan basis. Finally, like Detroit clubwomen, Murphy believed in using political power to effect social change.[96]

In all their activities addressing the problems brought on by massive urbanization and industrialization, clubwomen were certain that their counsel in these civic matters was crucial. Armed with the franchise, they set about to make their demands known. They were relegated to organizational, not leadership, positions in the political parties and were seldom successful candidates for public office. Consequently, while some joined and worked for the political parties, many others continued their political work within the framework of their clubs. This gave them control over the leadership and issues in their clubs but contributed to a diffused effort and pejorative stereotypes. Clubwomen themselves sometimes showed a preference for nonpolitical work. Most, however, wanted to be active participants in the political process because they believed that, as equal citizens, they had a responsibility to do so.

During the 1920s, clubwomen teamed up with other civic groups and contributed their organizational and networking ability to many successful projects. The 1931 centennial edition of the *Detroit Free Press* reported that it was "difficult to find any civic project, relating to the welfare of women and children and even of general import which the City Federation [Detroit Federation of Women's Clubs] had not helped to bring about."[97] At the same time, they were learning the limits of their enfranchised citizenship. In 1920s Detroit, women encountered a gendered politics and did not share political power equally within the city. Still, by the end of the decade, politicians like Mayor Frank Murphy sought out the support of Detroit's clubwomen. He appreciated their impressive organizational ability and respected their political opinions. He understood the city was run by both male and female citizens.

Conclusion

No effort is in vain; the reward is in the doing.

New Era Study Club Song, "Early History of the New Era Study Club"

In 1930, Detroit was mired in a deep economic depression. The city was confronted with all its previous municipal responsibilities plus an enormous public relief burden. In July of that year, the mayor, Charles Bowles, was recalled. In the subsequent election, Frank Murphy was elected mayor. Clubwomen supported Murphy because his philosophy of government was similar to theirs. When he declared his candidacy, he echoed Progressive Era concerns, saying that Detroit was "in ashes, a political ruin, burned to the ground by hate, by discord, by selfishness, by government put to corrupt and selfish ends." He promised to maintain his "conception of social and progressive justice."[1]

In opposing the business-sponsored candidate, white clubwomen displayed the same political independence they had in the 1923 Recorder's Court election. Although black and white clubwomen did not work together, both groups had strong supporters among them for Murphy. Murphy was a Democrat, but the president of the Detroit Women's Republican Club voted for him. African American women also voted independently of their leaders; Beulah Young pledged to "keep all the coloured people's votes in Detroit sewed up" for Murphy. Murphy received a majority, sometimes as high as 80 percent, in all the black precincts.[2]

Detroit women both black and white emerged from the 1920s as influential, but seldom crucial, players in Detroit politics. A 1931 article in *The Detroiter* described the progress twentieth-century cities had made in areas like public health, recreation, and education, all areas in which Detroit clubwomen had sponsored programs. The article predicted that "The political intelligence of the coming city will be better organized than at present, with women, labor and business representatives in council."[3] While such praise was certainly deserved, overall, clubwomen were unable to accomplish as much as they perhaps wanted to or could have.

The explanation for that qualified success lies in the methodological and ideological strategies Detroit clubwomen used in their civic activities. Clubwomen entered into municipal politics maintaining their club affiliations, through which they attempted to influence officials and public policy. The choice of many to confine political work to within the clubs had organizational and practical considerations. They had used this methodology successfully in appealing to local and state governments before suffrage. Within their organizations, they were able to control their agenda and their method of work. As white women oftentimes jealously guarded their programs, so, too, did black women who believed they had to compromise their goals when they affiliated with white women.[4] Even when black clubwomen offered overtures, they were never reciprocated.

Detroit clubwomen's political culture arose under circumstances that had changed by the time they acquired the franchise and yet they maintained many of the same strategies. For example, clubwomen's aversion to partisan politics may have been a strategic error, considering the fact that many political decisions were made within the parties. Furthermore, even when they joined parties, women's political independence caused male party regulars to regard them as suspect and unreliable. In the 1920s Detroit politics were vastly different than they had been only twenty years earlier with the advent of industrialization and a growing multiethnic and biracial population. Clubwomen took notice of these changes but did not significantly change their modus operandi.

Clubwomen's separate political traditions had methodological advantages as well as disadvantages. Pursuing political work alongside other club activities sometimes produced dissension within the ranks and created an overcrowded agenda where programs only received cursory attention. In addition, the press often marginalized club work by relegating news about their programs to the clubwomen's pages, leaving them vulnerable to pejorative stereotypes about women's political capabilities. Working often exclusively with other racially and socioeconomically similar clubwomen isolated them and clouded their judgment. Finally, clubwomen's tendency to scrutinize political issues kept them well informed but also impeded their ability to attend to pressing issues.

In Detroit clubwomen's political culture had ideological implications that both enhanced and hindered their political effectiveness. Within the urban context of 1920s Detroit, clubwomen successfully championed policies to protect women and children from the worst abuses of an industrial economy. They sought to reduce crime by creating a more moral environment and advocated for more humane forms of incarceration and punishment. Women also addressed the daily dangers of living in an urban society, raising public awareness of government's responsibility to ensure citizens' health, welfare, and safety. In addition, clubwomen had a certain moral clout when it came to these typically "women's" issues. As they gained respect for their opinions on issues related to women and children, however, this also limited their range of issues; overplaying maternalism could be disadvantageous as well.[5]

As clubwomen advocated policies that protected women and children, they also erred in believing that they spoke for all women. In the DFWC, there were a variety of religious women's clubs, a few African American ones, and some business and professional clubs but almost no ethnic or working-class women's organizations. In spite of the selective nature of Detroit's clubwomen, they believed that they had the exclusive right to speak for all. Detroit's white clubwomen advocated programs that had gendered notions rooted in class assumptions that dictated that most women avoid wage work. These class assumptions also had a racial component to them as white clubwomen facilitated wage work for African American women. White clubwomen had "unrealistic expectations of female unity, embedded in essentialist notions of womanhood."[6] This error was repeated by African American clubwomen as well, who felt they spoke for all African American women. Black clubwomen's policies and programs were also rooted in class terms when they stressed bourgeois ideology. They often misunderstood their working-class sisters. In addition, they clung to the perception that Victorian notions of female respectability would prove black women worthy of respect. This, in turn, would increase respect for the whole race. Their commitment to this idea persisted throughout the decade even as other African American women turned away from exclusive clubs to use militancy and promote economic nationalism.[7]

For Detroit's clubwomen, maintaining their clubs and pre-suffrage strategies for civic improvement was a logical choice because even though women had gained the franchise, politics was still dominated by men. Detroit women did not challenge the political structure but instead pursued public policies that stemmed from private needs.[8] Clubwomen's maternalist vision was really about power relations and the limited choices for women. Clubwomen looked to the state to provide a healthier, more moral environment for themselves and their families.[9]

The male monopoly of Detroit's business community with its profound influence on municipal politics provided an urban context that circumscribed clubwomen's political effectiveness. The city was grappling with enormous problems posed by its industrial and urban development in the early twentieth century. Detroit faced questions about what municipal services were necessary and how it would pay for them. There were also sensitive issues about public and private ownership. In this political-economic atmosphere, clubwomen's belief that they, too, were entitled to voice their demands was often greeted with marked hostility. Demands like smoke abatement became possible only when they appeared cost-effective. Clubwomen occasionally had access to powerful businessmen, like John Dodge, who helped finance the school milk program. More often, however, their ideas and reforms were received condescendingly or were met with resistance. In addition, Detroit clubwomen's fortunes were constrained by their limited access to the public media, which often portrayed them as incompetent and self-centered.

In spite of the many limitations placed on women's political effectiveness, Detroit's white clubwomen enjoyed some success in city and state political affairs. Their dogged determination to fully understand municipal matters forced a public airing of many issues. Their local organizational ability and pre-primary plans brought Detroit politics to the neighborhood block. The educational and get-out-the-vote campaigns encouraged learned and participatory city politics.

Clubwomen successfully sponsored legislation to make the work environment more suitable for women. They joined, and oftentimes led, campaigns against the high cost of living. They worked tirelessly for mothers' pensions and lobbied for Sheppard-Towner legislation and funding. They actively supported anti-gambling legislation and both Prohibition and Prohibition reform. Women worked to establish and thereafter supported the Women's Division of the Detroit Police Department. They investigated prisons and successfully defeated measures to reinstitute capital punishment in Michigan. They were considered meticulous, respected jurors. Within the city, they organized public awareness campaigns of such health dangers as rats and smoke. Clubwomen worked both legislatively and educationally for safety on Detroit streets and in Detroit homes. They successfully challenged the Republican domination of the state and helped elect Democrat Woodbridge Ferris to the U.S. Senate in 1922. Lastly, Detroit clubwomen followed their beliefs and helped elect Frank Murphy in both the crucial Recorder's Court election of 1923 and the important mayoral election in 1929. They achieved their successes often with other allies in the Detroit community.

The political history of Detroit's clubwomen in the 1920s has implications that reach beyond the city and help explain the political environment of the time. It shows how in spite of the franchise, women were only grudgingly accepted into the political process. Especially within the political parties, men were still in charge and only willing to grant women qualified participation, on male-defined terms. But political women, for their part, did not acquiesce to those demands; they simply continued to work as they had previously, in their clubs and associations. Women were not less political after suffrage. From their pre-suffrage experience, they understood that politics was male dominated. Thus, the vote was welcomed but not perceived as the end of the struggle for equal participation. Perhaps women misjudged the intransigence of men, but they knew the obstacles. In assessing their situation, women were selective about issues.

Detroit's black and white clubwomen fared differently in the 1930s. For white clubwomen, the adoption of federal welfare policies such as Social Security and Aid to Dependent Children vindicated their ideas about the state's responsibility for mothers and children.

In addition, women like Frances Perkins and Eleanor Roosevelt gave high-profile publicity to political women during the New Deal. African American clubwomen, on the other hand, suffered from their firm commitment to Victorian ideals. Victoria Wolcott has explained that in the future African American female respectability centered more on "self-worth, family survival and racial pride" than on the dated notions of bourgeois values held by clubwomen.[10] Black clubwomen could not adapt to the new public acceptance of sexuality or the male-dominated "New Negro" movement. Deborah Gray White has even concluded that the 1920s "crippled" the club movement.[11]

Despite the rather uneven rate of their political achievements, Detroit clubwomen had established a distinct presence in Detroit politics. Their experience reveals much about the political culture of the 1920s and women's role in it. Mass industrialization, mass immigration, and the doubling of the franchise all coincided in 1920s Detroit, making it an excellent environment to examine the role of urban and gendered variables on the activities of politically active clubwomen. The challenges remained for Detroit clubwomen, but they had moved toward fulfilling their promise.

Appendix: Directory of the Detroit Federation of Women's Clubs, 1926

Organized January 28, 1895
Charter Member of State Federation, 1895
Member of General Federation, 1916
Club House, Northwest Corner, Second and Hancock avenues

Past Presidents

Mrs. Frances G. Boynton
Miss Lydia Hopkins
Mrs. Pamela A. Patterson
Mrs. Andrew Howell
Mrs. John Walker
Mrs. Clara B. Arthur
Mrs. Clara C. Hickey
Mrs. W. H. Holden
Mrs. George G. Caron
Mrs. Delphine D. Ashbaugh
Mrs. W. R. Alvord
Mrs. C. R. Wilson
Mrs. Frederick G. Ray
Mrs. C. M. Novak
Mrs. Lillian S. Mathews

President Emeritus

Mrs. Delphine Dodge Ashbaugh

Honorary President

Mrs. Emma A. Fox

Officers, 1925–26

Mrs. Herbert F. Prescott, President
Mrs. Claire E. Swain, First Vice President
Mrs. George E. Phillips, Second Vice President
Mrs. Malcolm McKinnon, Recording Secretary
Mrs. A. H. Holman, Corresponding Secretary
Mrs. M. T. Wright, Treasurer
Mrs. Emma A. Fox, Official Parliamentarian

Executive Committee

Mrs. Arthur J. Lacy
Mrs. Geo. E. Doyle
Mrs. A. A. Hughes

Chairmen of Departments

Public Welfare Department

Mrs. W. L. Bullard, Chairman

DIVISIONS
Mrs. L. G. Cooper, Child Welfare
Mrs. Wm. B. Kelsey, Book and Periodical Committee
Mrs. Julien S. Connor, Public Health
Mrs. T. D. Moule, Public Safety

American Citizenship Department

Mrs. Joseph N. Krolik, Chairman

DIVISIONS
Mrs. Joseph N. Krolik, Legislative
Mrs. Ernst Wuesthoff, Civic
Mrs. George P. Fraser, Americanization

Applied Education Department

Miss Esther Cousins, Chairman

DIVISIONS
Miss Esther Cousins, Educational
Mrs. Walter A. Fisher, Conservation

Special Committee

Mrs. W. R. Alvord, American Home

Fine Arts Department

Mrs. Carl B. Chamberlain, Chairman

DIVISIONS

Mrs. J. Francis Quinn, Art
Mrs. Carl. B. Chamberlain, Music
Mrs. D. H. Bather, Drama and Literature Division

Chairmen of Committees

Miss Theo. McDonald, Finance
Mrs. George Seabold, House and Supply Committee
Miss Elizabeth Matheson, Federation History
Mrs. R. E. Huffman, Membership
Mrs. W. B. Taylor, Registration
Mrs. J. B. Whitley, Program
Mrs. C. J. Burgess, Auditorium
Mrs. G. W. Getzendanner, Pages
Mrs. J. Nelson Lewis, Reception
Mrs. Roland M. Athay, Music Program (Special)
Mrs. Herbert G. Wood, Social
Mrs. C. E. Sullivan, Scholarship

The Club Woman

Mrs. R. H. Ashbaugh, Managing Director
Mrs. W. R. Alvord, Editor
Mrs. F. L. Brandes, Associate Editor
Mrs. M. B. Sulzberger, Contributing Editor
Mrs. R. F. Callaway, Dramatic Editor
Mrs. Floyd G. Hitchcock, Art Editor
Mrs. O. E. Closson, Department Editor
Miss Ethel M. Francis, Advertising and Business Manager

Clubs

Afternoon Study Club

Mrs. Irwin Fullerton, President

American Association of University Women, Detroit Branch

Dr. Mary Thompson Stevens, President

Athena Delphian
Mrs. H. W. Chapman, President

Calean Study Club
Mrs. Harry D. Bumgardner, President

Canteen Club, Co. S., No. 2
Mrs. A. F. Squire, President

Catholic Study Club
Mrs. W. W. Warren, President

Cercle Dramatique
Mrs. Ralph Ainsworth, President

Clio Club
Mrs. Julia Finster, President

Club of Today
Mrs. G. B. Young, President

Community Club
Mrs. A. H. Holman, President

Coterie
Mrs. F. G. Hutchinson, President

Current Topic Club
Miss Rose Crysler, President

Dames of the Loyal Legion, Detroit Chapter
Miss Mary Lacey, President

Daughters of G.A.R., Gen. Alpheus S. Williams Fortress No. 1
Mrs. Ethel M. Burns, President

Daughters of G.A.R., Lawrence Reese Fortress No. 7
Mrs. Thomas Woollett, President

Daughters of Veterans, Adelaide Wallace Fairbanks Post Tent No. 16
Mrs. Blanche McEwen, President

Daughters of Veterans, Sarah M. W. Sterling Tent No. 3
Mrs. Florence Hamilton, President

Daughters of Veterans, Julia Mead Janes Tent No. 13
Mrs. Elizabeth Atkinson, President

Detroit Alliance Delta Delta Delta
Mrs. Carl B. Dolbeare, President

Detroit Branch, National Story Tellers' League
Miss Elizabeth Coolidge, President

Detroit Business and Professional Woman's Club
Miss Augusta M. Bookmyer, President

Detroit Circle, Florence Crittenton Home
Mrs. H. R. Daniels, President

Detroit Chapter, King's Daughters and Sons Home for Aged People
Mrs. Florence Darling, President

Detroit Chapter, Daughters British Empire
Mrs. S. L. McCombe, Regent

Detroit District Association of Michigan State Nurses Association
Miss Katherine Kimmick, President

Detroit Elementary Teachers' Association
Mrs. A. F. Wolfschlager, President

Detroit Federation W.C.T.U.

Mrs. Matie W. Jones, President

Detroit Girl Scout Officers' Association

Miss Helen M. McDonald, President

Detroit Home Economics Association

Miss Louise M. Clawson, President

Detroit Homemakers' Club

Mrs. Edward Harris, President

Detroit Industrial Club

Mrs. Frank Wolfe, President

Detroit New Century Club

Mrs. W. E. Collins, President

Detroit Parliamentary Law Club

Mrs. Emma A. Fox, President

Detroit Review Club

Miss Fanny Hasty, President

Detroit School of Expression Alumni Study Club

Mrs. Eva Bishop, President

Detroit Section of the Council of Jewish Women

Mrs. Joseph Welt, President

Detroit Sorosis

Mrs. John S. Siefert, President

Detroit Study Club

Mrs. A. L. Turner, President

Detroit Woman's Auxiliary, R.M.A.
Mrs. B. B. Thayer, President

Detroit Woman's Club
Mrs. Roland Cornell, President

Detroit Woman Principals' Club
Miss Mabel Redman, President

Detroit Woman's Swimming Assoc.
Mrs. Bess Kennedy, President

Detroit Woman Writers' Club
Mrs. Louise B. Clancy, President

Dial Club
Mrs. Herbert W. Mason, President

Diversity Literary Club
Mrs. Frank J. Roehm, President

Edna Chaffee Noble Alumni Association
Mrs. Tresa Merrill, President

Entre Nous Club
Mrs. John Bambrick, President

Friday Study Club
Mrs. Horace Biglow, President

Gavel Club
Mrs. C. R. Wilson, President

Good Cheer Club
Miss Ethel Munroe, President

Guardian Association of Campfire Girls
Mrs. I. W. Stuart, President

Highland Park Woman's Club
Mrs. J. J. Livingstone, President

Home Study Club
Mrs. C. U. Bear, President

Hypatia Club
Mrs. Ida Jones, President

International Kindergarten Union, Detroit Branch
Mrs. Ethelyn Woodruff, President

Knight Study Club
Mrs. M. J. Wright, President

League of Protestant Women
Mrs. Rowena Rice, President

Libri
Mrs. John McNeil Burns, President

Lincoln Study Club
Mrs. Howard Marsh, President

Margaret Foley Club
Lola McPherson, President

Michigan League for Crippled Children
Mrs. E. S. Leonard, President

New Colony Club
Mrs. W. F. Seeley, President

Nornae Study Club
Mrs. J. C. Goodale, president

Northeastern Woman's Club
Mrs. Harry V. Wilkie, President

Northwestern Woman's Club
Mrs. Philip Griffiths, President

Northwestern Welfare Club
Mrs. G. M. Fanning, President

North Woodward Woman's Club
Mrs. A. J. Coon, President

Outlook Club
Mrs. W. E. Brownlee, President

Palestine Woman's Association
Mrs. W. E. Gould, President

Parmenas Club
Mrs. Robert Wells, President

P.E.O. Chapter A
Mrs. W. Robertson, President

P.E.O. Chapter B
Mrs. G. F. Key, President

P.E.O. Chapter D
Mrs. C. W. Lemmon, President

P.E.O. Chapter F
Mrs. H. M Robbins, President

P.E.O. Chapter J
Mrs. Minnie L. Mills, President

Phi Theta Phi Sorority
Miss Edna G. Luths, President

Progressive Civic League
Mrs. Ruby Zahn, President

Progressive Delphian
Miss A. M. Block, President

Samaritan Club
Mrs. L. I. Coon, President

Shakespeare Study Club
Mrs. James Edwin Hancock, President

Sigma Tau Delta Sorority
Margaret Thompson, President

Sojourners Woman's Club
Mrs. George L. Hughs, President

Southeastern Woman's Club
Mrs. J. P. Selden, President

Southwestern Woman's Club
Mrs. I. V. Maurer, President

Spanish War Woman's Club
(no president listed)

Sunshine Club
Mrs. Elizabeth Holtz, President

Theta Lambda Sorority Alumnae Chapter
Ella Kunze, President

Thursday Study Club
Mrs. J. B. Pollock, President

Tuesday Musicale
Mrs. Leland B. Case, President

Twentieth Century Club
Mrs. James A. Hurst, President

Weekly Study Club
Mrs. Charles E. Wisner, President

Western Boulevard Child's Conservation League
Mrs. W. M. Washington, President

Wimodausis
Mrs. A. G. Kunz, President

Wolverine Study Club
Mrs. F. L. Munson, President

Woman's Aquatic Club
Mrs. Minnie May Baldwin, President

Woman's Historical Club
Mrs. E. C. Calvert, President

Women's Independent Voters Association
Mrs. Harriet Trix, President

Women's Research Club
Mrs. Frederick C. Massnick, President

Woman's Social Club
Mrs. J. Evo, President

The Auxiliary to the Children's Home of the Salvation Army
Mrs. Alfred Wilson, President

Woman's Auxiliary to the Detroit Florists' Club
Mrs. John Klang, President

Women's Club of the Service Flag
Mrs. C. A. Coolidge, President

Women's Triangle Club
Mrs. F. L. Wyckoff, President

Worthwhile Club of Highland Park
Mrs. W. M. Hallack, President

Zonta Club
Miss Winifred Sewell, President

Suburban Clubs

Archie Club
Mrs. S. Zimmerman, President

Brightmoor Woman's Club
Mrs. George Baird, President

Conservation and Improvement Circle
Mrs. Grant Wilcox, President

Clawson Woman's Club
Mrs. J. E. Mooney, President

Ladies' Literary Club, Wayne
Mrs. V. R. Hisey, President

Ladies’ Literary Club, Farmington
Mrs. Roy Brown, President

Ladies’ Literary Club, Mt. Clemens
Mrs. G. R. Schimmel, President

Trenton Woman’s Club
Mrs. N. A. Mans, President

Child Study Club, Redford
Mrs. W. R. Rosengarten, President

Woman’s Club, Redford
Mrs. Carl Wilcox, President

Women’s Club, Plymouth
Mrs. R. O. Chappel, President

Tuesday Study Club, Wyandotte
Mrs. R. B. Burrell, President

Winter Study Club, Dearborn
Mrs. Louis Ives, President

Woman’s Club, Royal Oak
Mrs. W.S. McDowell, President

Woman’s Literary Club, Birmingham
Mrs. C. C. Osborn, President

Wyandotte Delphian Chapter
Mrs. G. A. Lauffer, President

Woman’s Literary Club, River Rouge
Mrs. Annie Mills, President

Notes

Notes to Introduction

1. *Detroit Times,* February 21, 1919.

2. John B. Reid, "'A Career to Build, a People to Serve, a Purpose to Accomplish': Race, Gender and Detroit's First Black Women Teachers, 1865–1916," *Michigan Historical Review* 18:1 (1992): 22–23; Stephanie J. Shaw, *What a Woman Ought to Be and to Do: Black Professional Women Workers during the Jim Crow Era* (Chicago, 1996); Deborah Gray White, *Too Heavy a Load: Black Women in Defense of Themselves, 1894–1994* (New York, 1999).

3. Anne Firor Scott, *Natural Allies: Women's Associations in American History* (Chicago, 1993).

4. Sara Evans, "Women's History and Political Theory: Toward a Feminist Approach to a Public Life," in Suzanne Lebsock and Nancy Hewitt, eds., *Visible Women: News Essays on American Activism* (Urbana, 1993), 119–39.

5. Louise A. Tilly and Patricia Gurin, "Women, Politics, and Change," in Louise A. Tilly and Patricia Gurin, eds., *Women, Politics and Change* (New York, 1992), 6.

6. See Joanne L. Goodwin, "An Experiment in Paid Motherhood: The Implementation of Mothers' Pensions in Early Twentieth-Century Chicago," *Gender and History* 3 (Autumn 1992): 323–43; Anne Meis Knupfer, *Toward a Tenderer Humanity and a Nobler Womanhood: African-American Women's Clubs in Turn of the Century Chicago* (New York, 1996); Kathryn Kish Sklar, "The Historical Foundations of Women's Power in the Creation of the American Welfare State, 1830–1930," in Seth Koven and Sonya Michel, eds., *Mothers of a New World* (New York, 1993), 43–93; Theda Skocpol, *Protecting Soldiers and Mothers: The Political Origins of Social Policy in the United States* (Cambridge, 1992); Maureen A. Flanagan, "The City Profitable, The City Livable: Environmental Policy, Gender and Power in Chicago in the 1910s," *Journal of Urban History* 22 (January 1996): 163–90; and Maureen A. Flanagan, "Gender and Urban Political Reform: The City Club and the Woman's City Club of Chicago in the Progressive Era," *American Historical Review* (October 1990): 1032–50.

7. Susan Ware, *Partner and I: Molly Dewson, Feminism and New Deal Politics* (New Haven, 1987), xii, xvi, xviii, 91.

8. Melvin Holli, *Reform in Detroit: Hazen S. Pingree and Urban Politics* (New York, 1969); Raymond R. Fragnoli, "Progressive Coalitions and Municipal Re-

form: Charter Revision in Detroit, 1912–1918," *Detroit in Perspective: A Journal of Regional History* 4 (Spring 1980): 131; Wilma Henderson, ed., *Detroit Perspectives: Crossroads and Turning Points* (Detroit, 1991), 222–24; Jack D. Elenbaas, "The Boss of the Better Class: Henry Leland and the Detroit Citizens League, 1912–1924," *Michigan History* 58:2 (Summer 1974): 131–50; John C. Leggett, "Class Consciousness and Politics in Detroit: A Study in Change," *Michigan History* 48:4 (December 1964): 290–97; Jack D. Elenbaas, "The Excess of Reform: The Day the Detroit Mayor Arrested the City Council," *Michigan History* 54:1 (Winter 1970): 266–74; Arthur E. DeMatteo, "Organized Labor versus the Mayor: The Detroit Federation of Labor and the Revised City Charter of 1914," *Michigan Historical Review* 22:2 (Fall 1995): 63–97.

9. Megan Taylor Shockley, *"We too, are Americans": African-American Women in Detroit and Richmond, 1940–1954* (Urbana, 2004); Thomas J. Sugrue, *The Origins of the Urban Crisis: Race and Inequality in Post-War Detroit* (Princeton, 1996); Heather Ann Thompson, *Whose Detroit?: Politics, Labor and Race in a Modern American City* (Cornell, 2001).

10. Victoria W. Wolcott, *Remaking Respectability: African-American Women in Interwar Detroit* (Chapel Hill, 2001).

11. Jack D. Elenbaas, "Detroit and the Progressive Era: A Study of Urban Reform, 1900–1914" (Ph.D. diss., Wayne State University, 1968), 120.

12. Pamela Tyler, *Silk Stockings and Ballot Boxes: Women and Politics in New Orleans, 1920–1963* (Athens, GA, 1996), 14; Scott, *Natural Allies,* 153.

13. Lorraine Gates Schuyler, *The Weight of Their Votes: Southern Women and Political Leverage in the 1920s* (Chapel Hill, 2011), 7, 11.

14. Paula Baker, "The Domestication of Politics: Women and American Political Society, 1780–1920," in Vicki L. Ruiz and Ellen Carol DuBois, eds., *Unequal Sisters: A Multicultural Reader in U.S. Women's History,* 2nd ed. (New York, 1994), 91.

15. "A Brief History of the Detroit Federation of Women's Clubs," *1918–1919 Directory of the Detroit Federation of Women's Clubs,* pp. 9–11, Burton Historical Collection, Detroit Public Library (hereafter BHC).

16. Evans, "Women's History and Political Theory," 128.

17. Gayle Gullett, *Becoming Citizens: The Emergence and Development of the California Women's Movement, 1880–1911* (Urbana, 2000), 3.

18. Scott, *Natural Allies,* 142.

19. Maureen Flanagan, *Seeing with Their Hearts: Chicago Women and the Vision of the Good City, 1871–1933* (Princeton, 2002), 29.

20. Gullett, *Becoming Citizens.*

21. http://www.daahp.wayne.edu/1900_1949html

22. Arthur LaBrew, *300th Year Celebration: The Black Community, Its Music and the Fine and Secular Arts; The Detroit History That Nobody Knew (or bothered to remember) 1800–1900* (Detroit, 2001), 157.

23. Linda Gordon, *Pitied But Not Entitled: Single Mothers and the History of Welfare* (New York, 1994), 111–12, 124, 141–42.

24. Ruth Feldstein, *Motherhood in Black and White: Race and Sex in American Liberalism, 1930–1965* (Ithaca, 2000); Cheryl D. Hicks, *Talk with You Like a Woman: African American Women, Justice and Reform in New York, 1890–1935* (Chapel Hill, 2011); Molly Ladd-Taylor, *Mother-Work: Women, Child Welfare and the State, 1890–1930* (Urbana, 1994); Gwendolyn Mink, *The Wages of Motherhood: Inequality in the Welfare State, 1917–1942* (Ithaca, 1995).

25. Maureen A. Flanagan, "The Predicament of New Rights: Suffrage and Women's Political Power from a Local Perspective," *Social Politics: International Studies in Gender, State and Society* 2 (Fall 1995): 305–30.

26. Skocpol, *Protecting Soldiers and Mothers,* 2–3.

27. Nancy F. Cott, "Across the Great Divide: Women in Politics before and after 1920," in Tilly and Gurin, eds., *Women, Politics and Change,* 154–72.

28. Gladys E. Nauss, "Detroit Federation of Women's Clubs: A Study in Organizational Change" (Master's thesis, Wayne State University, 1949), 10.

29. Dorothy Salem, *To Better Our World: Black Women in Organized Reform, 1890–1920* (Brooklyn, 1990), 42.

30. Robin S. Peebles, "Detroit's Black Women's Clubs," *Michigan History* 70 (January–February 1986): 48; Joyce Haynes-Brooks, "Message from the President," Fiftieth Rededication Celebration, Detroit Association of Women's Clubs, BHC. For a comparison with Chicago black women's clubs, see Knupfer, *Toward a Tenderer Humanity and a Nobler Womanhood.*

31. Baker, "The Domestication of Politics," 97; Flanagan, "The Predicament of New Rights," 305–30; Kathryn Kish Sklar, *Florence Kelley and the Nation's Work: The Rise of Women's Public Culture, 1830–1900* (New Haven, 1995); Evans, "Women's History and Political Theory"; Scott, *Natural Allies,* 33.

32. Maureen Flanagan, *Charter Reform in Chicago* (Carbondale, 1987), *21;* James J. Connolly, *The Triumph of Ethnic Progressivism: Urban Political Culture in Boston, 1900–1925* (Cambridge, 1998).

33. Sarah Mercer Judson, "Cultivating Citizenship in the Kindergartens of Atlanta, 1890s–1920s," *Atlanta History* 41:4 (January 1998): 17–33; Glenda Gilmore, *Gender and Jim Crow: Women and the Politics of White Supremacy in North Carolina, 1890–1920* (Chapel Hill, 1996), 195–202.

34. The origin of this quote is in dispute, perhaps by Lotte Scharfman, president of the Massachusetts League of Women, at a later date (http://www.lwvma.org/cet.shtml, accessed August 10, 2011) or Marian Wright Edelman, African American lawyer (http://www.feminist.com/resources/quotes/democ.html).

35. Schuyler, *The Weight of Their Votes,* 11, 165.

36. "A Challenge and a Promise," 5.

Notes to Chapter 1

1. Sharon E. McHaney, "Securing the Sacred Right to Vote," *Michigan History Magazine* 75 (March/April 1991): 40.

2. Ibid., 41.

3. Alice Tarbell Crathern, *In Detroit . . . Courage Was the Fashion: The Contribution of Women to the Development of Detroit, 1701 to 1951* (Detroit, 1953), 117, 119.

4. Ibid., 118.

5. "Club History," Box 11, Manuscript Collection, Emma A. Fox Papers, BHC.

6. McCoy was born Mary Eleanor Delaney and attended a Freedmen's School in St. Louis. She moved to Detroit in 1875 upon her marriage to Elijah McCoy. Arthur Turner and Earl Moses, *Colored Detroit: A Brief History of Detroit's Colored Population and Directory of Their Businesses, Organizations, Professions and Trades* (Detroit, 1924), 15.

7. Turner and Moses, *Colored Detroit,* 15.

8. Clara B. Arthur, *Progress of Michigan Women* (Detroit, n.d., n.p.), 5, BHC.

9. Evans, "Women's History and Political Theory," 130.

10. "A Brief History of the Detroit Federation of Women's Clubs," 11.

11. Clara Arthur's concern for children had begun in New Brunswick, Canada, where she was the daughter of the first woman teacher there. Her educational background and civic interests were similar to those of many Detroit clubwomen. Arthur graduated from the New Brunswick Normal Training School in 1875. Shortly after her marriage and subsequent move to Detroit, she became a charter member of the Equal Suffrage Club and was elected president of the Michigan Equal Suffrage Association in 1906. She was a charter member of the progressive Twentieth Century Club and president of the DFWC. Detroit historian Clarence Burton described her as a tireless worker for equal suffrage and "community uplift." Clarence Burton, *The City of Detroit, Michigan, 1701–1922* (Detroit: S. J. Clarke, 1927), 5:147.

12. Crathern, *In Detroit,* 124–26.

13. Roy Rosenweig, *Eight Hours for What We Will: Workers & Leisure in an Industrial City, 1870–1920* (New York, 1983).

14. Dominick Cavallo, *Muscles and Morals: Organized Playgrounds and Urban Reform, 1880–1920* (Philadelphia, 1981), 38.

15. Scott, *Natural Allies,* 124–25.

16. Cavallo, *Muscles and Morals,* 1.

17. "Americanization Committee," *Club Woman* 12:1 (September 1919): 14.

18. Gullett, *Becoming Citizens;* Judith N. McArthur, *Creating the New Woman: The Rise of Southern Women's Progressive Culture in Texas, 1893–1918* (Chicago, 1998).

19. Melissa R. Klapper, *Small Strangers: The Experience of Immigrant Children in America, 1880–1925* (Chicago, 2007), 89–90. Such supervised play was expensive, so in 1906 like-minded people banded together to form the Playground Association of America with the goal of Americanization and instilling values in children like teamwork. Playgrounds had moral, social, and political elements as well. Reformers believed that new migrants needed training in group loyalty so they encouraged sports teams. They provided sandboxes and swings but also leadership training for team sports like baseball. Children and their families often

welcomed these opportunities. Reformers believed that children should work with other children rather than with their immigrant parents. They thought that immigrant families poorly prepared their children for the demands of a modern society. The children themselves often shunned organized playground activities that had strict schedules and assigned time for patriotic songs and supervised play. "Thirty-Five Years of Accomplishment, 1895–1929," pamphlet, p. 4, Detroit Federation of Women's Clubs, BHC.

20. Crathern, *In Detroit,* 127.

21. *Detroit Free Press,* March 21, 1906.

22. "Close Call for Bathhouse Item," unidentified newspaper clipping, Clara B. Arthur Scrapbook, BHC.

23. Sarah A. Grindley, "Club History, Historical Sketch, 1895–1935," *Club History, 1895–1935,* vol. 73, pp. 8–10, Manuscript Collection, Federation of Women's Clubs of Metropolitan Detroit, BHC.

24. *Detroit News Tribune,* February 18, 1906.

25. Grindley, "Historical Sketch," 9–10.

26. Nauss, "Detroit Federation of Women's Clubs," 93.

27. *Detroit News Tribune,* February 18, 1906.

28. Baker, "The Domestication of Politics," 85–102; Sklar, "The Historical Foundations of Women's Power," 43–78; Ladd-Taylor, *Mother-Work;* Mink, *The Wages of Motherhood.*

29. Skocpol, *Protecting Soldiers and Mothers,* 3, 48, 51, 160, 177, 331, 333, 343, 368; Sonya Michel, "The Limits of Maternalism: Policies toward American Wage-Earning Mothers during the Progressive Era," in Koven and Michel, *Mothers of a New World,* 277–320.

30. Elisabeth Israels Perry, "Women's Political Choices after Suffrage: The Women's City Club of New York, 1915–1990," *New York History* (October 1990): 417–34.

31. Elenbaas, "Detroit and the Progressive Era," 69.

32. DeMatteo, "Organized Labor versus the Mayor," 87–89.

33. Olivier Zunz, *The Changing Face of Inequality: Urbanization, Industrial Development and Immigrants in Detroit, 1880–1920* (Chicago, 1982), 311–12.

34. Elenbaas, "Detroit and the Progressive Era," 69.

35. Sidney Fine, *Frank Murphy: The Detroit Years* (Ann Arbor, 1975), 91.

36. Elenbaas, "Detroit and the Progressive Era," 89, 120.

37. Flanagan, "Gender and Urban Political Reform"; McArthur, *Creating the New Woman;* Gullett, *Becoming Citizens;* Connolly, *The Triumph of Ethnic Progressivism.*

38. "Thirty-Five Years of Accomplishment," 6.

39. Crathern, *In Detroit,* 129–31. Laura Freele Osborn graduated from a teacher's school, the Normal Training School, in Huntington, Indiana, her home state. She then taught for seven years in the Indiana and Illinois public schools. She moved to Detroit and joined the Twentieth Century Club because she was looking for some respite from raising three small children. She maintained a special interest in education and wrote a paper for the club on trade schools for girls.

For her research, she wrote to all the states to learn about the state of education throughout the nation. In this way, educational research became her passion. "Laura F. Osborn," *The Detroit Club Woman* 2 (December 1937): 4.

40. "Laura F. Osborn," 4.

41. Crathern, *In Detroit,* 132.

42. "Legislative Report," Minutes 1917–1918, Spring 1917, vol. 10, p. 728, Manuscript Collection, Federation of Women's Clubs of Metropolitan Detroit.

43. Mrs. George Johnston, president of the Twentieth Century Club, to Osborn, February 23, 1917, Manuscript Collection, Box 16, Correspondence, Laura Osborn Papers, BHC.

44. Reid, "'A Career to Build, a People to Serve, a Purpose to Accomplish,'" 22–23.

45. Ibid., 15n50.

46. Salem, *To Better Our World,* 78.

47. Nauss, "Detroit Federation of Women's Clubs," 68–73.

48. Elenbaas, "The Boss of the Better Class," 132, 133, 148.

49. Fine, *Frank Murphy,* 96.

50. Fragnoli, "Progressive Coalitions and Municipal Reform," 131; *Detroit News,* November 7, 1917.

51. "Report of the Legislative Department," [October 1917 and November 1917], Minutes 1917–1918, vol. 10, pp. 884, 921, Manuscript Collection, Federation of Women's Clubs of Metropolitan Detroit.

52. Liette Gidlow, *The Big Vote: Gender, Consumer Culture and the Politics of Exclusion* (Baltimore, 2004), 115–22.

53. Fragnoli, "Progressive Coalitions," 138–39.

54. "City Charter," Box 5, Manuscript Collection, League of Women Voters Papers, BHC.

55. Fragnoli, "Progressive Coalitions," 133–36.

56. Ibid., 136–39.

57. McHaney, "Securing the Sacred Right to Vote," 44.

58. *Michigan Suffragist* 1 (February 1914): 10.

59. "The Awakening of Woman," *National Association Notes* 19 (January 1917): 3, 13.

60. Turner and Moses, *Colored Detroit,* 15.

61. White, *Too Heavy a Load,* 103.

62. Arthur, *Progress of Michigan Women,* 16.

63. "Legislative Report," April 1917, Minutes 1917–1918, vol. 10, p. 727, Manuscript Collection, Federation of Women's Clubs of Metropolitan Detroit.

64. Manuscript Collection, Ella H. Aldinger, Box 1, Folder 2, Newspaper Clippings 1916–1923, *Detroit News,* April 1917 (date handwritten, not specific), Michigan Historical Collection at the Bentley Historical Library (hereafter MHC).

65. Crathern, *In Detroit,* 191.

66. "Resolution of Board of Directors of Detroit Federation of Women's Clubs," March 14, 1918, Minutes 1917–1918, vol. 10, p. 1245, Manuscript Collection, Federation of Women's Clubs of Metropolitan Detroit.

67. Ibid., 1249.

68. "Report of the Legislative Department," October 18, 1918, Minutes 1918–1920, vol. 11, pp. 55–56, Manuscript Collection, Federation of Women's Clubs of Metropolitan Detroit.

69. "Report of the Legislative Department," November 14, 1918, Minutes 1918–1920, vol. 11, p. 93, Manuscript Collection, Federation of Women's Clubs of Metropolitan Detroit.

70. McHaney, "Securing the Sacred Right to Vote," 45.

71. Minutes, May 9, 1918, Minutes 1918–1920, vol. 11, p. 23, Manuscript Collection, Federation of Women's Clubs of Metropolitan Detroit.

72. "Report of the Legislative Committee," December 6, 1918, Minutes 1918–1920, vol. 11, p. 129, Manuscript Collection, Federation of Women's Clubs of Metropolitan Detroit.

73. "Legislative Report," [December 1917 or January 1918], Minutes 1917–1918, vol. 10, p. 1181, Manuscript Collection, Federation of Women's Clubs of Metropolitan Detroit.

74. *Detroit News,* June 5, 1919.

75. McHaney, "Securing the Sacred Right to Vote," 45.

76. Kevin Boyle, *Arc of Justice: A Saga of Race, Civil Rights, and Murder in the Jazz Age* (New York, 2004), 202–6.

77. Nauss, "Detroit Federation of Women's Clubs," 29.

78. Crathern, *In Detroit,* 17.

79. Edith Alvord's personal calendar, Box 3, 1920–1921, Manuscript Collection, Edith Vosberg Alvord Papers, BHC.

80. Mrs. Helen Russell to Edith Alvord, May 20, 1920, Box 1, Folder 1, Manuscript Collection, Edith Vosberg Alvord Papers.

81. Nauss, "Detroit Federation of Women's Clubs," 16. (This research includes a map, but I do not have permission to reprint it.)

82. *Club Woman* 14 (January 1922): 245–46.

83. *General Index Sanborn Maps: Detroit* (New York, 1950).

84. Reid, "'A Career to Build, a People to Serve, a Purpose to Accomplish," 2–3. Meta Pelham taught public school in Detroit after graduating from Fenton Normal School in central Michigan. Later she had health problems and gave up teaching to become a journalist for the *Detroit Plaindealer.* Irving Garland Penn, *The Afro-American Press and Its Editors* (New York, 1891), 419–20.

85. Wolcott, *Remaking Respectability,* 39, 45–47, 150.

86. Deborah Gray White, "The Cost of Club Work, the Price of Feminism," in Lebsock and Hewitt, *Visible Women,* 247–64.

87. "Early History of the New Era Study Club" (typed manuscript, n.d.), Box 1, Club History, Club Song, Manuscript Collection of New Era Study Club, BHC.

88. Wolcott, *Remaking Respectability,* 54.

89. Ibid., 154.

90. Shaw, *What a Woman Ought to Be and to Do,* 8, 19, 69.

91. Gilmore, *Gender and Jim Crow,* 10–11.

92. Shaw, *What a Woman Ought to Be and to Do,* 219.

93. Ibid., 26, 93, 119.

94. "The Awakening of Woman," 4.

95. Michigan Colored Women's Club, Meta E. Pelham (biographical sketch), Box 1, Record Group 60–14, State Archives of Michigan. There is some evidence of cross-racial cooperation between black and white women, but it was hardly the norm. In Atlanta both black and white reformers were so convinced that kindergartens would spread the ideals of citizenship and lessen crime that they joined together in the Kindergarten Alumnae Association. They even joined forces in an appeal to incorporate kindergartens, both black and white, into the Atlanta school system. They used their votes in 1921 to pass a bond issue to raise the money needed to start the schools. In this effort they were only partially successful as black kindergartens were not approved by the city until 1945 (Judson, "Cultivating Citizenship in the Kindergartens of Atlanta," 17–33). In North Carolina black and white women worked together in integrated county councils during World War I to further national defense with projects like bond drives. They also organized home demonstrators who taught women of both races about health, nutrition, and soil conservation as part of their war work. But these white women did not pledge to champion voting rights for black women. At the war's end, white women in North Carolina saw the usefulness of cooperation with African American women but still believed in white supremacy (Gilmore, *Gender and Jim Crow,* 195–202).

96. Mrs. W. T. Francis, Chairman, Press Committee of the National Association of Colored Women's Clubs, to DFWC, May 5, 1916, vol. 73, *Club History;* Hester Keyes of Minnesota State Federation of Colored Women's Clubs to DFWC, May 9, 1916, Minutes 1917–1918, vol. 10, Manuscript Collection, Federation of Women's Clubs of Metropolitan Detroit.

97. *Twentieth Century Club of Detroit Bulletin* 1:4 (January [1917 or 1918]), Manuscript Collection, Emma A. Fox Papers.

98. "Meeting of the Executive Committee," December 11, 1921, Minutes 1922–1924, vol. 13, p. 245, Manuscript Collection, Federation of Women's Clubs of Metropolitan Detroit.

99. White, *Too Heavy a Load,* 104.

100. *Detroit News,* September 19, 1921.

101. Zunz, *The Changing Face of Inequality,* 286, 327, 338, 358–59.

102. Louise M. Young, *In the Public Interest: The League of Women Voters, 1920–1970* (New York, 1989), 182n43.

103. *Detroit Free Press,* November 13, 1919, and March 8, 1919.

104. *1900 Directory of the Detroit Federation of Women's Clubs, 1915–1916 Directory of the Detroit Federation of Women's Clubs,* and *Detroit Federation of Women's Clubs Annual Report, 1927–1928.*

105. *Detroit News,* October 9, 1921.

106. Elizabeth Gulley and Lillian Johnson, "Citizenship Activities of Some Detroit Women," *National Association Notes* 27 (April 1925): 9.

107. Elizabeth Gulley to Lucia Voorheis, August 26, 1924, Box 1, Correspondence 1924, Lucia Grimes Voorheis Papers, MHC.

108. Zunz, *The Changing Face of Inequality,* 286–87.

109. Lynda Ann Ewen, *Corporate Power and Urban Crisis in Detroit* (Princeton, 1978), 118.

110. "Detroit Population Statistics Reveal Many Unusual Facts," *The Detroiter* 22 (August 10, 1931): 8.

111. Quoted in Flanagan, "The City Profitable," 166–67.

112. "City Administrator Essays Solving Many Problems in 1920," *The Detroiter* 11 (January 3, 1920): 3.

Notes to Chapter 2

1. "Report of the Legislative Committee," April 1, 1918–March 31, 1919, Minutes 1918–1920, vol. 11, pp. 399–403, Manuscript Collection, Federation of Women's Clubs of Metropolitan Detroit.

2. Sklar, *Florence Kelley,* 151.

3. Gordon, *Pitied But Not Entitled,* 111–12, 124, 141–42.

4. In this regard, Detroit clubwomen fit Paula Baker's description of how women appealed to the state to alleviate the problems of an industrial society. Baker, "The Domestication of Politics," 97.

5. Shaw, *What a Woman Ought to Be and to Do,* 169, 173; White, *Too Heavy a Load,* 16.

6. Women in New Orleans stated that getting the vote gave them "the opportunity to define a new role for themselves" (Tyler, *Silk Stockings and Ballot Boxes,* 2). Women, in general, relied on their clubs for civic activity rather than electoral politics (Cott, "Across the Great Divide," 161). In Chicago, clubwomen continued to use their voluntary organizations but also used their franchise rights to elect people sympathetic to their agenda (Flanagan, "The Predicament of New Rights," 308). Women in California women realized the vote did not give women power immediately but was a vehicle toward power (Gullett, *Becoming Citizens,* 201–2). Civic-minded clubwomen especially felt the time had come to turn their wishes into public policy. Southern women "embraced the vote as a powerful weapon in their progressive arsenal" (Schuyler, *The Weight of Their Votes,* 135).

7. Kristi Andersen, "Women and Citizenship in the 1920s," in Tilly and Gurin, *Women, Politics and Change,* 185.

8. Perry, "Women's Political Choices after Suffrage," 418.

9. Andersen, "Women and Citizenship in the 1920s," 183, 187.

10. Elizabeth L. Gulley, "Education vs. Charity as a Club Woman's Program," *National Association Notes* 22:7 (April 1925): 1–2; Savonia Carson, "Michigan," *National Association Notes* 27 (January 1925): 13; Evelyn Brooks Higginbotham, "In Politics to Stay: Black Women Leaders and Party Politics in the 1920s," in Tilly and Gurin, *Women, Politics and Change,* 199–216.

11. Edith Alvord, "Club Women and Their Citizenship," address to Annual Meeting of North Dakota Federation of Women's Clubs, October 7, 1926, Box 6, Clippings and Writings, Folder 7, Manuscript Collection, Edith Vosburgh Alvord Papers.

12. *Detroit Times,* March 5, 1919.

13. Ibid.

14. Gulley and Johnson, "Citizenship Activities," 9.

15. "NAACP Elects Officers," *Detroit Contender,* November 15, 1920.

16. "Michigan Women Showing Keen Interest," *Michigan Citizen* 1 (January 10, 1920): 7.

17. Wilma Cavanaugh, "Women Get Control of County Convention before Car Leaves," n.d., Folder 2, Newspaper Clippings 1916–1933, Ella H. Aldinger Papers.

18. *Detroit News,* March 8, 1919.

19. Nancy Cott, *The Grounding of Modern Feminism* (New Haven, 1987), 104.

20. Schuyler, *The Weight of Their Votes,* 191.

21. Kristi Andersen, *After Suffrage: Women in Partisan and Electoral Politics before the New Deal* (Chicago, 1996), 11, 52–53, 59–60, 67–68.

22. Lillian Smith Mathews, "Woman as a Working Power," in *Detroit Federation of Women's Clubs, Directory, 1923,* 5.

23. Lillian Smith Mathews was born in Evansville, Indiana, in 1868 but moved to Detroit twenty-five years later upon her marriage. Reading Room File, *Detroit News,* July 29, 1927.

24. *Detroit Independent,* June 10, 1927.

25. Elizabeth L. Gulley to Lucia Grimes, August 26, 1924, Box 1, Correspondence 1924, Lucia Voorheis Grimes Papers.

26. Gulley, "Education vs. Charity," 2.

27. Lillian Johnson, "How Municipal Government Is Effected [*sic*] by the Entrance of Women into Politics," January 1923, Box 1, Folder 3, Manuscript Collection, Detroit Study Club, BHC.

28. Margaret McCall, "Lillian Johnson, as We Know Her," May 1952 meeting, Box 2, Folder 1, Manuscript Collection, Detroit Study Club.

29. White, *Too Heavy a Load,* 98.

30. Hazel V. Carby, *Reconstructing Womanhood: The Emergence of the Afro-American Woman Novelist* (New York, 1987), 18, 118.

31. Quoted in Hicks, *Talk with You Like a Woman,* 168.

32. *Report of the Mayor's Committee on Race Relations* (Detroit, 1926), BHC.

33. "Report of the Legislative Department," October 11, 1923, Minutes 1922–1924, vol. 13, p. 901, Manuscript Collection, Federation of Women's Clubs of Metropolitan Detroit.

34. "Report of the Civics Department," January 28, 1921, Minutes 1920–1922, vol. 12, p. 333, Manuscript Collection, Federation of Women's Clubs of Metropolitan Detroit.

35. Quoted in Wolcott, *Remaking Respectability,* 151.

36. Andersen, "Women and Citizenship in the 1920s," 189.

37. "Report of the Civics Department," January 28, 1921, p. 333.

38. Majorie Elaine Porter, "Club Programs Disclose Their Unity of Purpose," *Detroit News,* October 5, 1924.

39. Quoted in "Detroit League of Women Voters," *Detroit Federation of Women's Clubs: Directory, 1921–1922*, 67.

40. Young, *In the Public Interest*, 182n43; *Michigan Woman* 3 (1925): 14.

41. Ida M. Peppers was born in Springfield, Illinois, in 1876 and was educated in the Springfield public schools. She received advanced training in painting at the Episcopal Seminary of Springfield, but she was devoted to civic affairs she pursued within women's clubs. She was the chairman of the Legislative Department of the DFWC and organized and chaired the Wayne County Legislative Council, which was devoted to promoting legislation to benefit women and children. Later she was both the president of the Detroit LWV and the chairman of the Department of Efficiency in Government of the Michigan LWV. *Michigan Woman* 2–3 (1924–25): 28.

42. Majorie Elaine Porter, "Will Organize County League of Women Voters," *Detroit News*, January 13, 1924.

43. *Detroit News*, March 8, 1925.

44. Wolcott, *Remaking Respectability*, 150.

45. Gulley, "Education vs. Charity," 1.

46. "Early History of the New Era Study Club."

47. *Detroit Independent*, October 14, 1927.

48. [Grace] D. W. Murphy, "Women Voters and the Political Issues of the Day," November 30, 1927, Manuscript Collection, Detroit Sorosis Literary and Art Club Yearbook, 1927–1928, BHC.

49. Detroit Study Club, Yearbooks, 1924–1925, 1925–1926, 1926–1927, Box 7, Folder 1, Manuscript Collection, Detroit Study Club.

50. *Detroit People's News*, December 28, 1930.

51. Beulah Alexander Young was from Tennessee, where she graduated from Lane College. Upon her marriage to Dr. James Young, the couple moved to Detroit. In 1924 she was the only African American woman to graduate from the Detroit Conservatory of Music. She helped organize the Junior NAACP and was in the choir of the Second Baptist Church. *Michigan Chronicle*, June 28, 1986.

52. Nathaniel Leach, *Reaching Out to Freedom: The Second Baptist Connection* (N.p., 1988), 50.

53. *Detroit People's News*, December 28, 1930. Later, the Political Leaders Assembly helped elect Charles D. Diggs Sr. to the state senate in 1936. *Michigan Chronicle*, June 28, 1986.

54. Andersen, "Women and Citizenship in the 1920s," 189–93.

55. "Report of the Board of Directors," October 6, 1921, Minutes 1920–1922, vol. 12, p. 783, Manuscript Collection, Federation of Women's Clubs of Metropolitan Detroit.

56. *Detroit News*, January 27, 1924.

57. William P. Lovett to Executive Board of Detroit Citizens League, September 9, 1924, Box 3, Manuscript Collection, Detroit Citizens League, Additional Papers, BHC.

58. "A Woman's Viewpoint," *Club Woman* 13 (September 1920): 46.

59. *Detroit News*, March 4, 1923.

60. "The Drive to Register Women," *Club Woman* 13 (October 1920): 16–17.

61. "Non-Voters Are Traitors," *Michigan Citizen* 3 (September 23, 1922): 5.

62. *Detroit News*, October 19, 1924.

63. Michael McGerr, *The Decline of Popular Politics: The American North, 1865–1928* (New York, 1986), 196.

64. "Crude Attacks on City Courts Arouses Anger—Voters Flock to Registration Office to Offset Massing of Negroes," *Detroit Free Press*, March 16, 1923.

65. R. L. Bradby, "Special to Members," *Second Baptist Herald*, September 2, 1928.

66. Gulley and Johnson, "Citizenship Activities," 9.

67. Gidlow, *The Big Vote*, 2, 4, 189.

68. "Legislative Council of Michigan Women," *Club Woman* 15 (March 1923): 422.

69. *Detroit News*, November 29, 1925.

70. *Detroit News*, December 4, 1925.

71. Ibid. Laura Cramer, who was nominated for the City Commission of Highland Park, was not only a clubwoman but a highly qualified candidate. She held degrees from the University of Michigan and Columbia University and had been a teacher in the Highland Park Schools for fifteen years. She was interested in the health and well-being of children. She organized the Child Health Day and was chairman of the Building Committee of the Highland Park YWCA. She was the president of the Hypatia Club as well as a member of the Women's City Club. Although she was nominated, she was not elected. *Detroit Free Press*, March 9, 1941.

72. *Detroit News*, January 15, 1926.

73. *Detroit News*, January 22, 1926.

74. *Detroit News*, February 17, 1926.

75. *Detroit News*, October 23, 1927.

76. "Our Poor Registration System," *Detroit Citizen*, May 1928.

77. "Bill for Permanent Registration," *Michigan Woman* 6 (September 1928): 26.

78. "History of the Passage of the Law in Michigan," Box 4, Manuscript Collection, League of Women Voters, BHC.

79. *Detroit News*, November 18, 1928.

80. "History of the Passage of the Law in Michigan."

81. *Detroit News*, November 18, 1928.

82. "History of the Passage of the Law in Michigan."

83. *Detroit News*, February 7, 1926.

84. Ibid. Pearl Graves (Mrs. Charles M.) Novak was an educated, politically active clubwoman. She graduated (as did her grandmother, mother, and later her daughter) from Olivet College. Upon her marriage and move to Detroit, she quickly became a leader in many women's clubs. She was president of the Detroit New Century Club, Women's Association of North Woodward Congregational Church, and the State Congregational Women's Union. She was also a member of the Twentieth Century Club and a board member of the YWCA. She was presi-

dent of the DFWC when women acquired the ballot and as such, she was often invited to Lansing to voice her opinion on women's issues. "Some of Our Past Presidents," *The Detroit Club Woman* 1 (January 1937): 6, 20.

85. Shaw, *What a Woman Ought to Be and to Do,* 13, 37, 189, 210.

86. *Detroit News,* November 3, 1925.

87. *Detroit News,* November 7, 1926.

88. Perry, "Women's Political Choices after Suffrage," 421.

89. Mildred Lane Simpson to Pliny Marsh, March 23, 1919, Manuscript Collection, Detroit Citizens League, Additional Papers.

90. Pliny Marsh to Mildred Lane Simpson, May 26, 1919, Manuscript Collection, Detroit Citizens League, Additional Papers.

91. "The Drive to Register Women."

92. *Detroit News,* May 14, 1919.

93. Ibid.

94. Ella Aldinger, MLWV Report of State Convention, Resolutions, December 1924, Box 1, Folder 1, Manuscript Collection, Ella H. Aldinger Papers.

95. *Detroit News,* July 22, 1928.

96. *Detroit News,* October 12, 1924.

97. *Detroit News,* May 18, 1930.

98. Senora D. Smith, telephone conversation with author, January 22, 2001.

Notes to Chapter 3

1. Robyn Muncy, *Creating a Female Dominion in American Reform, 1890–1935* (New York, 1991), 103; Andersen, *After Suffrage,* 189.

2. McArthur, *Creating the New Woman,* 31, 33, 55–56, 77–79; Flanagan, *Seeing with Their Hearts;* Gullett, *Becoming Citizens;* Scott, *Natural Allies;* Tyler, *Silk Stockings.*

3. Sklar, "The Historical Foundations of Women's Power," 68.

4. Eileen Boris, "Reconstructing the 'Family': Progressive Reform and the Problem of Social Control," in Noralee Frankel and Nancy S. Dye, eds., *Gender, Class Race and Reform in the Progressive Era* (Lexington, 1991), 73, 73–82.

5. Kathleen M. Blee, *Women of the Klan: Racism and Gender in the 1920s* (Berkeley, 1991), 155–56.

6. JoEllen McNergney Vinyard, *Right in Michigan's Grassroots: From the KKK to the Michigan Militia* (Ann Arbor, 2011), 43.

7. James A. Geschwender, *Class, Race and Worker Insurgency: The League of Revolutionary Black Workers* (New York, 1977), 64.

8. Boyle, *Arc of Justice,* 9–10.

9. James R. Grossman, *Land of Hope: Chicago, Black Southerners and the Great Migration* (Chicago, 1989), 262–63.

10. William M. Tuttle Jr., *Race Riot: Chicago in the Red Summer of 1919* (New York, 1970), vii, 21.

11. Mrs. Leslie Morton Stone to DFWC, April 15, 1923, vol. 68, 1922–

1924, Manuscript Collection, Federation of Women's Clubs of Metropolitan Detroit.

12. Scrapbook of Harriet Barrier, Box 2, Folder 8, pp. 32–33, Manuscript Collection, Detroit Study Club.

13. Minutes 1918–1923, January 24, 1921, Manuscript Collection, Detroit Woman's Club, BHC.

14. "Remedy Must Be Found for Conditions Disclosed by Americanization Committee—Board of Commerce Committee Appointed to Deal with Negro Housing Situation as Shown by Preliminary Investigation into Deplorable Conditions in Sections Inhabited by Colored Population," *The Detroiter* 11 (December 19, 1919): 2. Earlier in 1904 the DFWC's corresponding secretary made an appeal to the similarly classed Detroit Study Club for a donation to establish lectures for the poor. The money would be provided for lectures for "those who have hitherto been limited in their ambitions and deprived of all means of a higher culture." Mrs. Fran[k] M. Nichols, Corresponding Secretary for DFWC, to Detroit Study Club, January 12, 1904, Scrapbook of Harriet Barrier 1898–1928, Box 2, Folder 6, Manuscript Collection, Detroit Study Club.

15. Forrester B. Washington, "The Detroit Newcomers' Greeting," *The Survey* 38 (April 1917–September 1917): 334.

16. David M. Katzman, *Before the Ghetto: Black Detroit in the Nineteenth Century* (Urbana, 1973), 162–63.

17. Wolcott, *Remaking Respectability,* 47.

18. Gulley, "Education vs. Charity," 1.

19. Hicks, *Talk with You Like a Woman,* 13–14.

20. Kevin K. Gaines, *Uplifting the Race: Black Leadership, Politics and Culture in the Twentieth Century* (Chapel Hill, 1966), 94, 113, 169.

21. White, *Too Heavy a Load,* 110–12.

22. Johnson, "Municipal Government."

23. Resolution #4 by Mrs. J. Nelson Lewis, Thirty-Third Annual Convention of the MSFWC, October 18–21, Saginaw, MI, Box 4, 1907–1935, Manuscript Collection, Edith Vosburgh Alvord Papers.

24. Majorie Elaine Porter, "Glorifying the Home This Year's Club Aim," *Detroit News,* September 20, 1928.

25. Lillian Mathews, "Woman as a Working Power," *Detroit Federation of Women's Clubs: Directory, 1923,* 5.

26. *Detroit News,* January 19, 1923.

27. *Detroit News,* October 29, 1922.

28. *Detroit News,* February 11, 1923.

29. Cott, *Grounding of Modern Feminism,* 120–27.

30. Clara Mengler, "Women Workers of Michigan," *Magazine of the Women's City Club* 5 (January 1926): 35.

31. Yearbook 1923–1924, Box 7, Folder 1, Manuscript Collection, Detroit Study Club.

32. Unidentified newspaper clipping, April 13, 1920, Box 3, Folder 3, Manuscript Collection, Detroit Sorosis Club.

33. "Annual Report of the Civics Department," April 29, 1921, Minutes 1920–1922, vol. 12, p. 653, Manuscript Collection, Federation of Women's Clubs of Metropolitan Detroit.

34. *Detroit News*, November 23, 1919.

35. "Report of the Public Health Committee," December 11, 1924, Minutes 1924–1925, vol. 14, p. 367, Manuscript Collection, Federation of Women's Clubs of Metropolitan Detroit.

36. "Annual Report of the American Citizenship Department," April 27, 1928, Minutes 1927–1928, vol. 17, p. 298, Manuscript Collection, Federation of Women's Clubs of Metropolitan Detroit.

37. *Detroit News*, April 11, 1919.

38. *Detroit News*, April 8, 1922.

39. "Reform Begins at Home," *Club Woman* 17:1 (September 1924): 38.

40. *Bulletin of Women's City Club*, June 1924.

41. James C. Cahill, "Employment of Males and Females Under 18—Hours of Labor, 5330, Act #341 as Amended August 14, 1919," *Michigan Compiled Laws of 1915, Annotated Supplement 1922* (Chicago, 1922), 522.

42. Clara Mengler, "Night Work for Women in Industry," *Magazine of the Women's City Club* (May 1926): 35, 41.

43. MacDonald had been a public school teacher but after her marriage listed her occupation as "housewife." She was the president of the Women's Taxpayer's League and president of the Women Citizens' League. Jessie B. MacDonald, "Candidates for the Primary October 6: What They Are and What They Stand For," *Michigan Woman* 2–3 (1924–25): 26.

44. *Detroit News*, January 7, 1922.

45. "Reminiscences on the 30th Anniversary of the Detroit Study Club," March 2, 1929, Manuscript Collection, Box 2, Folder 2, Detroit Study Club.

46. "History of Michigan State Association of Colored Women," Manuscript Collection, Box 9, Folder 4, Detroit Study Club.

47. Wolcott, *Remaking Respectability*, 95.

48. Edith V. Alvord, "Equal Opportunities for Women Wage Earners," *Club Woman* 13:3 (November 1920): 150.

49. Richard W. Thomas, *Life for Us Is What We Make It: Building Community in Detroit, 1915–1945* (Bloomington, 1992), 222.

50. "Report of Executive Committee," November 6, 1928, Minutes 1928–1929, vol. 18, p. 65, Manuscript Collection, Federation of Women's Clubs of Metropolitan Detroit.

51. Mink, *The Wages of Motherhood*, 51, 120.

52. Reading Room File, *Detroit News*, November 26, 1946.

53. *Detroit News*, January 19, 1921.

54. *Detroit News*, February 9 and 25, 1921.

55. Ibid.

56. *Detroit News*, March 20, 1921.

57. "Report of the Legislative Department," January 10, 1923, Minutes

1922–1924, vol. 13, p. 325, Manuscript Collection, Federation of Women's Clubs of Metropolitan Detroit.

58. "Report of the Civic Division," February 26, 1926, Minutes 1925–1926, vol. 15, pp. 545–47, Manuscript Collection, Federation of Women's Clubs of Metropolitan Detroit.

59. Michel, "The Limits of Maternalism," 299–307; Mink, *The Wages of Motherhood,* 8; Ladd-Taylor, *Mother-Work,* 141, 202.

60. Mink, *The Wages of Motherhood,* 39; Ladd-Taylor, *Mother-Work,* 149.

61. Michel, "The Limits of Maternalism," 299–307; Mink, *The Wages of Motherhood,* 8; Ladd-Taylor, *Mother-Work,* 141, 202.

62. Mink, *The Wages of Motherhood,* vii, 26, 28–29; Ladd-Taylor, *Mother-Work,* 5, 46, 50, 141.

63. "Report of the Civic Department," March 13, 1924, Minutes 1922–1924, vol. 13, pp. 1427–34, Manuscript Collection, Federation of Women's Clubs of Metropolitan Detroit.

64. Muncy, *Creating a Female Dominion in American Reform,* 103.

65. Minnie Cage, "Eye Bills, Mrs. Alvord Tells Clubs," *Detroit Times,* December 28, 1930.

66. "Report of the Legislative Department" and "Report of the Legislative Department, Special Meeting," January 28, 1921, and February 9, 1921, Minutes 1920–1922, vol. 12, pp. 327, 399–403, Manuscript Collection, Federation of Women's Clubs of Metropolitan Detroit.

67. *Detroit News,* February 11, 1923.

68. "Report of the Legislative Department," n.d., Minutes 1922–1924, vol. 13, Manuscript Collection, Federation of Women's Clubs of Metropolitan Detroit.

69. Mrs. Arthur Wallace, "Annual Report of the Department of Legislation," *Club Woman* 15 (June 1923): 610, 627, 628.

70. Dr. Richard Olin to Mrs. Arthur Wallace, May 5, 1923, Minutes 1922–1924, vol. 13, Manuscript Collection, Federation of Women's Clubs of Metropolitan Detroit.

71. Blanche M. Haines, "Work in Michigan under Sheppard-Towner Act," *Club Woman* (November 1923): 151.

72. See also Muncy, *Creating a Female Dominion in American Reform;* Skocpol, *Protecting Soldiers and Mothers;* and Sklar, "The Historical Foundations of Women's Power."

73. Lillian Smith, "What Michigan Has Done for Its Babies: The Scope and Result of the Work Done with Sheppard-Towner Funds," *Michigan Woman* (January 1929): 21–24.

74. Mink, *The Wages of Motherhood,* 73.

75. Cott, *Grounding of Modern Feminism,* 98, 249.

76. Alice Ames (Mrs. Thomas) Winter, "Mrs. Winter Replies to the *Dearborn Independent,*" *Club Woman* 16:9 (May 1924): 524–26, 558; Ladd-Taylor, *Mother-Work,* 171.

77. "Report of the Legislative Department," November 1, 1933, vol. 13, p.

963, and November 9, 1923, Minutes 1922–1924, vol. 13, pp. 1013–15, Manuscript Collection, Federation of Women's Clubs of Metropolitan Detroit.

78. Mary Church Terrell, "Report of the National Chairman on Legislation," *Convention, Minutes, 1926,* National Association of Colored Women Fifteenth Biennial Session, Oakland, CA, August 1–5, 1926, 75–76.

79. *Club Woman* (May 1922): 477. In Michigan in the 1920s, there was legislation already on the books that regulated child labor. Children under the age of eighteen could not work more than nine hours for six consecutive days or ten hours in any one day. Furthermore, children under the age of sixteen could not work in factories or canneries between 6:00 p.m. and 6:00 a.m. These laws did not apply to agriculture or household labor. "Report of the Legislative Special Meeting," February 9, 1921, Minutes 1920–1922, vol. 12, p. 403, Manuscript Collection, Federation of Women's Clubs of Metropolitan Detroit; "Report of the Legislative Department," November 1, 1933, vol. 13, p. 963, and November 9, 1923, vol. 13, pp. 1013–15.

80. "Amendment Is Sought to Stop Child Labor," *Detroit News,* December 9, 1923.

81. "Child Labor," handwritten, no name, MS League of Women Voters and Mrs. Craig Miller to Julia Lathrop, September 30, 1924, both in Box 4, Manuscript Collection, League of Women Voters, BHC.

82. "Child Labor."

83. "The Children's Amendment in Michigan by Bulletin #2 of Legislative Council of Michigan Women," *The Club Women* (April 1925): 495.

84. Mrs. F. C. Aldinger, "What the 1925 Legislature Did," *Michigan Woman* 3 (Summer 1925): 16.

Notes to Chapter 4

1. Baker, "The Domestication of Politics," 91, 92, 95, 97.

2. Gullett, *Becoming Citizens,* 99, 107.

3. Nancy F. Cott, *The Bonds of Womanhood: Woman's Sphere in New England, 1780–1835* (New Haven, 1977), 153.

4. Perry, "Women's Political Choices after Suffrage," 434.

5. Kenneth D. Rose, *American Women and the Repeal of Prohibition* (New York, 1996), 138.

6. The Detroit Citizens League admitted women after they achieved suffrage. The league's executive board was enlarged on June 10, 1919, to include Mrs. Frank S. Bigler and Mrs. Charles A. Strelinger as members. The board continued to be dominated by men throughout the 1920s (Detroit Citizens League, Box 2, Manuscript Collection, Additional Papers). In their membership drive of January 1919, while admitting women, they emphasized that four hundred men were listed as new members. "Big League Meeting Thursday January 16th," *Civic Searchlight* 6 (January 1919): n.p., BHC.

7. Tera W. Hunter, *To 'Joy My Freedom: Southern Black Women's Lives and*

Labors after the Civil War (Cambridge, 1997), 139.

8. Washington, "The Detroit Newcomers' Greeting," 335.

9. White, *Too Heavy a Load*, 128–30, 141.

10. Carby, *Reconstructing Womanhood*, 18, 168.

11. Gaines, *Uplifting the Race*, 4, 17, 106.

12. Hicks, *Talk with You Like a Woman*, 13, 55.

13. *Detroit News*, March 4, 1922.

14. Ibid.

15. Wolcott, *Remaking Respectability*, 121–26, 195–97.

16. "Report of the MLWV Convention 1922: Resolutions for 1922," Box 1, Folder 1, 1922–1923, Ella H. Aldinger Papers.

17. *Detroit News*, September 7, 1922.

18. *Detroit News*, October 4, 1922.

19. *Detroit News*, March 4, 1923.

20. Mrs. Arthur Wallace, "Annual Report of the Legislative Department," *Club Woman* (June 1923): 610.

21. *Detroit News*, April 15, 1925.

22. *Detroit News*, September 7, 1927.

23. *Detroit News*, November 16, 1920.

24. *Detroit Citizen*, April 1921, p. 9.

25. *Detroit News*, January 2, 1921.

26. *Detroit News*, January 5, 1921. Murray's "municipal welfare workers" bear a striking resemblance to Boston's "street mothers" in Sarah Deutsch's research. Deutsch explains how in 1909 the Boston Equal Suffrage Association and the Good Government Association wanted female officers to play a role similar to that described by Murray. Consequently, Detroit women were advocating policies that had been proposed by women in other cities. Sarah Deutsch, *Women and the City: Gender, Space and Power in Boston, 1870–1940* (New York, 2000), 73.

27. Mary E. Odem, *Delinquent Daughters: Protecting and Policing Adolescent Female Sexuality in the United States, 1885–1920* (Chapel Hill, 1995), 4.

28. *Detroit News*, February 17, 1921.

29. Hicks, *Talk with You Like a Woman*, 13–14, 185.

30. Gaines, *Uplifting the Race*, 93.

31. Hazel V. Carby, "'It Jus Be's Dat Way Sometime': The Sexual Politics of Women's Blues," in Vicki L. Ruiz and Ellen Carol DuBois, eds., *Unequal Sisters: A Multicultural Reader in U.S. Women's History*, 2nd ed. (New York, 1994), 330–41.

32. "Open Meeting with Miss Virginia Murray, Head of Women's Division of the Police Department," November 4, 1921, Yearbook 1921–1922, Box 7, Folder 1, Manuscript Collection, Detroit Study Club.

33. Wolcott, *Remaking Respectability*, 154. Detroit African-American History Project of Wayne State University, "Detroit Historical Events Timeline," http://www.daahp.wayne.edu/1900-1949.html (accessed August 10, 2011).

34. James D. Inches to Mrs. Pearl Novak, June 24, 1921, Correspondence 1920–1922, vol. 67, Manuscript Collection, Federation of Women's Clubs of Metropolitan Detroit.

35. Grindley, "Club History," pp. 41–42.

36. *Detroit News*, October 9, 1921.

37. *Detroit News*, November 3, 1921.

38. Ibid.

39. Recommendation to Mayor Couzens from DFWC, Correspondence 1920–1922, vol. 67, Manuscript Collection, Federation of Women's Clubs of Metropolitan Detroit.

40. "Minutes," January 30, 1923, Minutes 1922–1924, vol. 13, p. 460, Manuscript Collection, Federation of Women's Clubs of Metropolitan Detroit.

41. *Detroit News*, February 11, 1923.

42. *Detroit News*, June 27, 1926.

43. George E. Worthington, "Prostitution in Detroit," Box 14, Manuscript Collection, Detroit Citizens League, Additional Papers.

44. Wolcott, *Remaking Respectability*, 107.

45. Couzens to Novak, February 24, 1922, Correspondence 1920–1922, vol. 67, Manuscript Collection, Federation of Women's Clubs of Metropolitan Detroit.

46. "Report of the Legislative Department," April 12, 1923, Minutes 1922–1923, vol. 13, p. 664, Manuscript Collection, Federation of Women's Clubs of Metropolitan Detroit.

47. Worthington, "Prostitution in Detroit."

48. "The Awakening of Woman," 4.

49. Gulley, "Education vs. Charity," 1.

50. Detroit African-American History Project of Wayne State University, "Detroit Historical Events Timeline."

51. These homes were like those established by other African American women with similar motivations and fears. In 1897 Virginia Earle Matthews founded the Woman's Loyal Union in New York City with other middle-class black women, who started the White Rose Mission Settlement for the black community there. The mission provided industrial and domestic education as well as temporary lodging for migrants. Hicks, *Talk with You Like a Woman*, 100.

52. Gaines, *Uplifting the Race*, 82–83.

53. Wolcott, *Remaking Respectability*, 65, 69, 106, 154.

54. Clara Downey, "Report of the Civic Department," November 11, 1921, Minutes 1920–1922, Manuscript Collection, Federation of Women's Clubs of Metropolitan Detroit. The DFWC did nothing to assist in the dismantling of the buffet flats. This reflects a similar attitude of white clubwomen in Atlanta. During World War I they were worried about preserving working-class white girls' morality. At the same time, they were indifferent about African American women's morals or safety. Sarah Mercer Judson, "'Leisure Is a Foe to Any Man': The Pleasures and Dangers of Leisure in Atlanta during World War I," *Journal of Women's History* 15:1 (Spring 2003), http://www.jstor.org/ (accessed August 13, 2011).

55. "Minutes of the Regular Meeting," January 3, 1922, Box 3, Folder 3, Manuscript Collection, Detroit Sorosis Club.

56. Hicks, *Talk with You Like a Woman,* 175.

57. Lillian Bateman Johnson, "Looking Backward," speech delivered March 19, 1948, Lillian Bateman Johnson Collection, Box 2, Folder 2, Manuscript Collection, Detroit Study Club.

58. Rosalyn Terborg-Penn, "African-American Women's Networks in the Anti-Lynching Crusade," in Noralee Frankel and Nancy Dye, eds., *Gender, Class, Race and Reform in the Progressive Era* (Lexington, 1991), 148–59.

59. Terrell, "Report of the National Chairman on Legislation," 74–75.

60. "Meeting of the Executive Committee," December 11, 1921, Minutes 1922–1924, vol. 13, p. 245, Manuscript Collection, Federation of Women's Clubs of Metropolitan Detroit.

61. LaVerne Lane Betts, "Concerning the Age of Consent," *Club Woman* 14:8 (April 1922): 425–26.

62. Grindley, "Club History," p. 12.

63. Frances Knight, "The Law and the Woman," *Club Woman* 14:6 (February 1922): 281–82.

64. *Detroit News,* April 1, 1922.

65. "Court Social Worker Mistreats Is Charged," unidentified newspaper, Zahn-Reading Room File, BHC.

66. "Report of the Civic Department," November 3, 1921, Minutes 1920–1922, vol. 12, p. 881, Manuscript Collection, Federation of Women's Clubs of Metropolitan Detroit.

67. Ibid., 905.

68. William Lovett to Edith Alvord, January 18, 1922, Box 1, Folder 1, Manuscript Collection, Edith Vosburgh Alvord Papers.

69. Alvord to Lovett, January 23, 1922, Box 1, Folder 1, Manuscript Collection, Edith Vosburgh Alvord Papers.

70. Leigh Ann Wheeler, *Against Obscenity: Reform and the Politics of Womanhood in America, 1873–1935* (Baltimore, 2004), 47, 74, 101–3.

71. Fine, *Frank Murphy,* 108.

72. Ibid., 100.

73. *Detroit News,* April 1, 1923.

74. Charles Campbell to Detroit merchants, [1920], Box 14, Correspondence, Manuscript Collection, Detroit Citizens League, Additional Papers.

75. *Detroit Free Press,* March 16, 1923.

76. *Detroit News,* April 1, 1923.

77. Fine, *Frank Murphy,* 123, 126, 137.

78. Ibid., 104, 111.

79. *Detroit News,* April 3, 1923. Recorder's Court results (the first six were elected): Murphy (77,444); Jeffries (71,635); Faust (71,621); Keidan (71,088); Cotter (69,871); Stein (60,639); Heston (52,806); Marsh (51,674); Kent (46,230); Speed (35,508); Baxter (31,784); Lee (31,336). *Detroit News,* April 3, 1923.

80. Quoted in Fine, *Frank Murphy,* 116.

81. Minutes, January 28, 1921, Minutes 1920–1922, vol. 12, p. 309, Manu-

script Collection, Federation of Women's Clubs of Metropolitan Detroit.

82. "Campaign against Capital Punishment—Progressive Civic League of Detroit Waging Battle against Bill in Legislature," unidentified newspaper clipping, Zahn-Reading Room File.

83. *Detroit News,* February 11, 1923.

84. *Michigan Woman* (Spring 1925): 25; *Detroit News,* March 13, 1925.

85. Fine, *Frank Murphy,* 102, 137.

86. *Detroit News,* January 25, 1927.

87. *Detroit News,* February 27, 1929.

88. "Minutes of Board of Directors Meeting," April 1929, Minutes 1928–1929, vol. 18, Manuscript Collection, Federation of Women's Clubs of Metropolitan Detroit; *Detroit News,* February 27, 1929.

89. *Lansing Journal,* June 26, 1923.

90. Elva M. Forncrook, Assistant Chief Probation Officer, Dept. of Probation/Dept. of Probation Records and Circuit Courts, to Lillian Mathews, January 24, 1924, Minutes 1922–1924, vol. 68, Manuscript Collection, Federation of Women's Clubs of Metropolitan Detroit.

91. *Detroit News,* January 27, 1920.

92. R. Zahn to John A. Russell, president of Detroit Board of Commerce, n.d., Zahn-Reading Room File.

93. Circular, n.d., Zahn-Reading Room File.

94. *Detroit News,* February 2, 1924.

95. Ruby Zahn, "Club Members Visit Jail," *Twentieth Century Club Magazine* (January 1927): 3–8.

96. Mary E. O'Brien, "Progressive Civic League," *Club Woman* (January 1927): 288–89, 295–96. The Progressive Civic League's work with women's prisons conforms to similar women's clubs' behavior in Boston where women saw themselves as rescuers and strove to maintain their moral authority. It was this moral authority that was the basis for their original public work. The women attempted to re-create a home atmosphere; Detroit women did so with flowers and fruit in the prisons. Deutsch, *Women and the City,* 72–72.

97. Julia K. Jaffray, "The Michigan Jails," *Club Woman* 19:5 (June 1927): 658–61.

98. Ella Aldinger to Lucia Grimes, May 28, 1927, Box 2, Papers 1912–1932, Manuscript Collection, Lucia Voorheis Grimes Papers.

99. "Women's First Lesson in Crafty Politics," *Michigan Citizen* (April 1926): 5–6.

100. *Detroit News,* April 6, 1919.

101. *Detroit News,* April 27, 1919.

102. DFWC to James Couzens, February 1, 1922, Minutes 1920–1922, vol. 12, Manuscript Collection, Federation of Women's Clubs of Metropolitan Detroit.

103. *Detroit News,* December 20, 1920.

104. *Detroit Times,* February 10, 1919.

105. Ibid. Delphine Dodge Ashbaugh was born in Niles, Michigan, and

was the sister of automobile manufacturers John and Horace Dodge. She was a member of the Detroit Review Club and later served as its president. Like many clubwomen, she devoted her life to club work and public service. She founded the Auxiliary to the Salvation Army and was president of both the DFWC and Michigan State Federation of Women's Clubs from 1914 to 1916. During World War I she was appointed director of the Red Cross for Michigan and the state chairman of the Women's Liberty Loan Drive. She founded and edited the *Club Woman* and was superintendent of the Michigan Industrial Home for Girls. *History of the Michigan State Federation of Women's Clubs, 1895–1953* (published by state federation), 191–92.

106. *Detroit News,* May 18, 1919.

107. Michigan Compiled Laws, 1915, vol. 3, sec. 1, chap. 262, p. 5356.

108. Boyle, *Arc of Justice;* Forrester Washington, "Child Welfare," *Twentieth Century Club of Detroit Bulletin* 1:4 (January [1917 or 1918]): n.p.

109. [Eleanor] L. Hutzel, "Probation for the Wayward Minor over Seventeen Years of Age," *Michigan Woman* (November 1926): 26, 28.

110. *Detroit News,* January 2, 1927. Two years later, Eleanore Hutzel reported in the *Michigan Woman* that the Wayward Minor Court (established after the passage of the bill), a division of the Probate Court, was only for problems that had not yet become criminal. If someone over seventeen committed a felony, he would go to a criminal court. Between January 1 and May 15, 1923, there were three hundred cases before the Wayward Court. They were mostly out-of-towners who were looking for work and when finding none drifted into the bad areas of the city. Between December 1927 and December 1928, there were 126 cases of female Wayward Minors. Hutzel felt that the Wayward Minor provisions had taken people "off the wrong track" and on the right one. Eleanore L. Hutzel, "The Wayward Minor Court—Is Helping the Problem Boy and Girl in Wayne County," *Michigan Woman* (June 1929): 27–32.

111. *Detroit News,* December 12, 1929.

112. *Detroit News,* June 28, 1930; Rose, *American Women and the Repeal of Prohibition,* 2, 91. Helen Hall Newberry (Mrs. Henry Bourne) Joy, the national vice chairman of WONPR, had a long, distinguished life in club and civic work. Born into a family whose ancestors arrived on the *Mayflower,* Newberry was educated at the Detroit Female Seminary and the Hahn Detroit Conservatory of Music. She married the son of the president of the Michigan Central Railroad, Henry Bourne Joy. As such, she had grown up in a privileged family whose money came from the pre-automobile industry. Her husband, however, was president of the Packard Motor Company. She was a charter member of the Wayne County Red Cross and did relief service during the Spanish-American War, World War I, and World War II. Her interest in prohibition reform mirrored that of her husband, who came to a similar conclusion about the efficacy of the law. Helen Hall Newberry Joy, *Historical and Genealogical Record of the Michigan Daughters of the American Revolution, 1940–1952* (Adrian, 1952), 29.

113. *Detroit Free Press,* September 18, 1931.

114. Grace C. Root, *Women and Repeal: The Story of the Women's Organization for National Prohibition Reform* (New York, 1934), 140.

115. Ibid., 140–41.

116. Rose, *American Women and the Repeal of Prohibition,* 147.

Notes to Chapter 5

1. Quoted in Flanagan, "The City Profitable," 175.

2. Evans, "Women's History and Political Theory," 129.

3. Civics Department annual report, *Club Woman* 13 (June 1921): 585.

4. *National Association Notes* 19 (January 1917): 13.

5. Yearbook 1922–1923, Box 7, Folder for yearbooks, Manuscript Collection, Detroit Study Club.

6. Grindley, "Club History," p. 4.

7. Michigan Compiled Laws 1915, vol. 3, sec. 1, chap. 262, p. 5375.

8. *Report of the Mayor's Committee on Race Relations,* 12.

9. Minutes 1920–1922 pp. 243, 291–95, Manuscript Collection, Federation of Women's Clubs of Metropolitan Detroit.

10. Ibid.

11. *Annual Report: City of Detroit, 1919–1920* (n.p., n.d.), 110; *Annual Report: City of Detroit, 1921* (n.p., n.d.), 178; *Annual Report: City of Detroit 1922,* 238; Deutsch, *Women and the City,* 220.

12. Wheeler, *Against Obscenity,* 73, 95, 113, 181.

13. Meg Jacobs, *Pocketbook Politics: Economic Citizenship in Twentieth Century America* (Princeton, 2005), 21, 66.

14. Martha Ray (Mrs. F. G.) to Mayor James Couzens, December 19, 1919, vol. 66, Correspondence 1919–1920, Manuscript Collection, Federation of Women's Clubs of Metropolitan Detroit.

15. Mayor Couzens to Martha Ray, January 19, 1920, vol. 66, Correspondence 1918–1976, Manuscript Collection, Federation of Women's Clubs of Metropolitan Detroit.

16. Martha Ray to Mayor James Couzens, January 25, 1920, vol. 66, Correspondence 1918–1976, Manuscript Collection, Federation of Women's Clubs of Metropolitan Detroit; Edith Watkins Dunk, "Why a Woman Should Be Sent to Congress," *Club Woman* 12 (August 1920): 159. Martha Ray's actions demonstrated the public importance she attached to her club work. She was born in Ridgeway, Lenawee County, Michigan. She attended the University of Michigan for three years and finished her bachelor's degree thirty years later. Throughout her life she typified the interests of many clubwomen and devoted herself to both education and club work. She was the girls' advisor at Highland Park High School for five years and the student advisor and home visitor for the Northville School District for another three years. She was president of the DFWC from 1918 to 1920, as well as president of the New Century Club. Her interest in the high cost of living stemmed from her position in the DFWC as well as her con-

cerns about the home in a modern urban environment. Martha Lawton Ray, *The Detroit Club Woman* 1:4 (February 1937): 4, 14.

17. Jacobs, *Pocketbook Politics*, 70–73.

18. Lizabeth Cohen, *A Consumers' Republic: The Politics of Mass Consumption in Postwar America* (New York, 2003), 21.

19. *Twentieth Century Club of Detroit Bulletin* 3 (April 1919), Manuscript Collection, Emma Fox Papers.

20. *Detroit News*, January 11, 1920.

21. Ibid.

22. Johnson, "Municipal Government."

23. "Annual Report of the Legislative Committee," Minutes 1920–1922, vol. 12, p. 855, Manuscript Collection, Federation of Women's Clubs of Metropolitan Detroit.

24. "Thirty-Five Years of Accomplishment," 16.

25. George Engel, "Spring Is Here—Clean Up," *Club Woman* 12:8 (April 1920): 443–44.

26. *Detroit News*, December 7, 1919.

27. *Detroit News*, March 22, 1925.

28. Ibid.

29. John C. Dancy, "A Brief Survey of Negro Life Today in Detroit," in Turner and Moses, *Colored Detroit*, 54–55.

30. Hunter, *To 'Joy My Freedom*, 195.

31. Grace G. Gray, "The Americanization Committee," *Club Woman* 12:9 (May 1920): 550.

32. *The Detroiter* 14:38 (July 16, 1923): 6.

33. *Report of the Mayor's Committee on Race Relations*, 5.

34. *The Detroiter* 14:38 (July 16, 1923), 6.

35. Hicks, *Talk with You Like a Woman*, 9, 253.

36. Gertrude Wallace, "Report of the Legislative Department," May 13, 1924, Minutes 1922–1924, vol. 13, p. 1453, Manuscript Collection, Federation of Women's Clubs of Metropolitan Detroit.

37. Hicks, *Talk with You Like a Woman*, 28; Gaines, *Uplifting the Race*, 180; Washington, "The Detroit Newcomers' Greeting," 335.

38. Wolcott, *Remaking Respectability*, 134.

39. Dancy, "A Brief Survey," 52.

40. "Save Detroit from Smoke Loses," *Club Woman* 19 (November 1926).

41. *Detroit News*, December 16, 1923.

42. "Report of Community Service," January 15, 1925, Minutes 1924–1925, vol. 14, p. 433, Manuscript Collection, Federation of Women's Clubs of Metropolitan Detroit.

43. David Stradling, *Smokestacks and Progressives: Environmentalists, Engineers and Air Quality in America, 1881–1951* (Baltimore, 1999), 3–4.

44. Dorothy Pudrith, "To Smoke or Not to Smoke," *Michigan Woman* 6 (February 1928): 25–27.

45. *Detroit News*, January 13, 1925, February 6, 1927, March 10, 1926,

September 25, 1921.

46. *Detroit News,* April 3, 1928.

47. Harry L. Shearer, "The Civic Housekeeping of Mrs. Detroit Taxpayer," *Michigan Woman* 8 (January 1930): 17, 28.

48. Charles E. Boyd, "The City's Problems," *The Detroiter* 19 (January 9, 1928): 5.

49. *Michigan Woman* 6 (January 1928): 23.

50. John W. Chandler, "The Widening of Woodward Avenue," *Michigan Woman* 4 (January/February 1926): 8, 9, 22–23.

51. *Detroit News,* June 23, 1920.

52. Ibid.

53. Maureen A. Flanagan, "Gender and Urban Political Reform: The City Club and the Woman's City Club of Chicago in the Progressive Era," *American Historical Review* 95:4 (October 1990): 1036.

54. *Detroit News,* October 14, 1928.

55. *Detroit News,* May 5, 1929.

56. *Detroit News,* October 14, 1928, November 17, 1929, November 22, 1929.

57. "Rapid Transit for Detroit," *Magazine of the Woman's City Club* 9 (March 1929): 19.

58. Minutes, March 25, 1929, Manuscript Collection, Detroit's Woman's Club.

59. *Detroit News,* April 2, 1929.

Notes to Chapter 6

1. "Detroit Welcomes State Federation of Women's Clubs in Annual Gathering," *Detroit Free Press,* October 15, 1923, Box 1, Folder 1, Manuscript Collection, Edith Alvord Papers.

2. Annual Meeting, North Dakota Federation of Women's Clubs, Wahpeton, North Dakota, October 7, 1926, Department of American Citizenship, Box 6, Clippings and Writings, Folder & Writings, Manuscript Collection, Edith Alvord Papers.

3. *Lansing State Journal,* May 15, 1922, Folder 2, News Clippings 1916–1923, Ella H. Aldinger Papers.

4. White, *Too Heavy a Load,* 51–52.

5. Gaines, *Uplifting the Race,* 43.

6. "Detroit Women of Prominence," *Woman's Bulletin,* June 1928.

7. "What the Women Are Doing," *Michigan Citizen* 5 (September 27, 1924): 4.

8. *Detroit Times,* February 21, 1919.

9. *Detroit News,* November 11, 1919.

10. "GOP Ingham Convention at Mason, 'Ladylike,'" February 12, [1919], Folder 2, News Clippings, 1916–1923, Manuscript Collection, Ella H. Aldinger Papers.

11. "To the Loyal Republicans of Detroit," *Detroit Republican Party Brochure,* September 13, 1920.

12. "New Voters—Should Not Be Deceived by the Methods of the Republicans," *Michigan Citizen* 3 (December 13, 1919): 3.

13. Cecille Pratt, "The Michigan Woman in Politics," *Michigan Citizen* 1 (December 13, 1919): 7.

14. Freeman, *A Room at a Time,* 7, 109, 110, 119.

15. Andersen, *After Suffrage,* 114.

16. Mary Holland Kinkaid, "Democrats Give Women Full Share in Party," *Michigan Citizen* 5 (February 2, 1924): 4. This bears out the research of Maureen Flanagan, who explained that in Chicago, the political institutions had certain male-dominated structures that were well established before the enfranchisement of women. Flanagan, "The Predicament of New Rights."

17. "Democratic Women of State Federation Hold Inspiring Meeting at Lansing, October 13th," *Michigan Citizen* (May 1926): 8. Nationally, the Democrats had women do work within the Women's Division of the Democratic National Committee. Under the leadership of Molly Dewson, local women reported to their clubs about what was happening nationally. It was called the Reporter Plan and it linked women's issue-oriented approach to active grassroots organizations. "The Women Have Set an Example," *Michigan Citizen* (November 8, 1924): 1; Susan Ware, *Partner and I: Molly Dewson, Feminism and New Deal Politics* (New Haven, 1987), 169, 198.

18. *Detroit News,* October 17, 1920.

19. Grace Stephens (Mrs. W. H.) Jobe, "Democratic Women's Clubs Determined to Carry On," *Michigan Citizen* (January 1925): 5.

20. Freeman, *A Room at a Time,* 225.

21. Hallie Q. Brown, "Republican Colored Women of America," *National Association Notes* 27 (December 1924): 1.

22. Carson, "Michigan," 13.

23. Lillian Johnson, "Report on Colored Women in Politics," October 28, 1924, Box 2, Folder 3, Manuscript Collection, Detroit Study Club.

24. Thomas, *Life for Us Is What We Make It,* 262. The nature of urban politics in other cities resulted in a difference in political party affiliation. In Chicago, for instance, from the early twentieth century, there was always a small number of African Americans who voted Democratic, and contested elections drew some African Americans into voting Democratic. See Douglas Bukowski, *Big Bill Thompson, Chicago and the Politics of Image* (DeKalb, IL, 1998).

25. Schuyler, *The Weight of Their Votes,* 91–92, 114, 224; Fine, *Frank Murphy,* 231.

26. *Women in Politics* (August 1931): 2–3.

27. "A Word to the Women," *Women in Politics* (December 1931).

28. "Detroit Welcomes State Federation of Women's Clubs in Annual Gathering," *Detroit Free Press,* October 16, 1923, Box 1, Folder 1, Manuscript Collection, Ella H. Aldinger Papers.

29. *Detroit News,* March 29, 1919.

30. "Laura Freele Osborn," Box 20, Biography Folder, Manuscript Collection, Laura Osborn Papers.

31. *Detroit News,* March 6, 1919: Devine, 12,431; Biddle, 11,133; Maybee, 8,253; Grimes, 7,410.

32. *Detroit News,* March 29, 1919; "Report of the Legislative Department," Minutes 1918–1920, vol. 11, Manuscript Collection, Federation of Women's Clubs of Metropolitan Detroit.

33. *Detroit News,* April 18, 1919. At the state level, however, Michigan elected the only female member to a State Agricultural Board in April 1919—Mrs. Dora Stockman, a farm woman living about a mile northwest of Lansing. She was also the first woman elected to a state office in Michigan. She believed her success lay in the fact that women were the prime consumers in the family. Because women spent ninety cents of every dollar, women were "practically, therefore politically, interested in health, education and wages." Her academic training in nutrition and home economics led to her interest in educating urban women that in order for their farm counterparts to have the same standard of living as women in the city, the latter needed to be willing to pay higher prices for food. She believed that the overarching agenda for Michigan women should be to provide a healthy, economical diet for their families. In addition, since women spent a large percentage of male earned income, they needed to be politically involved with issues that ultimately affected the home. *Detroit News,* May 18, 1919.

34. *Detroit News,* October 7, 1925.

35. Andersen, *After Suffrage,* 111.

36. Deutsch, *Women and the City,* 262.

37. *Detroit News,* March 4, 1923.

38. Alvord was born in Rochester, New York, but shortly afterward moved to Grand Rapids, Michigan. She graduated from Olivet College and taught Latin for four years in Indiana. "Edith Vosburgh Alvord," *The Detroit Club Woman* 1 (June 1937): 4–5.

39. Grant Hudson to Edith Alvord, August 16, 1922, Box 1, Folder 1, Manuscript Collection, Edith Alvord Papers.

40. "Legislative Department," *Detroit Federation of Women's Clubs: Directory, 1919–1920,* 9.

41. *Club Woman* 14 (September 1921): 128.

42. *Detroit Citizen* 2 (March/April 1922): 11.

43. Carson, "Michigan," 13.

44. Andersen, "Women and Citizenship in the 1920s," 189–93.

45. *Detroit News,* November 7, 1922.

46. *Detroit News,* May 11, 1924.

47. *Detroit News,* November 7, 1926.

48. Terrell, "Report of the National Chairman on Legislation," 76, 78.

49. Ida Mae Bell, "Why the Negro Should Register and Vote," *Detroit Independent,* June 10, 1927.

50. Minutes 1922–1924, vol. 13, p. 282, Manuscript Collection, Federation of Women's Clubs of Metropolitan Detroit.

51. *Detroit News,* November 20, 1920.

52. *Detroit News*, October 2, 1923.

53. *Detroit News*, March 2, 1924.

54. *Detroit News*, December 2, 1928.

55. *Detroit News*, January 25, 1925.

56. "Report of the Executive Committee," March 30, 1925, Minutes 1924–1925, vol. 14, pp. 727–33, Manuscript Collection, Federation of Women's Clubs of Metropolitan Detroit.

57. Unnamed (perhaps Kathleen Hendrie McGraw, president of the Michigan Branch of the National Woman's Party) to Edna Prescott, [1925], Box 1, Correspondence 1925–1928, Lucia Voorheis Grimes Papers; "Women's Place in Industry," *Twentieth Century Club Magazine* (April 1920): 11.

58. Mrs. F. C. Aldinger, "What the 1925 Legislature Did," *Michigan Woman* 3 (Summer 1925): 26, 27. At first glance, it seems that the experience of Edna Prescott might actually move her to be a more vigorous proponent of equal rights for women. She was born in Ann Arbor, Michigan, but went to Columbus, Ohio, for a course in Kindergarten Normal Training School. She taught kindergarten for two years in Ann Arbor before marrying and moving to Detroit. At that time the Detroit School Board was looking for kindergarten teachers and although fully qualified, Prescott was ineligible because she was married. However, she volunteered to teach the whole year without payment because she really loved the job. Prescott, while experiencing discrimination as a married woman, failed to grasp the economic impact such laws had on women without financial resources. Apparently her financial circumstances were advantageous; she spent the rest of her life in volunteer and club work. "Some of Our Past Presidents—Edna Henion Prescott," *Club Woman* (January 1937): 6.

59. "Report to the Members of the Legislative Council of Michigan Women," May 28, 1927, Box 2, Papers 1912–1932, Lucia Voorheis Grimes Papers.

60. Beth Fay Adams, "What Was Done by the State Legislature," *Michigan Woman* 7 (July/August 1929): 26.

61. *Detroit News*, December 20, 1925.

62. *Detroit News*, December 2, 1928.

63. *Detroit News*, December 9, 1928.

64. Janie Porter Barrett, "National Executive Board Meeting, May 2, 1925," *National Association Notes* 27 (June 1925): 1.

65. Marjorie Elaine Porter, "Undue Flattery Costly to Givers' Self-Respect," *Detroit News*, November 18, 1928.

66. *Detroit News*, December 4, 1927.

67. *Detroit News*, October 26, 1924.

68. Garnet Warfel, "Women Candidates Talk Short and to the Point," *Detroit News*, August 15, 1930.

69. *Detroit News*, November 4, 1928.

70. "Annual Legislative Division, Minutes," May 7, 1928–May 7, 1929, Minutes 1928–1929, vol. 18, Manuscript Collection, Federation of Women's Clubs of Metropolitan Detroit.

71. "Report of the Legislative Division, Minutes," 1929–1930, Minutes

1929–1930, vol. 19, Manuscript Collection, Federation of Women's Clubs of Metropolitan Detroit.

72. Schuyler, *The Weight of Their Votes,* 8, 165, 189–96.

73. Ibid., 2, 10.

74. Linda Culpepper, *Detroit News*, e-mail message to author, April 28, 2010.

75. *Detroit Contender,* May 7, 1921; *Detroit Independent*, September 10, 1927, October 14, 1927.

76. Lillian Johnson, "The Newspaper's Part in the Life of Detroit," November 13, 1925, Box 2, Folder 3, Manuscript Collection, Detroit Study Club.

77. Irvine Garland Penn and Frederick Douglass, *The Afro-American Press and Its Editors* (New York, 1891), 419–20.

78. Meta E. Pelham, "Miss Meta Pelham, Custodian of Douglass Funds, Expresses Sound Sentiment," *National Association Notes* 27 (April 1925): 6. Pelham was born in Virginia but moved to Detroit at a young age. She was the valedictorian at her Detroit high school and attended the Fenton College Normal School (Central Michigan). Penn and Douglass, *The Afro-American Press and Its Editors,* 419–20.

79. Turner and Moses, *Colored Detroit,* 68.

80. Michigan Colored Women's Club, Box 1, Record Group 60-14, State Archives of Michigan.

81. *Michigan Chronicle,* June 28, 1986. Evelyn Brooks Higginbotham noted the importance of the black press and women in "In Politics to Stay," 203–5.

82. Thomas, *Life for Us Is What We Make It,* 115.

83. Fine, *Frank Murphy,* 201–4, 246.

84. Berneice Collins to DFWC, December 9, [no year], Minutes 1929–1930, vol. 19, Manuscript Collection, Federation of Women's Clubs of Metropolitan Detroit. Jean Chamberlain was a good choice to head unemployment relief. She was born in Parkersburg, West Virginia, where she completed high school and graduated from the Sines Business Institute of Parkersburg. Her understanding of unemployment in Michigan was so respected that Governor Brucker appointed her to the Michigan Unemployment Commission. But she had other interests as well. She was on the Recorder's Court Jury Commission for six years as well as the House of Corrections Commission. In addition to her appointed positions she was president of the DFWC from 1928 to 1930. Jean B. Chamberlain, *Club Woman* 3 (October 1938): 9.

85. *Detroit News,* October 26, 1930.

86. Lent D. Upson, "Next Year's Legislature," *Michigan Woman* 8 (September 1930): 11, 14–15; *Detroit News,* November 16, 1930.

87. *Detroit News,* April 13, 1930.

88. *Detroit News,* October 12, 1930.

89. Meeting Minutes, January 30, 1930, Minutes 1929–1930, vol. 19, Manuscript Collection, Federation of Women's Clubs of Metropolitan Detroit.

90. *Detroit News,* December 14, 1930; Wolcott, *Remaking Respectability,* 217.

91. Wolcott, *Remaking Respectability,* 209–10.

92. Ibid.

93. Detroit Public Library, "Housewives' League of Detroit," http://Detroit.lib.mi.us/Urban_Houswives/hid.html (accessed January 14, 2012). Darlene Clark Hine, "The Housewives' League of Detroit: Black Women and Economic Nationalism," in Lebsock and Hewitt, *Visible Women,* 223–41.

94. Detroit Public Library, "Housewives' League of Detroit."

95. Fine, *Frank Murphy,* 206–7, 209.

96. Ibid., 217, 225–26. Murphy enjoyed a good relationship with clubwomen. He appointed Caroline Parker of the Detroit branch of the American Civil Liberties Union (ACLU) to the House of Corrections Commission. Josephine Gomon, a former teacher and liberal thinker, influenced Murphy's politics and became the assistant secretary to the mayor. Beulah Young, publisher of the Detroit *People's News,* claimed she would keep black voters in Detroit for Murphy. Later she was a member of Murphy's Mayors Women's Committee. Ibid., 216, 217, 221–22, 230, 231.

97. *Detroit Free Press,* May 10, 1931.

Notes to Conclusion

1. Fine, *Frank Murphy,* 214, 215, 219.

2. Ibid., 222, 240.

3. Lent D. Upson, "The City of Tomorrow," *The Detroiter* 22 (February 9, 1931): 6.

4. White, *Too Heavy a Load,* 104.

5. Ruth Mosher Place, "The Hand That Wields the Ballot," *Club Woman* 19:1 (September 1926): 18.

6. Wheeler, *Against Obscenity,* 95.

7. Wolcott, *Remaking Respectability,* 176–80.

8. Evans, "Women's History and Political Theory," 132; Flanagan, "The City Profitable," 165, 168.

9. Sarah Deutsch, "Learning to Talk More Like a Man: Boston Women's Class-Bridging Organizations, 1870–1940," *American Historical Review* 97:2 (April 1992): 404; Scott, *Natural Allies,* 158.

10. Wolcott, *Remaking Respectability,* 95.

11. White, *Too Heavy a Load,* 110–13, 141.

Selected Bibliography

A Note on Sources

The Burton Historical Collection of the Detroit Public Library houses the minutes, correspondence, and published works of many Detroit women's clubs. The collections are both manuscript and published materials. The Burton also holds biographical collections of significant Detroit clubwomen. African American women's clubs have only limited records at the Burton. Mrs. Senora D. Smith, the historian for the Detroit Association of (Colored) Women's Clubs (DAWC), explained that there were few club records for the 1920s. Smith noted that the DAWC did not own a clubhouse until 1941 and therefore rarely maintained its manuscripts outside of individual presidents, secretaries, etc. The Detroit African American newspapers of the time have a few extant editions on microfilm at the Burton, but otherwise are not kept in area collections. The clubwomen saw needs in the community, and took care of them. At the time, they didn't think it was necessary to keep records. Therefore, the description of African American women's club activities in Detroit is uneven and conclusions about these activities remain tenuous.

Investigating the activities of women during the 1920s presents problems identifying these women, as women. In the newspapers and official club publications, they are referred to almost exclusively by their husband's names. Therefore, women's first names will be used, if possible. Otherwise, they will be listed under their husband's name, as was the custom at the time.

Primary Sources

Archival and Manuscript Collections

Burton Historical Collection, Detroit Public Library, Detroit, Michigan

- Annual Report (City of Detroit)
- Edith Vosburgh Alvord Papers
- Clara B. Arthur, Scrapbook
- Detroit Citizens League
- Detroit Community Club
- Detroit Sorosis Club
- Detroit Study Club

Detroit Woman's Club
Federation of Women's Clubs of Metropolitan Detroit
Emma Fox Papers
Lillian Bateman Johnson Papers
League of Women Voters
Michigan Equal Suffrage Association
New Era Study Club
Laura Osborn Papers
Zahn-Reading Room File
Zonta Club

Michigan Historical Collections, Bentley Historical Library, Ann Arbor, Michigan
Ella H. Aldinger Papers
Lucia Voorheis Grimes Papers

Michigan State University Libraries Collections, East Lansing, Michigan
National Association of Colored Women's Clubs, Records
The National Notes

State Archives of Michigan, Bureau of Michigan History, Lansing, Michigan
Michigan Colored Women's Club

Newspapers

Detroit Contender
Detroit Free Press
Detroit Independent
Detroit Journal
Detroit News
Detroit People's News
Detroit Times
Detroit Tribune
Lansing State Journal
Michigan Chronicle
The Owl

Magazines, Journals, Directories, and Pamphlets

Civic Searchlight (Detroit Citizens League)
Club Woman (Detroit Federation of Women's Clubs)
Colored Detroit, 1924: A Brief History of Detroit's Colored Population (Detroit, 1924)
Courier (Michigan Republicans)
Detroit Citizen (Progressive Community Magazine)
Detroit Federation of Women's Clubs Directory
Detroiter (Chamber of Commerce)
Magazine of the Woman's City Club
Michigan Citizen (Michigan Democrats)
Michigan Suffragist (Michigan Equal Suffrage Association)

Michigan Woman (Michigan League of Women Voters)
Twentieth Century Club Magazine
Woman's Bulletin
Women in Politics

Published Primary Sources

Arthur, Clara B. *Progress of Michigan Women.* Detroit: N.p., n.d.

Cahill, James C. "Employment of Males and Females under 18—Hours of Labor, 5330, Act #341 as amended August 14, 1919." *Michigan Compiled Laws of 1915, Annotated Supplement 1922.* Chicago, 1922.

Grennell, Judson. "What Michigan Women Should Know about Voting." Waterford, 1919.

Laws of Michigan Relating to Women. Lansing, 1916.

Report of the Mayor's Committee on Race Relations. Detroit, 1926.

Secondary Sources

Books and Articles

Andersen, Kristi. *After Suffrage: Women in Partisan and Electoral Politics before the New Deal.* Chicago, 1996.

———. . "Women and Citizenship in the 1920s." In Louise Tilly and Patricia Gurin, eds. *Women, Politics and Change.* New York, 1990.

———. "Women and the Vote in the 1920s: What Happened in Oregon." *Women and Politics* 14:4 (1994) 43–56.

Babson, Steve. *Working Detroit.* New York, 1984.

Baker, Paula. "The Domestication of Politics: Women and American Political Society, 1780–1920." In Vicki L. Ruiz and Ellen Carol DuBois, eds. *Unequal Sisters: A Multicultural Reader in U.S. Women's History.* New York, 1994.

Barrett, Paul. *The Automobile and Urban Transit: The Formulation of Public Policy in Chicago, 1900–1930.* Philadelphia, 1983.

Blair, Karen. *The Torchbearers: Women and Their Amateur Arts Associations in America, 1890–1930.* Bloomington, 1994.

Bowen, Louise de Koven. *Growing Up with a City.* New York, 1926.

Boyle, Kevin. *Arc of Justice: A Saga of Race, Civil Rights, and Murder in the Jazz Age.* New York, 2004.

Brown, Dorothy M. *Setting a Course: American Women in the 1920s.* Boston, 1987.

Buechler, Stephen M. *The Transformation of the Woman Suffrage Movement: The Case of Illinois, 1850–1920.* New Brunswick, NJ, 1986.

Buenker, John D. *Urban Liberalism and Progressive Reform.* New York, 1973.

Carby, Hazel V. *Reconstructing Womanhood: The Emergence of the Afro-American Woman Novelist.* New York, 1987.

Crathern, Alice Tarbell. *In Detroit . . . Courage Was the Fashion: The Contribution of Women to the Development of Detroit, 1701–1951.* Detroit, 1953.

Cavallo, Dominick. *Muscles and Morals—Organized Playgrounds and Urban Reform, 1880–1920.* Philadelphia, 1981.

Cohen, Lizabeth. *A Consumers' Republic: The Politics of Mass Consumption in Postwar America.* New York, 2003.

Connolly, James J. *The Triumph of Ethnic Progressivism: Urban Political Culture in Boston, 1900–1925.* Cambridge, 1998.

Conot, Robert. *American Odyssey: A Unique History of America Told through the Life of a Great City.* New York, 1974.

Cott, Nancy. "Across the Great Divide: Women in Politics before and after 1920." In Louise A. Tilly and Patricia Gurin, eds., *Women, Politics and Change.* New York, 1990.

———. *The Bonds of Womanhood: Woman's Sphere in New England, 1780–1835.* New Haven, 1977.

———. *The Grounding of Modern Feminism.* New Haven, 1987.

Crooks, James B. *Politics and Progress: The Rise of Urban Progressivism in Baltimore, 1895–1911.* Baton Rouge, 1968.

Curry, Lynne. *Modern Mothers in the Heartland: Gender, Health, and Progress in Illinois, 1900–1930.* Columbus, 1999.

DeMatteo, Arthur E. "Organized Labor versus the Mayor: The Detroit Federation of Labor and the Revised City Charter of 1914." *Michigan Historical Review* 22 (Fall 1995): 63–92.

Deutsch, Sarah. "Learning to Talk More Like a Man: Boston Women's Class-Bridging Organizations, 1870–1940." *American Historical Review* 97:2 (April 1992): 379–404.

———. *Women and the City: Gender, Space and Power in Boston, 1870–1940.* New York, 2000.

DuBois, Ellen Carol. "Working Women, Class Relations, and Suffrage Militance: Harriot Stanton Blatch and the New York Woman Suffrage Movement, 1894–1907," in Marjorie Spruill Wheeler, ed. *One Woman, One Vote: Rediscovering the Woman Suffrage Movement.* Troutdale, OH, 1995.

Elenbaas, Jack D. "The Boss of the Better Class: Henry Leland and the Detroit Citizens League, 1912–1924." *Michigan History* 58 (Summer 1974): 131–50.

———. "The Excess of Reform: The Day the Detroit Mayor Arrested the City Council." In Wilma Henderson, ed., *Detroit Perspectives: Crossroads and Turning Points.* Detroit, 1991.

Engelmann, Larry D. "A Separate Peace: The Politics of Prohibition Enforcement in Detroit, 1920–1930." *Detroit in Perspective* 1 (Autumn, 1972): 51–73.

Evans, Sara. "Women's History and Political Theory: Toward a Feminist Approach to a Public Life." In Suzanne Lebsock and Nancy Hewitt, eds., *Visible Women: New Essays on American Activism.* Urbana, 1993.

Ewen, Lynda Ann. *Corporate Power and Urban Crisis in Detroit.* Princeton, 1978.

Feldstein, Ruth. *Motherhood in Black and White: Race and Sex in American Liberalism, 1930–1965.* Ithaca, 2000.

Fine, Sidney. *Frank Murphy: The Detroit Years.* Ann Arbor, 1975.

Finegold, Kenneth. *Experts and Politicians: Reform Challenges to Machine Politics in*

New York, Cleveland and Chicago. Princeton, 1995.

Firebaugh, Glenn, and Kevin Chen. "Vote Turnout of Nineteenth Amendment Women: The Enduring Effect of Disfranchisement." *American Journal of Sociology* 100 (January 1995): 972–96.

Flanagan, Maureen A. *Charter Reform in Chicago*. Carbondale, 1987.

———. "The City Profitable, the City Livable: Environmental Policy, Gender and Power in Chicago in the 1910s." *Journal of Urban History* 22 (January 1996): 163–90.

———. "Gender and Urban Political Reform: The City Club and the Woman's City Club of Chicago in the Progressive Era." *American Historical Review* 95:4 (October 1990): 1032–50.

———. "The Predicament of New Rights: Suffrage and Women's Political Power from a Local Perspective." *Social Politics: International Studies in Gender, State and Society* 2 (Fall 1995): 305–30.

———. *Seeing with Their Hearts: Chicago Women and the Vision of the Good City, 1871–1933*. Princeton, 2002.

Fragnoli, Raymond R. "Progressive Coalitions and Municipal Reform: Charter Revision in Detroit, 1912–1918." *Detroit in Perspective* 4 (Spring 1980): 119–42.

Freedman, Estelle B. *Their Sisters' Keepers: Women's Prison Reform in America, 1830–1930*. Ann Arbor, 1981.

Freeman, Jo. *A Room at a Time: How Women Entered Party Politics*. New York, 2000.

Gaines, Kevin K. *Uplifting the Race: Black Leadership, Politics, and Culture in the Twentieth Century*. Chapel Hill, 1966.

Gidlow, Liette. *The Big Vote: Gender, Consumer Culture and the Politics of Exclusion*. Baltimore, 2004.

Goodwin, Joanne L. "An Experiment in Paid Motherhood: The Implementation of Mothers' Pensions in Early Twentieth-Century Chicago." *Gender and History* 3 (Autumn 1992): 323–43.

Gordon, Linda. *Pitied But Not Entitled: Single Mothers and the History of Welfare*. New York, 1994.

———. *Woman's Body, Woman's Right: A Social History of Birth Control in America*. New York, 1974.

Green, Elna C. *Southern Strategies: Southern Women and the Woman Suffrage Question*. Chapel Hill, 1997.

Gullett, Gayle. *Becoming Citizens: The Emergence and Development of the California Women's Movement*. Urbana, 2000.

Hawley, Ellis. *The Great War and the Search for a Modern Order*. 2nd ed. New York, 1992.

Hays, Samuel P. "The Politics of Municipal Reform in the Progressive Era." *Pacific Northwest Quarterly* 54 (October 1964): 157–69.

Henderson, Wilma. "The Progressives and Other Reformers." In Wilma Henderson, ed., *Detroit Perspectives: Crossroads and Turning Points*. Detroit, 1991.

Heyda, O. P. Marie. "Senator James McMillan and the Flowering of the Spoils

System." *Michigan History* 54 (Fall 1970): 183–200.

Hicks, Cheryl D. *Talk with You Like a Woman: African American Women, Justice and Reform in New York, 1890–1935.* Chapel Hill, 2011.

Higginbotham, Evelyn Brooks. "In Politics to Stay: Black Women Leaders and Party Politics." In Louise A. Tilly and Patricia Gurin, eds., *Women, Politics and Change.* New York, 1990.

———. *Righteous Discontent: The Women's Movement in the Black Baptist Church, 1880–1920.* Cambridge, 1993.

Hine, Darlene Clark. "The Housewives' League of Detroit: Black Women and Economic Nationalism." In Suzanne Lebsock and Nancy Hewitt, eds., *Visible Women: New Essays on American Activism.* Urbana, 1993.

Holli, Melvin, ed. *Detroit.* New York, 1976.

———. "Mayoring in Detroit, 1824–1985: Is Upward Mobility the 'Impossible Dream'?" *Michigan History* 13 (Spring 1987): 1–15.

———. *Reform in Detroit: Hazen S. Pingree and Urban Politics.* New York, 1969.

Hunter, Tera W. *To 'Joy My Freedom: Southern Black Women's Lives and Labors after the Civil War.* Cambridge, 1997.

Hyde, Charles K. Review of *Detroit Street Railways,* vol. 1, 1863–1922. *Detroit in Perspective* 7 (Fall 1983): 84–85.

Jacobs, Meg. *Pocketbook Politics: Economic Citizenship in Twentieth Century America.* Princeton, 2005.

Judson, Sarah. "Cultivating Citizenship in the Kindergartens of Atlanta, 1890s–1920s." *Atlanta History* 41 (January 1998): 17–30.

———. " 'Leisure Is a Foe to Any Man': The Pleasures and Dangers of Leisure in Atlanta during World War I." *Journal of Women's History* 15:92 (Spring 2003). http://www.jstor.org/ (accessed August 13, 2011).

Katz, Sherry, J. "A Politics of Coalition: Socialist Women and the California Suffrage Movement, 1900–1911." In Marjorie Spruill Wheeler, ed., *One Woman, One Vote: Rediscovering the Woman Suffrage Movement.* Troutdale, OH, 1995.

Katzman, David M. *Before the Ghetto: Black Detroit in the Nineteenth Century.* Urbana, 1973.

Klapper, Melissa R. *Small Strangers: The Experience of Immigrant Children in America, 1880–1925.* Chicago, 2007.

Knupfer, Anne Meis. *Toward a Tenderer Humanity and a Nobler Womanhood: African American Women's Clubs in Turn of the Century Chicago.* New York, 1996.

Kolko, Gabriel. *Main Currents in Modern American History.* New York, 1984.

Kornbluh, Mark Lawrence. *Why America Stopped Voting: The Decline of Participatory Democracy and the Emergence of American Politics.* New York, 2000.

Koven, Seth, and Sonya Michel, eds. *Mothers of a New World.* New York, 1993.

LaBrew, Arthur. *300th Year Celebration: The Black Community, Its Music and the Fine and Secular Arts; The Detroit History That Nobody Knew (or bothered to remember) 1800–1900.* Detroit, 2001.

Ladd-Taylor, Molly. *Mother-Work: Women, Child Welfare and the State, 1890–1930.* Urbana, 1994.

Leach, Nathaniel. *Reaching Out to Freedom: The Second Baptist Connection.* N.p., 1988.

Lebsock, Suzanne, and Nancy Hewitt, eds. *Visible Women: New Essays on American Activism*. Urbana, 1993.

Leggett, John C. "Class Consciousness and Politics in Detroit: A Study in Change." *Michigan History* 48 (December 1964): 287–300.

Love, Nancy S. "Ideal Speech and Feminist Discourse: Habermas Re-Visioned." *Women and Politics* 11:3 (1991): 101–22.

McArthur, Judith N. *Creating the New Woman: The Rise of Southern Women's Progressive Culture in Texas, 1893–1918*. Urbana, 1998.

———. "Minnie Fisher Cunningham's Back Door Lobby in Texas: Political Maneuvering in a One-Party State." In Marjorie Spruill Wheeler, ed., *One Woman, One Vote: Rediscovering the Woman Suffrage Movement*. Troutdale, OH, 1995.

McBride, Genevieve G. *On Wisconsin Women: Working for Their Rights from Settlement to Suffrage*. Madison, 1993.

McGerr, Michael E. *The Decline of Popular Politics: The American North, 1865–1928*. New York, 1986.

McHaney, Sharon E. "Securing the Sacred Right to Vote." *Michigan History Magazine* 75 (March/April 1991): 38–45.

Michel, Sonya. "The Limits of Maternalism: Policies toward American Wage-Earning Mothers during the Progressive Era." In Seth Koven and Sonya Michel, eds., *Mothers of a New World*. New York, 1993.

Miller, Kristie. *Ruth Hanna McCormick: A Life in Politics, 1880–1944*. Albuquerque, 1992.

Miller, Zane. *Boss Cox's Cincinnati: Urban Politics in the Progressive Era*. New York, 1968.

Mink, Gwendolyn. *The Wages of Motherhood: Inequality in the Welfare State, 1917–1942*. Ithaca, 1995.

Montgomery, David. *The Fall of the House of Labor*. Cambridge, 1987.

Muncy, Robyn. *Creating a Female Dominion in American Reform, 1890–1935*. New York, 1991.

Murphy, Marjorie. *Blackboard Unions: The AFT and the NEA, 1900–1980*. Ithaca, 1990.

Peebles, Robin S. "Detroit's Black Women's Clubs." *Michigan History* 70 (January–February 1986): 48.

Perry, Elisabeth Israels. *Belle Moskowitz: Feminine Politics and the Exercise of Power in the Age of Alfred E. Smith*. New York, 1987.

———. "Women's Political Choices after Suffrage: The Women's City Club of New York, 1915–1990." *New York History* (October 1990): 417–34.

Reed, James. "Doctors, Birth Control and Social Values, 1830–1970." In Judith Walzer Leavitt, ed., *Women and Health in America*. Madison, 1984.

Root, Grace C. *Women and Repeal: The Story of the Women's Organization for National Prohibition Reform*. New York, 1934.

Rose, Kenneth D. *American Women and the Repeal of Prohibition*. New York, 1996.

Ruiz, Vicki L., and Ellen Carol DuBois. *Unequal Sisters: A Multicultural Reader in U.S. Women's History*. 2nd ed. New York, 1994.

Salem, Dorothy. *To Better Our World: Black Women in Organized Reform, 1890–1920*. Brooklyn, 1990.

Sarvasy, Wendy. "Beyond the Difference versus Equality Policy Debate: Postsuffrage Feminism, Citizenship, and the Quest for a Feminist Welfare State." *Signs: Journal of Women in Culture and Society* 17 (Winter 1992): 329–62.

Schiesl, Martin J. *The Politics of Efficiency: Municipal Administration and Reform in America, 1800–1920*. Berkeley, 1977.

Shockley, Megan Taylor *"We too, are Americans": African-American Women in Detroit and Richmond, 1940–1954*. Urbana, 2004.

Schuyler, Lorraine Gates. *The Weight of Their Votes: Southern Women and Political Leverage in the 1920s*. Chapel Hill, 2006.

Scott, Anne Firor. *Natural Allies: Women's Associations in American History*. Urbana, 1991.

Shaw, Stephanie J. *What a Woman Ought to Be and to Do: Black Professional Women Workers during the Jim Crow Era*. Chicago, 1996.

Sklar. Kathryn Kish. *Florence Kelley and the Nation's Work: The Rise of Women's Public Culture, 1830–1900*. New Haven, 1995.

———. "The Historical Foundations of Women's Power in the Creation of the American Welfare State." In Seth Koven and Sonya Michel, eds., *Mothers of a New World*. New York, 1993.

Skocpol, Theda. *Protecting Soldiers and Mothers: The Political Origins of Social Policy in the United States*. Cambridge, 1992.

Stradling, David. *Smokestacks and Progressives: Environmentalists, Engineers and Air Quality in America, 1881–1951*. Baltimore, 1999.

Sugrue, Thomas J. *The Origins of the Urban Crisis: Race and Inequality in Post-War Detroit*. Princeton, 1996

Tager, Jack. *The Intellectual as Urban Reformer: Brand Whitlock and the Progressive Movement*. Cleveland, 1968.

Terborg-Penn, Rosalyn. "African-American Women's Networks in the Anti-Lynching Crusade." In Noralee Frankel and Nancy Dye, eds., *Gender, Class, Race and Reform in the Progressive Era*. Lexington, 1991.

Thomas, Richard W. *Life for Us Is What We Make It: Building Black Community in Detroit, 1915–1945*. Bloomington, 1992.

Thompson, Heather Ann. *Whose Detroit?: Politics, Labor and Race in a Modern American City*. Cornell, 2001.

Tilly, Louise A., and Patricia Gurin, eds. *Women, Politics and Change*. New York, 1990.

Tyler, Pamela. *Silk Stockings and Ballot Boxes: Women and Politics in New Orleans, 1920–1963*. Athens, GA, 1996.

Ware, Susan. *Beyond Suffrage: Women and the New Deal*. Cambridge, 1991.

———. *Partner and I: Molly Dewson, Feminism and New Deal Politics*. New Haven, 1987.

Wheeler, Leigh Ann. *Against Obscenity: Reform and the Politics of Womanhood in America, 1873–1935*. Baltimore, 2004.

———. "From Reading Shakespeare to Reforming Burlesque: The Minneapolis

Woman's Club and the Women's Welfare League, 1907–1920." *Michigan Historical Review* 25 (Spring 1999): 45–75.

Wheeler, Marjorie Spruill. *New Women of the New South: The Leaders of the Woman Suffrage Movement in the Southern States.* New York, 1993.

———, ed. *One Woman, One Vote: Rediscovering the Woman Suffrage Movement.* Troutdale, OH, 1995.

White, Deborah Gray. "The Cost of Club Work, the Price of Black Feminism." In Suzanne Lebsock and Nancy Hewitt, eds., *Visible Women: New Essays on American Activism.* Urbana, 1993.

———. *Too Heavy a Load: Black Women in Defense of Themselves, 1894–1994.* New York, 1999.

Wolcott, Victoria W. *Remaking Respectability: African American Women in Interwar Detroit.* Chapel Hill, 2001.

Zunz, Olivier. *The Changing Face of Inequality: Urbanization, Industrial Development and Immigrants in Detroit, 1818–1920.* Chicago, 1982.

Dissertations and Theses

Elenbaas, Jack D. "Detroit and the Progressive Era: A Study of Urban Reform, 1900–1914." Ph.D. diss., Wayne State University, 1968.

Gidlow, Liette Patricia. "Getting Out the Vote: Gender and Citizenship in an Age of Consumer Culture." Ph.D. diss., Cornell University, 1997.

Nauss, Gladys E. "Detroit Federation of Women's Clubs." Master's thesis, Wayne State University, 1949.

Wolcott, Victoria Widgeon. "Remaking Respectability: African-American Women and the Politics of Identity in Interwar Detroit." Ph.D. diss., University of Michigan, 1995.

Index

Page numbers in italics refer to illustrations

www.ingramcontent.com/pod-product-compliance
Lightning Source LLC
LaVergne TN
LVHW010355080826
844660LV00016B/974/J

* 9 7 8 0 8 1 4 3 3 8 1 5 5 *